Arctic Shipping

This book considers both the present state of Arctic shipping and possible future trends with reference to the various sectors of maritime transportation: cruise tourism, container traffic and bulk shipping. Ports are analysed as tools that support the strategies of coastal states to foster the development of resource extraction, enhance the attractiveness of Arctic shipping lanes and enable the control of maritime activities through coast guard deployment.

The aim of this book is to draw a picture of the trends of Arctic shipping. How is traffic evolving in Canada's Arctic, or along the Northern Sea Route? Are there significant differences between bulk and container shipping segments when considering the Arctic market? How are the ports and the hinterland developing and what are the strategies behind those? How is the legal framework shaping the evolution of maritime transportation? The contributors to this book consider all of these questions, and more, as they map out the prospects for Arctic shipping and analyse in detail the development of Arctic shipping as a result of multi-variable interactions.

This book will be key reading for industry professionals and post-graduate students alike.

Frédéric Lasserre is Professor in the Geography Department at Laval University, Canada and heads the Quebec Council for Geopolitical Studies. He was Project Director with Canada's ArcticNet research network between 2010 and 2015.

Olivier Faury is an Assistant Professor at EM Normandie in Le Havre. He completed his PhD in 2016 on the economics elements that may increase the attractiveness of the Northern Sea Route comparing to the Suez Canal Route. Since July 2016, he has been working on the Arctic with a focus on the legal, risk, shipping and port parameters.

Routledge Studies in Transport Analysis

Maritime Networks
Spatial Structures and Time Dynamics
Edited by César Ducruet

Inland Waterway Transport
Challenges and Prospects
Bart Wiegmans and Rob Konings

Evaluating High-Speed Rail
Interdisciplinary Perspectives
Edited by Daniel Albalate and Germà Bel

The Airline Profit Cycle
A System Analysis of Airline Industry Dynamics
Eva-Maria Cronrath

Advances in Shipping Data Analysis and Modeling
Tracking and Mapping Maritime Flows in the Age of Big Data
Edited by César Ducruet

Maritime Mobilities
Edited by Jason Monios and Gordon Wilmsmeier

U.S. Freight Rail Economics and Policy
Are We on the Right Track?
Edited by Jeffrey T. Macher and John W. Mayo

Arctic Shipping
Climate Change, Commercial Traffic and Port Development
Edited by Frédéric Lasserre and Olivier Faury

For a complete list of titles in this series, please visit: www.routledge.com/Routledge-Studies-in-Transport-Analysis/book-series/RSTA

Arctic Shipping

Climate Change, Commercial Traffic
and Port Development

**Edited by Frédéric Lasserre
and Olivier Faury**

LONDON AND NEW YORK

First published 2020
by Routledge
2 Park Square, Milton Park, Abingdon, Oxon OX14 4RN

and by Routledge
605 Third Avenue, New York, NY 10017

First issued in paperback 2021

Routledge is an imprint of the Taylor & Francis Group, an informa business

British Library Cataloguing-in-Publication Data
A catalogue record for this book is available from the British Library

Library of Congress Cataloging-in-Publication Data
Names: Lasserre, Frédéric, 1967– editor. | Faury, Olivier, editor.
Title: Arctic shipping : climate change, commercial traffic and port
    development / edited by Frédéric Lasserre and Olivier Faury.
Description: Abingdon, Oxon ; New York, NY : Routledge, 2020. |
    Series: Routledge studies in transport analysis ; 12 | Includes
    bibliographical references and index.
Identifiers: LCCN 2019033601 (print) | LCCN 2019033602 (ebook) |
    ISBN 9781138489431 (hardback) | ISBN 9781351037464 (ebook)
Subjects: LCSH: Shipping—Arctic regions.
Classification: LCC HE752.A68 A73 2020 (print) | LCC HE752.A68 (ebook) |
    DDC 387.509163/2—dc23
LC record available at https://lccn.loc.gov/2019033601
LC ebook record available at https://lccn.loc.gov/2019033602

ISBN 13: 978-0-367-77760-9 (pbk)
ISBN 13: 978-1-138-48943-1 (hbk)

Typeset in Times New Roman
by Apex CoVantage, LLC

Contents

Contributors

Mawuli Afenyo is currently with the University of Manitoba (UM) where he researches subjects focused on Arctic shipping, oil spills and climate change adaptation to ports. He is part of the projects 'GENICE' (Microbial Genomics for Oil Spill Preparedness in Canada's Arctic marine environment). He is also an Instructor at the Asper School of Business of UM. Prior to joining UM, he received his PhD in engineering from the Memorial University of New-foundland, Canada. He also worked at the Joint Centre of Excellence for Arctic Shipping and Operations. Further, he worked on projects at the Centre for Risk, Integrity and Safety Engineering (C-RISE). Dr. Mawuli has also been a visiting scholar at the University of Helsinki, Finland and has attended and presented research findings at major international conferences on Arctic shipping and technology.

Olga Alexeeva is Associate Professor of Chinese History at the University of Quebec in Montreal (UQÀM), Canada. She earned her PhD in Chinese studies at the University of Paris VII-Denis, France and has held a postdoctoral fellowship at Laval University, Canada. Her current research interests focus on the history of contemporary China with particular reference to China's environmental issues and energy security. She has also written on a range of related topics pertaining to China's strategy in the Arctic.

Yann Alix. Since 2011, Dr. Yann Alix is General Delegate of the SEFACIL Foundation which aims to set up, lead and animate a unique international think tank of excellence around strategic and prospective analysis on themes related to the future of maritime transport, ports and logistics. Since 2012, Dr. Yann Alix is the founder and director of the book collection *Les Océanides*, as well as Co-founder and Co-director of Afrique Atlantique since 2017. After receiving his PhD from Concordia University and his doctorate in transport geography from Caen University, Prof. Alix started a career as consultant for Maritime Innovation in Rimouski, Canada (2000–2004) and has been appointed as Head of the Logistics Department at Normandy Business School (2005–2007). He was Director of the Port Training Institute (IPER) from 2007 to 2010. He has published many professional reports in the Americas, Europe and Africa as well as papers in academic journals. Last released are *The Future Belongs to*

Fluidity (2014), *The New Age of the Wood* (2015) and *Histoires courtes maritimes et portuaires. D'Afrique et d'ailleurs* (2016).

Kristin Bartenstein is a professor at the Faculty of Law of the Université Laval, Quebec. The focus of her work is on international law, in particular on the Law of the Sea and on international environmental law. She holds degrees from the Ludwig-Maximilians-Universität (Munich, Germany) and the Université Panthéon-Assas (Paris, France) as well as a LLD from the Université Laval. Much of her work has centered on Arctic issues, including Arctic navigation and environmental protection as well as several aspects of Arctic governance. She is the lead investigator of an interdisciplinary research project on the impacts of the Polar Code on Canadian regulation of Arctic shipping. She is a member, *inter alia*, of the Institut Québécois des Hautes Études Internationales (HEI) where she had been serving as the Director of the international studies programs between 2015 and 2017.

Pierre Cariou is Senior Professor at Kedge Business School, France. He is Visiting Professor at Shanghai Maritime University and the World Maritime University in Malmö, Sweden. Prior to this, he held the French Chair in Maritime Affairs at the World Maritime University in Malmö, Sweden, where he was in charge of shipping and port management specializations. From 2001 to 2004, he was Associate Professor in Economics at the University of Nantes (France). He completed his PhD in 2000 on liner shipping strategies and has since then contributed to several reports for private companies, the French Parliament, the Port Authorities of Nantes and Marseille, Casino Group, NATIXIS Bank of CMA CGM. His main research interests are shipping/port economics, maritime safety and environmental protection on which he has published more than 80 scientific papers.

Alex Champagne-Gélinas is a PhD candidate in urban studies at the Urbanization Culture Society Research Centre of the Institut National de la Recherche Scientifique (INRS) in Montreal. His PhD research focuses on energy transition and the spatial evolution of port regions. He also works with the Interuniversity Research Centre on Enterprise Networks, Logistics and Transportation (CIRRELT) on subjects related to maritime transportation, port-hinterland logistics, Chinese overseas investments and climate changes. He holds a master's degree in geography from the University of Montreal.

Claude Comtois is Professor at Montreal University and Scientific Advisor for Transport Canada's Port Working Group. His teaching and research addresses issues of port and maritime transport. He is the author or the co-author of over 100 scientific publications and 250 communications. He currently supervises projects on the competitiveness of port systems, the configuration of ocean transit networks, adaptation measures of maritime transport to climate changes and Arctic transport systems.

Brigitte Daudet is an expert on land issues and processes in urban management. She holds a postgraduate degree from the University of Caen Lower

Normandy, and was Lecturer at the University of Caen Lower Normandy (MRSH, CRESO). After a career with consulting firms, she was appointed as the Head of Urban Policy at the City of Luneville, and was afterwards Director of Projects for the Urban Community of Troyes, in charge of managing urban renewal projects. She has joined EM Normandie in 2007 as Senior Lecturer in Territory Development Management, conducted seminars on project management and created as well a round of professional conferences on territorial issues. Since the end of 2016, Brigitte Daudet has undertaken a PhD in Management Science on Port Governance in France and Ivory Coast at the IAE of Caen.

Jackie Dawson is a professor at the University of Ottawa, Department of Geography, Environment and Geomatics. She holds the Canada Research Chair (CRC) in Environment, Society and Policy and is a member of the Global Young Academy and the College of the Royal Society of Canada. She is an applied scientist working on the human and policy dimensions of environmental change in ocean and coastal regions. Her specific research interests include polar tourism and Arctic marine transportation trends and governance.

Olivier Faury is an assistant professor at EM Normandie in Le Havre. He completed his PhD in 2016 on the economics elements that may increase the attractiveness of the Northern Sea Route comparing to the Suez Canal Route. Before, he had worked 13 years as a Sales Manager including 11 years in the international transport industry in France as well as in Morocco for various companies such as SDV or STEF International. Since July 2016, he is still working on the Arctic issue and provides lectures on road, maritime transportation and logistics in bachelor and master I and II programs.

Laurent Fedi holds a juris doctorate in maritime law from the Faculty of Law at Aix-Marseille University (France). He started his professional career in a ship brokerage company. Since 2007, he has been Associate Professor at KEDGE Business School (Marseilles Campus, France). He directed the Maritime Department for eight years. He lectures on maritime law (safety, security and environmental protection) and business law at different levels of education. He currently leads different research projects, notably on the IMO Polar Code, on the evolution of maritime law on ships' air pollution and on the reform of port governance in the Mediterranean area. He has already published more than 40 scientific papers.

Changmin Jiang is Associate Professor at the Asper School of Business in the University of Manitoba, Canada. With his PhD degree in management science from the University of British Columbia, Canada, his major research area is transportation and logistics, which in particular involves economic and policy analysis. His studies focus on the competition and cooperation within and between different transport sectors, including air, rail and maritime.

Ronan Kerbiriou is GIS, Transport and Logistics Studies Engineer since 2012 at UMR IDEES laboratory, University of Le Havre. He is in charge of developing and keeping up to date the Geographic Information System of Devport. This GIS is regrouping data and information about logistic operation of the Seine valley and, more broadly, Europe. He carries out studies and shares his expertise with project partners (Port of Le Havre, CRITT TL, Sefacil Fondation, Haropa) to improve goods transport efficiency and development of the Seine valley port.

Suzanne Lalonde is a professor of International Law and the Law of the Sea at the Law Faculty of the University of Montreal and a research associate with the ArcticNet network of excellence in Canada. She holds a PhD in public international law from the University of Cambridge, King's College, obtained in 1997 under the supervision of James Crawford. Her publications and research focus on core international legal principles, especially those pertaining to sovereignty and the determination of boundaries on land and at sea, with a particular emphasis on the Arctic. She is the Canadian member of the International Law Association Committee currently investigating state practice in relation to straight baselines, a member of the Canadian Arctic Security Working Group and Co-editor of the journal *Ocean Development and International Law*.

Frédéric Lasserre worked as Consultant with the European Observatory of Geopolitics (OEG, Lyon, France) on the political and economic transformations of Central and Eastern Europe after the fall of the Berlin Wall; then as a Foreign Language Instructor in Japan. Between 1996 and 2001 he acted as Advisor in International Affairs on Asian Desks at the Quebec Ministry of Trade and Industry; and then with Investissement Québec, the Crown corporation responsible for the promotion of foreign investment in Quebec. He is Professor since 2001 in the Department of Geography at Laval University (Quebec, Canada), and a researcher with the Institut québécois des Hautes études internationales (IQHEI). He acted as Project Director with the ArcticNet research network between 2010 and 2015. He conducted extensive research in the field of maritime border disputes, water management and on the Arctic geopolitics, and published 23 books and over 120 refereed articles. He has coordinated since 2008 a multidisciplinary research team on the impacts of climate change on the governance of the Arctic, in particular with respect to navigation, resources and sovereignty disputes. In 2010 he published *Passages et mers arctiques. Géopolitique d'une région en mutation* [*Passages and Arctic Seas. Geopolitics of a Changing Region*], Presses de l'Université du Québec.

Alexandre Lavissière is Core Faculty in the fields of logistics, transportation, supply chain, international business and strategy. He obtained his MS and PhD in management from Kedge Business School. His research interests are in international trade, logistics and transportation, and more specifically Free Ports, dry ports, port management and airport handling. He was a Consultant in strategy for ten years for several companies and international institutions in more than 20 countries. He has participated and managed research projects for several governments, the World Bank and mineral companies. For two years, he was in charge of research projects at the Institute of Port Education and Research (IPER).

Yufeng (Travis) Lin is a research assistant at the Asper School of Business of the University of Manitoba, Canada. He earned his MSc from the University of Manitoba. He excels in transport sustainability, climate change adaptation and resilience, infrastructure planning and management, operation management and Arctic shipping.

Qiang Meng is currently Professor in the Department of Civil and Environmental Engineering at National University of Singapore. His research mainly focuses on transportation network modeling and optimization, shipping and intermodal freight transportation analysis, and quantitative risk assessment of transport operations. He has published more than 170 articles in the leading transportation and logistics journals. He is now Co-editor-in-Chief of *Transportation Research Part E* and Associate Editor of *Transportation Research Part B*.

Arild Moe is a research professor at the Fridtjof Nansen Institute in Norway, an independent social science research institute specializing in international energy, environmental and resource management politics. His degree is from the University of Oslo where he studied political science, Russian language and public law. Most of his research has been devoted to Russia, especially the energy sector and energy politics. Starting with participation in the Japanese-Russian-Norwegian International Northern Sea Route Programme (INSROP) he has conducted studies related to Arctic shipping. Moe is also involved in analyses of broader Arctic policy issues and recently directed a project studying the interests of Asian countries in the Arctic.

Adolf K.Y. Ng is Professor at the Asper School of Business of the University of Manitoba, Canada. Also, he is Vice President of the Hong Kong-Canada Business Association (Winnipeg Section). He earned his PhD from University of Oxford, UK, and he excels in transport geography, climate change adaptation and resilience, infrastructure planning and management, organizational change, global supply chains and Arctic shipping. He is a Senior Editor of *European Journal of International Management*, an Associate Editor of *Maritime Policy & Management* and *Asian Journal of Shipping and Logistics* and a Council Member of the International Association of Maritime Economists (IAME).

Jean-François Pelletier began his career as Transportation Analyst for Marine Policy and Programs of Transport Canada in Ottawa. He was then employed as Logistics Analyst for an emerging research center focusing on applied logistics. In parallel, he began teaching logistics at the Institut Maritime du Québec (IMQ) and eventually moved full time to this institution. At the IMQ, he quickly integrated the research team of Maritime Innovation where he conducted numerous applied research functions in the maritime logistics field. In 2007, he was hired as research associate and professor for the Institut portuaire d'enseignement et de recherche (IPER) in Le Havre, France. His duties for the

IPER consisted in providing training in port management issues and strategies as well as conducting applied research projects. He returned to Maritime Innovation in 2010 where he concentrated on applied research work for the marine industry. He joined CPCS in 2011 and provides strategic advice on transportation issues.

Arnaud Serry is Associate Professor in Geography at the University of Le Havre Normandy, specializing in maritime transport geography. Having held a position of Logistics Officer in an import-export business, his different missions led him to work in different aspects of transportation. He is also responsible for the project DEVPORT (www.devport.fr), which is based on the constitution of a Geographic Information System (GIS) dedicated to the Seine axis and which is oriented towards economic geography. His current research topics focus on three main areas: maritime transport in the Baltic Sea, the Seine valley and Normandy region and broader works on maritime transport including connections with modern technologies in the maritime world (AIS, LNG).

Brian Slack obtained his bachelor's degree from the London School of Economics and obtained master and doctorate degrees from McGill University. His professional career has been anchored by a position he held at Concordia University, where he is Distinguished Professor Emeritus. He has also held visiting positions at universities around the word. In 2003, he was awarded the Ullman Award for contribution to transport geography by the American Association of Geographers and in 2004 was awarded an honorary doctorate by the University of Le Havre. He has undertaken numerous scientific research studies applied to maritime and intermodal transport. He is a renowned expert on the relationship between traffic and infrastructures. He has served as Consultant for several port planning projects in Canada. Besides, he has a solid experience on maritime and rail transport in Europe, East Asia and Australia.

Pierre-Louis Têtu is working at the Unité Mixte de Recherche en Sciences Urbaines (UMR-SU/Urban Science Joint Research Unit [USJ-RU]) at Laval University, Quebec as a Research Professional for the Mobility and Transportation Unit while also a Part-Time Teacher in the Department of Geography, Environment, Geomatics of the University of Ottawa. From 2017 to 2019, Pierre-Louis was a Postdoctoral Fellow at the University of Ottawa. Funded by the Social Sciences and Humanities Research Council (SSHRC) of Canada Talent Program, he was involved in the Environment, Society, Policy Group (ESPG) led by Jackie Dawson. Dr. Têtu holds a PhD in Geographical Sciences from Laval University (Quebec, Canada) and specializes in policy and governance dimensions of transportation, extractive industries and shipping in the Arctic.

Dimitrios Theocharis is currently a PhD candidate in Cardiff Business School and his research topic is on the economic feasibility and environmental assessment of Arctic shipping. His research interests are in the areas of maritime transport, shipping economics and sustainability. After the completion of his undergraduate studies, he studied shipping and transport operations at a post-graduate level. Being passionate about research, he subsequently embarked on a PhD under a UK ESRC 3 + 1 Studentship. He holds a BSc in economics from Democritus University of Thrace, an MSc in international transport from Cardiff Business School and an MSc in Social Science Research Methods from Cardiff University.

Jérôme Verny is Professor at NEOMA Business School (France), as well as the Founder and Scientific Director of MOBIS, the international research institute for transport and innovative supply chain of NEOMA Business School. After earning a BS and a MS in economic geography & graduate engineering from the Higher School of Transport (Paris) and from the Transport, Planning, Environment Department at the National Advanced Civil Engineering School (ENPC, Paris), he received his PhD in transport and logistics from the Lille North of France University. He has worked internationally for the last 15 years with firms and public institutions in order to implement logistics innovations and performance optimization. Jerome's research interests mainly cover the fields of economic and transportation geography and international trade. In 2009, Dr. Verny was named the Young Researcher of the Year by OECD's International Transport Forum (ITF), with 52 ministers from ITF member countries present at Leipzig to witness his award. He manages several international research projects related to transportation and international trade. He has held various responsibilities within public and private organizations.

Chuanbei Zhou obtained her master's degree in transportation systems and management from National University, and her bachelor degree in logistics engineering in Dalian Maritime University (China). She is currently working in the Centre for Maritime Studies at the National University of Singapore.

Preface

Arctic shipping – where are we now

The use of Arctic shipping routes as a short cut between the Atlantic and the Pacific is an old dream. The first journey through the Northeast Passage was carried out by the Swedish explorer Adolf Erik Nordenskiöld 1878–79, whereas the Norwegian Roald Amundsen sailed through the Northwest Passage in 1903–06. However, it took still many years before the Arctic passages became a realistic option for international commercial shipping.

Whereas the NWP remained marginal as a shipping route, the Soviet Union created a special administration for the area between the Kara Gate and the Bering Strait calling it the Northern Sea Route and developed shipping as an important element in the conquest of Northern Siberia. From the early 1960s nuclear-powered icebreakers – a unique achievement – were used to escort convoys of cargo ships with a light ice class in and out of Siberia. Transits along the whole passage between east and west were few and far between and the whole area closed for foreign shipping. This changed with the speech Mikhail Gorbachev gave in Murmansk in 1987 where he called for international cooperation in the Arctic generally and in shipping specifically. In early 1991 the Northern Sea Route was officially opened for international shipping. Thus, it was political decisions, influenced by a re-assessment of the security situation and expectations for economic benefits that changed the conditions.

Soviet authorities enthusiastically supported an international research programme – INSROP, clarifying conditions for shipping in the Arctic, navigational, legal, environmental, technological, commercial, or political.[1] However, political declarations do not by themselves spur commercial interest. The response of international shipping was lukewarm – to say the least. The Soviets did not set up a convincing regulatory and administrative framework, and, most importantly, the general impression was that the ice situation made regular commercial navigation unpredictable and unsafe. This mood changed with the publication of reports documenting a receding ice cover, at the same time as the USGS 2008 assessment of the hydrocarbon potential in the Arctic attracted worldwide attention. Very rapidly, the Arctic became a hot topic. The changes in the natural conditions and understanding of the resource base gave way to expansive scenarios for shipping activity in the region.

In Russia, there was now a realization that something had to be done with the conditions for navigation, if the county were to reap benefits from the growing international interest in Arctic shipping. In 2010, discussions with potential international users were carried out and more flexible administrative treatment and lower icebreaker escort fees introduced, on a trial basis. The same year the first voyage through the Northern Sea Route with a foreign vessel, not visiting a Russian port, was carried out. The new regulations were written into law from 2013. The years up to then saw a rapid increase in international transits, but the absolute numbers were still very small. Some of the voyages clearly had an experimental character, many of the ships were in ballast. Even if many had the impression that Arctic shipping was booming, a firm basis for international transits was far from being established.

The Russian efforts developing international transits were spearheaded by Atomflot – the state-owned nuclear icebreaker fleet – which was required to cover some of its operational costs from escort fees. They saw new opportunities but were also driven by neediness. Technological developments had put the time-honoured Soviet convoy model – and Atomflot's business model – under pressure. New ships were developed for autonomous navigation, some of them double acting, which means that they can turn and be used for icebreaking on their own. Atomflot's largest customer Norilsk Nickel acquired its fleet of ice-strengthened cargo ships and annulled their contract with Atomflot in 2008, denying them of important income. International transits seemed like a promising alternative income source. However, the fees actually paid by the shipping companies were not quite up to expectation. In the new system, the fees were negotiable and international users, who could use alternative southern routes, were unwilling to pay high rates. Also the volume of trans-Arctic shipping sank from 2014. Partly this has been ascribed to a more uncertain international situation, but it probably had more to do with other developments.

The lure of Arctic transit shipping is always explained by shorter distance compared to the southern route. But distance in itself is not decisive for commercial calculations. It is comparative costs that matter. Distance affects costs since it means less time spent on a voyage and less fuel used. But these factors matter less when the freight market is lousy – as it has been for several years – meaning that it is cheap to charter a vessel, and if the fuel price is low – as it has been since 2014. In this situation the relative attraction of Arctic transit is reduced.

Fortunately for Atomflot a new customer arrived. The development of the liquid natural gas project on the eastern side of the Yamal Peninsula in Northwest Siberia – Yamal LNG – started only in 2013. The LNG plant and construction of the port in Sabetta entailed an explosion in transports of materials and equipment into Siberia, in many cases with help of icebreakers. With the start of gas production in December 2017 a new era in Arctic shipping began. The project included construction of 15 specially designed 299-meter-long LNG carriers able to break more than 2 meters of ice on their own. The carriers, which depart every 40 hours with their cargo, are owned and operated by various shipping joint ventures; 14 of them have international owners. Despite their icebreaking capabilities the project involves extensive use of Atomflot's icebreakers, notably to keep a channel open in the ice-infested waters along the peninsula. A channel permits higher speed and predictable sailing time for the very costly carriers. It also means that a firm income source for the icebreaker fleet has been found. In the coming years further LNG developments in the same region are expected. In fact, for some years the icebreaking capacity may be fully employed by LNG projects.

The LNG projects are also connected to another major development – the rise of Asia in Arctic affairs. Chinese companies are heavily involved in Yamal LNG and China is a major recipient of the gas. Chinese companies are part owners of most of the LNG carriers. But Chinese shipping companies have also looked closely for transit opportunities and a Chinese company opened a regular cargo route through the Arctic in 2018. Frequency and volumes are modest, but it shows a willingness to check out a niche market. Other big container companies remain sceptical of Arctic transit, since the corridor will continue to be seasonal still for many years and drifting ice can disturb individual journeys and make just-in-time schedules impossible; besides there are no real markets along the way.

As of now the commercial euphoria over Arctic shipping developments has subsided. Few, if any, will talk about the NSR as a new Suez Canal now. The NWP has remained little utilized for international traffic, mainly because of complicated natural conditions and environmental concerns, but also because the Canadian government has not supported it. However, an increase in destinational shipping connected to resource extraction in the Canadian Arctic can be seen.

Even with a more sober assessment of the potential there are interesting developments underway which require new research and analysis. Economic assessments under new, realistic assumptions is badly needed, not least the impact of international markets. Understanding the interlinkages between shipping and industrial development projects and ports connecting sea routes to inland waterways is another theme where more can be done. A very new development, calling for evaluation, is large-scale cruise tourism, especially in the Canadian Arctic.

Many factors will continue to impact Arctic shipping. In this brief introduction, political, environmental, technological, as well as commercial factors have been mentioned. Combining analysis of these drivers with establishment of new regulations safeguarding the natural environment and people in the Arctic remain a challenge for analysts as well as practitioners.

Arild Moe
Fridtjof Nansen Institute, Norway

Note

1 Douglas Brubaker, R., & Claes Lykke, R. (2010). A review of the International Northern Sea Route Program (INSROP) – 10 years on. *Polar Geography*, *33*(1–2), 15–38.

Introduction

Olivier Faury

The exploitation of the Arctic Ocean is a potential source of benefits for various industries, at the forefront of which are those related to shipping and extraction.

The recent attempts by COSCO and MAERSK to test transit along the Northern Sea Route (NSR) and the numerous academic articles published over recent years, tend to show the global interest toward the navigability of this ocean. Sailing though the Arctic may represent, in regards of the origin and destination, a 40% distance shortcut compared to conventional shipping lanes either through the Panama or Suez Canals. This shortcut may, hence, represent a time and fuel saving for shipowners, whether they deal in containers or bulk trade.

The Arctic area is also considered for its oil and gas resources with 22% of the world's reserves to be discovered, with however most of them located within the Exclusive Economic Zone of coastal states. Likewise, the Arctic is rich in minerals. One could mention, as an example, the nickel coming from Norilsk in Siberia or the numerous mines being developed in the Canadian Arctic.

The use of the Arctic Ocean as a transit lane and the exploitation of the mines and oil and gas fields are not the only source of potential economic development. The cruise industry has to be considered as one of them. The journey of the *Crystal Serenity* cruise ship through the Canadian Arctic has already attracted the interest of academics. Other cruisers have started to invest in polar-class vessels such as the French cruiser Ponant or its competitors, Hurtigruten and Lindblad. However, several cruise ships were blocked in September 2018 and could not enter the Northwest Passage (NWP), forcing the cruise companies to cancel the voyages. Although the Arctic is an area with a considerable economic potential, it also remains an ocean with numerous economic and geographic constraints.

One of the most serious obstacles lies in the ice extent and thickness. Even if sea ice melts at an accelerated pace due to global warming, no academic predicts an ice-free ocean on a year-round basis, meaning that ships will meet drifting ice in spring and fall; this is turn represents a critical risk for vessel integrity requiring ships to break through ice in winter. The seasons will keep bringing back a long period of darkness and extreme cold that are a danger for ships and crew members and may influence their ability to react properly to an emergency.

The variation of sea-ice extent and thickness, and the complexity to forecast it, is a major limitation to transit and more precisely to container shipping driven by just-in-time constraints. Thus, the use of the Arctic for sealift seems to be more interesting for bulk transportation even though most of the analyses done by academics have focused on containers. Sea ice, unforgiving weather and inaccurate charts make for more complex navigation. Remoteness, though not Arctic-specific but a major constraint, adds to the complexity rescuers would face in the event of an accident.

Because of the extreme climate conditions, navigation within the Arctic implies considering numerous aspects, such as ships dedicated to the area with a specific hull and engine power, and crew with extensive experience and skills for ice-infested waters. Depending on the ice conditions as well as the vessel's ice class, the shipowner may be asked by underwriters to be assisted by an icebreaker.

Yet all these specificities have a cost that hampers the economic development of the Arctic. These constraints to shipping in Arctic waters entail higher costs that are considered as being a significant economic factor to analyse when sailing within the Arctic, along with constraints on the reliability of just-in-time deliveries for container shipping.

Moreover, climate does act negatively not only on navigation, but also on the cost of infrastructures. Ports are one of the main pillars of Arctic development, since they serve the triple purpose of safety, economic development and maintenance of national sovereignty. Until now, their low number and density has not secured navigation and has not provided a place for vessels damaged by the ice, an analysis shared by underwriters and academics. The remoteness of oil, gas and mineral fields represents a challenge for the modernization, maintenance, building or the profitability of ports. One example of this is the port of Sabetta.

Due to the low resilience of the environment and to the risks weighing upon sailors and ships, a legal framework has been enforced. January 2017 saw the implementation of the Polar Code (PC) as a new constraining tool to govern navigation within polar waters. It inscribes itself in the continuity of the previous international codes and conventions, but the prophylactic aspect of this code is unprecedented, as it integrates numerous years of risk management. Yet the question of potential conflict between national regulations and the new born PC may exist and have an impact on risk management of this area.

As explained above, the Arctic is a complex system impacted by external factors (economic and climate) but also by internal parameters such as port networks and legal framework. The purpose of this book is to provide a global vision of this ocean by considering these parameters. To do so, this book is organized in three parts dealing with navigation, legal framework and ports.

The first portion focuses on shipping aspects. The first chapter "Weather Constraints on Ships Serving Coastal Settlements in Nunavik, 1993 to 2016" stresses the impact of climate conditions, other than ice, on the navigation within the Canadian part of the Arctic, and this since the onset of climate change. The second chapter, "Approaches of the Profitability of Arctic Shipping in the Literature" provides an overview of the analyses done on the Arctic in recent years. The author highlights that most of them deal with containers and are concentrated on cost analysis. The third one, "Modeling the Profitability of Liner Arctic Shipping" analyses the attractiveness of the Arctic for the transportation of containers. In this case the author looks at the impact the different types of fuel may have with different pairs of Origin/Destination. In addition, the fourth one "An Economic Analysis on the NSR Viability of an Ice-Class 1A Oil Tanker Vessel" investigates the profitability of the NSR in the case of bulk transportation and looks at the way economic parameters such as fuel, icebreaker fees and freight rate impact it. The fifth chapter, "Compared Transit Traffic Analysis along the NSR and the NWP" analyses the evolution of the different existing cargo flows along both the NSR and NWP. The overview integrates the origin and destination of the different cargo loaded and the type of ships for a period between 2011 and 2016. The last chapter dealing with shipping navigation, "The Evolution and Relative Competitiveness of Global Arctic Cruise Tourism Destinations" emphasizes the economic potential of the cruise shipping within the Arctic. To do so, authors provide a global vision of the cruise industry within the Arctic. If the development of the cruise industry shall have a positive economic impact, it may also have a disruptive influence upon local communities and face challenges such as the lack of non-homogenous infrastructures.

The second part of this book deals with the legal framework and this section is composed of two chapters. "Arctic Shipping Law from Atomised Legislations to Integrated Regulatory Framework: The Polar Code (R)Evolution?" focuses on the way the code project has evolved over the years and is integrated within the international legal framework. If the first chapter of this part is concentrated on the relation between the PC and the international framework, the second one, "Shipping in the Canadian and Russian Arctic: Domestic Legal Responses to the Polar Code", explores the way the national legal frameworks react with the PC.

Finally, the third and last part of this book provides an analysis of the development of Arctic ports. First, "An Analysis of the Arctic Ports" offers an overview of the existing ports, the manner in which they provide a safe place for the maintenance of vessels and the way they interact within the same country in order to ease the exportation of cargo and the supply of local communities. "Analysis of the Russian Arctic Port System Using AIS Data", the second chapter, focuses on the Russian part of this area. It demonstrates how Russian ports have integrated Arctic constraints in order to ease the exportation of raw materials. "Free Ports as a Tool to Develop the Navigation in the Arctic" tackles the issue of the relevance of Free Ports within the Arctic and suggests that the implementation of such a tool may offer the possibility to settle population and provide a sustainable economic development, independent from the exploitation of raw materials. The last chapter sheds light on the development of the Port of Churchill on Hudson Bay, in the Canadian subarctic region, once considered the gateway to the Arctic Bridge sea route, and now struggling to find a viable business model.

Part I

The economics of Arctic shipping

1 Weather constraints on ships serving coastal settlements in Nunavik, 1993 to 2016

Claude Comtois, Brian Slack and
Alex Champagne-Gélinas

Introduction

Maritime transport plays a key role in the economy of Nunavik, the territory north of the 55th parallel in Quebec. While the entire territory lies south of the Arctic Circle, its character and climate possess Arctic characteristics, especially because the coast is ice-bound for more than half the year. It comprises 14 Inuit communities situated along the coast, and a private port facility at Deception Bay that serves two mining operations (see Figure 1.1). There are no road connections between the villages and the outside world. Air transport provides passenger connections and the means to ship high-value goods such as electronics, small appliances and fresh food. All other goods depend on marine connections. There is a major difference between Deception Bay and the villages. Deception Bay provides berths for ocean-going ships, particularly bulk carriers involved in the shipments of minerals produced at the mines located inland over 100 km from the port. It also handles supplies for the mining operations, particularly fuel oil, general supplies and building materials. The port infrastructures permit shipping throughout the year. The villages, on the other hand, possess no formal port infrastructures, and navigation is restricted by seasonal ice conditions in both the approaches and the landing areas. Petroleum products need to be transferred through flexible hoses that are extended between the ships anchored offshore and the land-based storage facilities. Non-liquid products have to be unloaded from the ships to barges that transfer the freight onto the beaches where the cargo is lifted ashore. Service is entirely seasonal. Because of these distinctions the chapter focuses on marine transport serving the 14 communities.

The climate of the Arctic is changing and is predicted to change still further. There is considerable attention being paid as to how shipping will change too (Pizzolato, Howell, Derksen, Dawson, & Copland, 2014). The focus of much of this attention is being devoted towards the possibilities of exploiting the Arctic Ocean as a short cut to link Pacific and Atlantic markets. Most of the literature is optimistic, based on climate change model predictions (Melia, Haines, & Hawkins, 2016; Smith & Stephenson, 2013), and on recent changes in ice conditions (Prowse et al., 2009). Others take a more cautious approach based on shipping knowledge (Lasserre & Pelletier, 2011). There is some research on shipping

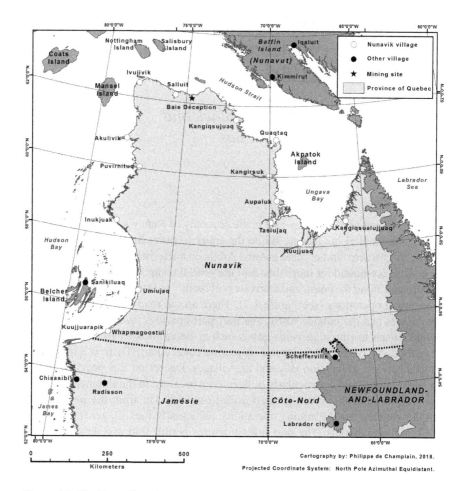

Figure 1.1 The Nunavik region

between the Canadian Arctic and outside markets involving the exploitation of mineral resources (Pizzolato et al., 2014; Giguère, Comtois, & Slack, 2017). Literature on coastal shipping is largely composed of industry publications (Dunn, 2015; Streiger, 2016; Spears, 2016). Academic research is quite limited (Brooks & Frost, 2012). While all of the cited literature stresses the importance of ice conditions, the question of how other elements of Arctic weather impact on shipping operations has been largely ignored. Ice is not the only environmental challenge faced by shipping and to ignore other weather constraints means that forward projections of marine transport in the Arctic are not realistic.

The objective of this chapter is to examine how marine operations in Nunavik are impacted by weather. It begins by providing a brief overview of coastal shipping in Nunavik: the characteristics of the fleet and how the villages are served. It goes on to analyse how coastal shipping in Nunavik is influenced by several key weather conditions whose importance was raised by the captains of vessels engaged in servicing the villages. Information was obtained through a detailed analysis of ships logs, and hourly and daily weather data from Environment Canada from 1993 to 2016.

Overview of shipping in Nunavik

The 14 villages in Nunavik depend on coastal shipping for the majority of their needs. The ships are loaded mainly in the Montreal region but also in Quebec City and Newfoundland. The ships then sail up the coast of Labrador and into the Hudson Strait to access the villages in Ungava Bay and on the east coast of Hudson Bay. It should be noted that the ships also serve villages on the west coast of Hudson Bay and in Nunavut. Shipping services are seasonal. The shipping season extends for 168 days from mid-June to the end of November. The actual frequency of services vary, with more intense services towards the beginning and end of the season (see Figure 1.2). Although there has been a great deal of discussion of recent shrinkage of Arctic ice cover, the length of the actual shipping season for coastal shipping has changed only modestly, with some recent earlier arrivals in late June, but there is great variability in the date of the last sailing in November (see Figure 1.2).

None of the villages possess port infrastructures. The vessels anchor offshore and the cargoes are transported to the shore by different methods that depend on the type of cargo. For fuels, a flexible hose is extended from the tankers with the aid of an ancillary tug boat offloaded from the vessel to the land-based pipelines that serve fuel storage facilities. In several villages safe anchorage may be 2 km from the shore. For general cargo vessels, tugs and barges must first be offloaded from the ship and then the actual freight is discharged onto the barge or pontoon, with the assistance of the tug, and thence to a floating dock or onto the beach for unloading. All these activities are dependent on suitable weather conditions.

Since there is a considerable time difference between vessel departures from the south and vessel arrivals in Nunavik, and because the number of services is constrained by the short navigation season, organising the services is highly complex.

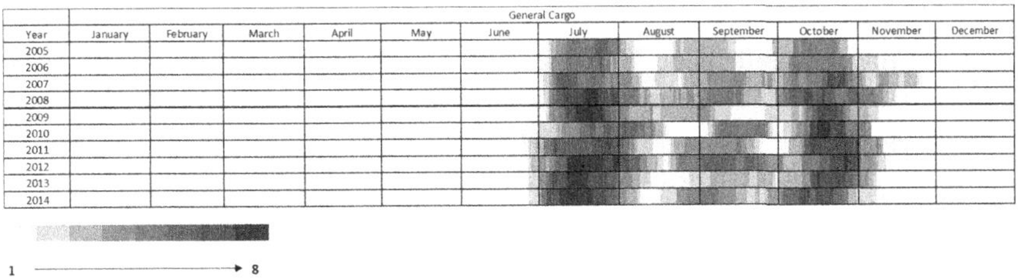

Figure 1.2 Frequency of shipping service in Nunavik

In the case of fuel supplies, the communities must ensure that all the needs for heating, electricity generation and transport for the year are planned correctly. For general cargo it is even more complex, because building materials, vehicles, certain foodstuff and personal items must be anticipated and ordered months in advance. With such a wide range of types of goods carried most are now containerised, except certain large capital equipment and project cargo that requires special storage and handling.

In 2016, over 200 000 litres of fuels were transported to Nunavik. Fuel shipments to the villages of Nunavik are provided by Petro Nav, a subsidiary of Groupe Desgagnés. The ships that serve the 14 Nunavik villages are small tankers (<10 000 gross registered tons [GRT]), because of the need to find a safe anchorage as close as possible to the shore. The number of vessels deployed each season has grown from two to three, and each vessel makes typically four voyages per navigation season between the refineries, Nunavik and other settlements in the Arctic. In 2014 Petro Nav stationed one of its largest tankers (75 000 GRT) to serve as an offshore storage facility in Diana Bay near the village of Quaqtaq. The goal was to reduce the number of trips the smaller tankers would have to make back to the St Lawrence ports. The company repeated the operation in 2015, but it was not continued in 2016. The experiment was deemed not to be a success. The costs of using a large ship as a floating storage facility over many weeks were high, particularly in terms of operating and insurance costs. In addition, it required additional transfers between ships, a cost and safety consideration.

There are no precise data on general cargo shipments in Nunavik, but we estimate that the annual traffic is approximately 150 000 tons. Both general cargo and fuel shipments are growing, in part due to the high population growth in the villages (almost double the rate of the province of Quebec as a whole) and the upgrading of housing and public facilities, but also due to the increased motorisation of Inuit society: including trucks, snowmobiles, all-terrain vehicles, etc.

Two shipping lines serve Nunavik on a regular basis with general cargo. Nunavut East Arctic Shipping (NEAS) maintains regular services to the 14 villages during the shipping season, and also makes calls at Deception Bay and several other settlements in Nunavut. Five vessels with capacities of 5 000 to 13 000 GRT are deployed. Their individual itineraries vary throughout the season. The Groupe Desgagnés maintains services to the Eastern Arctic with five vessels of between 7 000 and 17 000 GRT. Again the services include calls at Deception Bay and Nunavut as well as at the villages of Nunavik.

Three other carriers have, on occasion, made calls in Nunavik over the last ten years, including FedNav, McKeil Marine and Wagenborg Shipping. Usually, these are not regular services but special deliveries involving project cargo that requires special handling because of its dimensions or weight.

The shipping industry in coastal Nunavik has several distinctive features. First are the small scale of individual shipments and the total volume of trade. Second are the high costs due to the small size of the trade and the considerable imbalance between imports and exports. All the villages import far more than they ship out, resulting in vessels making the return trips largely without a revenue cargo.

Third are the challenges of the Arctic environment where various weather conditions constrain the efficiency of shipping operations. Even though shipping rates to Nunavik are high compared with almost anywhere else in the world, they are nevertheless far cheaper than by air, the only other way to access the villages. Published rates reveal that general freight shipped from Montreal to Nunavik is ten times more costly by air than by sea (rates published on the web sites of First Air [2017] and NEAS [2017]).

Measuring weather conditions that impact on shipping

The issue of weather and other environmental challenges confronting Arctic shipping is one of the most important topics that arose out of our interviews with captains of cargo ships that have sailed in Arctic waters over many years and with shipping company officials. These actors represent an exceptional resource for understanding the operational and commercial difficulties of sailing in Arctic waters. In this study, we have been fortunate to obtain the cooperation of all the major shipping lines serving Nunavik. Not only have we been able to obtain an understanding of shipping from the perspectives of some of the captains who each have had more than 20 years of sailing experience in the Arctic, but we have transcribed the individual logs of the vessels of one of the companies that has been engaged in Arctic services for more than 40 years. This database records the positions of ships and lengths of stay in ports of call, as well as weather and sea conditions during their transits. We have used the logs to follow the movement of the ships as well as the lengths of time they spend at each village. While the logs record actual weather conditions at specific places and at specific times, there is no indication of how representative these conditions are over the shipping season as a whole. For this reason, we have had to turn to weather data from Environment Canada.

Although the climate record of Environment Canada goes back to 1953, observations from some villages were not collected until later. In order to get comparable data for all villages, the official records of weather conditions between 1993 and 2016 are used in this study. The ships captains that were interviewed spoke of the extreme local variability in weather conditions, especially between the offshore waters and the land. By comparing data from the ships' logbooks with the data from Environment Canada, we found that the weather stations of most villages recorded similar enough data with the log books to be used for our analysis. In the cases of Ivujivik, Kuujuaq and Salluit the weather observations are recorded at the airports that are many kilometres inland, and these villages were excluded because the differences between the land-based data and the offshore data.

A day-long workshop was held on July 27, 2017 involving team members, climatologists and representatives from three shipping lines to assess the degree of impact of weather on shipping operations. Three types of weather conditions were identified as having particular impacts on the safety and security of the vessels at anchor and while engaged in transferring cargoes between ship and shore. First, is poor visibility which is produced by a number of weather conditions such as fog, blizzards or intense rainfall. Whatever its cause, poor visibility is a constraint on operations, since it is important that those on board can see what is taking place between the vessel and activities on land. This has both safety and operational efficiency dimensions. Second is wind, which has a very important effect on the safety of the ships at anchor. It is also is an important consideration affecting the ability to transfer cargoes between the vessels and the barges that carry general cargoes to the shore, as well as the flexible hoses that are laid out for fuel transfers. Third are freezing temperatures. Ice is a major navigational hazard, and freezing temperatures may affect the safety of personnel during loading and unloading.

Visibility

Visibility is measured by the Meteorological Optical Range (MOR) (Dunlop, 2008). MOR is the distance at which an object or light can be clearly discerned. It is a scale that varies from MOR 0 ('dense fog') where visibility is less than 50 yards to MOR 9 ('exceptional visibility') where objects further away than 30 miles may still be seen. In this study we use MOR 2 as our threshold for poor visibility. Described as 'fog', this level is reached when objects beyond 600 yards (548,6 m) are not visible.

Shipping is impacted in a number of ways when poor visibility is encountered. At sea in Arctic waters, speeds are reduced, because 'growlers' (small floating ice floes) are not detectible by radar. In harbour, ship discharging operations may be halted or delayed because of the poor visibility between ship and shore. For example, under MOR 2 conditions, deploying hoses from ship to shore is not permitted, and if the hose has already been deployed all pumping operations must be interrupted.

Here, MOR 2 conditions are presented as the number of days of occurrence as a proportion of the 168 day-long shipping season for the period 1993–2016.

Daily occurrence of poor visibility during the shipping season

During the navigation season poor visibility is encountered on average nearly 9% of days, which equates to a mean of 15 days. This is a rate of occurrence that is comparatively low. However, when poor visibility is encountered it can have important consequences on ship operations. Figure 1.3 indicates that average annual variations from one year to the next are modest, but over the most recent years there has been greater variability, and a slight upward trend has occurred since 1993.

Variations between villages

There are very important differences between the villages (see Table 1.1). Inukjuak and Kuujjuarapik experience poor visibility most frequently, at more than one standard deviation above the mean, the equivalent of 23 days during the shipping season. In Quaqtaq and Umiujag poor visibility is encountered on 21

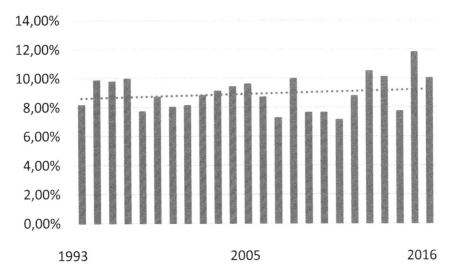

Figure 1.3 Frequency of days with visibility ≤ MOR 2 (% of shipping season)

Table 1.1 Frequency of visibility, wind and freezing temperature conditions during the shipping season 1993–2016 (% of shipping season)

	Visibility MOR ≤2	Wind Force ≥5	Wind Force ≥7	Days <0c
Akulivik	2,2	22,50	1,77	20,68
Aupaluk	4,5	17,30	1,06	18,93
Inukjuak	14,8	30,12	2,17	17,39
Kangiqsualujjuaq	5,2	5,22	0,31	20,38
Kangiqsujuaq	11,0	26,2	4,60	25,97
Kangirsuk	10,8	12,85	1,38	22,02
Kuujjuarapik	14,3	21,14	1,10	13,21
Puvirnituq	7,8	28,32	2,46	21,04
Quaqtaq	12,7	28,92	9,54	24,26
Tasiujaq	0,7	23,71	5,40	18,84
Umiujaq	12,2	21,29	2,87	15,25
Average	8,7	21,6	2,96	19,82
St. deviation	4,9	7,49	0,03	3,70

days on average. At the other extreme are Tasiujaq and Akulivik where poor visibility is experienced on only two days during the shipping season which is below one standard deviation from the mean. The spread between two days per shipping season and 23 days is a very important difference for shipping operations. General location appears to play no role in the incidence of poor visibility, since there are both high and low occurrence villages on both Hudson and Ungava Bays. Local site conditions are the determining factors.

Wind speed

Wind is measured according to the Beaufort Scale (Dunlop, 2008). Two sets of wind speed values are presented. The first is based on wind speeds equal to and above Beaufort Scale 5. This indicates that wind speeds are recorded at over of 29 km/h. The second is Beaufort Scale 7 where winds in excess of 50 km/h occur, a level that is referred to as 'near gale' with waves between 4 m and 5,5 m in height.

The coasts of Nunavik are windy. During the navigation season one day in five on average experience winds in excess of Beaufort Scale 5. At this level of wind speed, ships are barred from approaching the villages. If they are already at anchor, discharging cargo can continue, but depending on wind direction and tidal conditions it might be halted.

At Beaufort Scale 7 all ship transfers must be terminated, and when there are sustained winds reaching Scale 8, the ships must move and find shelter.

Daily occurrence of winds equal or greater than Force 5 and 7 during the shipping season

With the notable exception of the first year of record and the most recent year, the overall yearly trend of Beaufort Scale 5 wind speeds in Nunavik have been constant (see Figure 1.4). There has been little change over the years from 1994 to 2015.

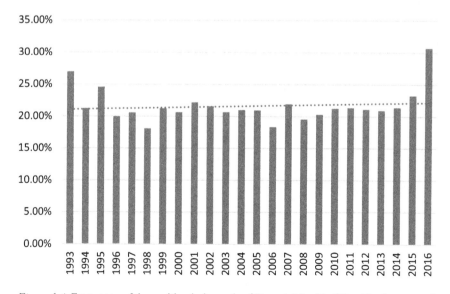

Figure 1.4 Frequency of days with wind speeds of Force ≥5 (as % of the shipping season)

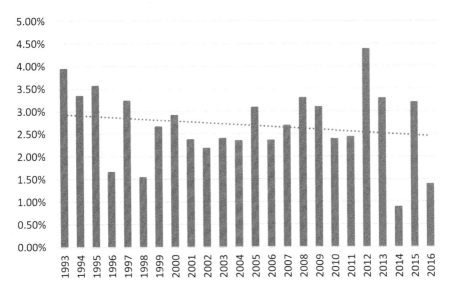

Figure 1.5 Frequency of days with wind speeds Force ≥7 (as % of the shipping season)

At Beaufort Scale 7 all shipping operations are halted. On average these conditions are encountered during only 2.96% of the shipping season (the equivalent of 5 days). Although the average occurrence is low the results reveal greater variability year to year than the Scale 5 winds. Overall, a slight lower trend of occurrence of Scale 7 winds between 1993 and 2016 is indicated (see Figure 1.5).

The results reveal that all parts of Nunavik are exposed to wind and that its occurrence has not changed significantly over the last 22 years. There are no regional differences in occurrence, indicating that villages in Hudson Bay, Hudson Strait and Ungava Bay are exposed to comparable episodes of wind occurrence.

Variations between villages

On average villages experience Force 5 winds on 21.6% of the shipping season (or 36 days). With three exceptions, the individual averages for villages over the period cluster around the overall mean (see Table 1.1). Inukjuak is the windiest village, experiencing the frequency of Beaufort Scale 5 winds more than one standard deviation above the mean or 51 days. Two villages record the least frequency of wind: Kangiqsualujjuaq where average Force 5 winds occur two standard deviations below the overall mean or five days during the shipping season a year and Kangirsuk where the occurrence is one standard deviation below the mean, or 21 days.

Again there are very considerable differences between the overall means of villages with Force 7 winds. Four villages experience Force 7 winds less frequently than the others. Kangiqsualujjuaq again is the least windy village, experiencing near gale conditions on only one day per season. For Aupaluk, Kangirsuk and Kuujjuarapik Force 7 winds are encountered on approximately two days per year. At the other end of the scale, Quaqtaq experiences Force 7 winds on 16 days during the shipping season, while Tasiujaq (nine days) and Kangiqsujuaq (eight days) are other exposed villages. Quaqtaq appears to be particularly exposed to gale force winds. It is among the villages with the highest records of Force 5 winds, but not quite reaching one standard deviation above the mean, but its experience of Force 7 places it as an extreme case (see Table 1.1). In examining the individual average of all yearly means of Force 7 winds for Quaqtaq its scores are always above the averages of all the villages, but in 2000, 2008 and 2012 the differences were pronounced, indicating episodes of unusual gale frequencies.

Wind speed differences clearly reflect local site configurations. The villages recording lower than average strong winds are on protected sites. Kangiqsualujjuaq is located on the eastern side of Ungava Bay on a deep but narrow north-south inlet in which there is a natural embayment on the eastern shore which provides a south-facing settlement site that is surrounded by hills. Kangirsuk is on the western part of Ungava Bay on a north shore of an embayment deep in an east-west aligned river estuary. The site is south facing and is surrounded by hills. On the other hand Kuujjuarapik is the most southerly settlement in Nunavik, and is located on the northwest shore at the mouth of an estuary on the eastern shore of Hudson Bay. Unlike the other two low-wind incidence villages there are no immediate hills providing protection to Kuujjuarapik.

Of the two windiest villages Quaqtaq is sited on a west-facing bay open to winds from across the fetch of Hudson Bay, while Tasiujaq is on the west shore of Ungava Bay at the head of a northeast-facing channel that funnels winds from across the Bay.

Freezing temperatures

This value is based on the number of days during the shipping season when the maximum temperatures fail to rise above 0c. It is clear that this metric is very general and open to broad interpretations. Several other measures relating to cold weather were considered, such as the incidence of freezing rain, and the duration of cold spells, but were found to be wanting either because directly recorded data is unavailable or because the incidence during the shipping season was found to be highly irregular from one year to the next. Sea-ice conditions during the navigation season were available for only three of the selected villages. The metric employed here merely indicates that frosts will occur, that exposed pools of water will freeze, that any precipitation will fall as snow, the rate of melting of shore or surface sea ice may be reduced. Its availability does provide means of comparing the differences between villages regarding the incidence of potentially adverse thermal conditions.

The potential impacts of freezing temperatures on shipping depend on their intensity and duration. Coatings of ice and frost on the vessels may represent a safety hazard for personnel and reduce the efficiency of equipment. At its most severe, coatings of ice may cause problems for communication antennas. On shore, hoar frost and ice represent challenges to the operation of equipment and vehicles and the safety of personnel.

Daily occurrence of temperatures equal or greater than 0c during the shipping season

For Nunavik the mean incidence of days of freezing temperatures between 1993 and 2010 in the 11 villages as a proportion of the shipping season is 20,5% or 34 days. While Figure 1.5 reveals a slight cyclical pattern of occurrences between 1993 to 2010, in fact the totals vary from year to year in a narrow range (see Figure 1.6). There is little evidence of a recent decline in the number of freezing days during the shipping season.

VARIATIONS BETWEEN VILLAGES

There are differences between villages in terms of the number of days with freezing temperatures (see Table 1.1). Kangiqsujuaq experiences the greatest number of freezing days during the shipping seasons with 44 days, or more than one standard deviation above the mean. It is the most northerly settlement of those selected. The villages with the shortest number of freezing days are Kuujjuarapik (22 days) and Umiujaq (26 days) that are one standard deviation below the mean. These are

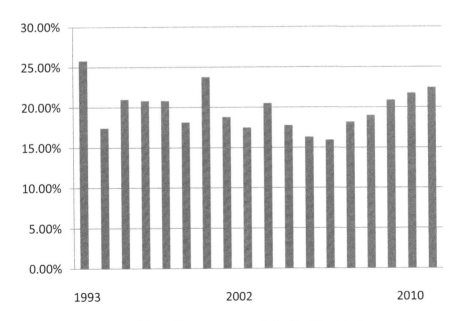

Figure 1.6 Frequency of days with temperatures ≤0c (as % of the shipping season)

the two most southerly located villages on Hudson Bay. A strong meridional relationship exists therefore for this variable, unlike the more site-determinant factors affecting the distribution of the other variables.

Comparison with weather observations from logbooks

In the logs there were 784 observations of MOR 0 to 2. This total represents 5,2% of the 14 980 separate records of visibility contained in the log books. This score is lower than the climate averages from Environment Canada, which reports a frequency of 8.4%. A different situation is revealed when wind speeds obtained from the logs are compared with climate means. The logs indicate that out of 29 461 wind speed entries 30,5% are equal or higher than Force 5, and 7,2% are of Force 7 or higher. The climate records are 21,6% and 2,96% respectively.

These differences arise from the fact that ships only record weather data when they are anchored near the villages. If the weather is good, they discharge faster and stay for a shorter amount of time. When the weather is bad, operations are slowed, and the ships stay longer. This means that there are necessarily more records in the logbooks when the weather is bad than when the weather is good. There is also the fact that while we have included weather data from villages where the airports are relatively close to the village, fog and wind are weather elements that are notoriously variable by site, particularly at the interface of land and sea. While the ships logs are recording conditions that actually occurred during each visit we are forced to use the official climate reports because the log-based data at present is not broken down village by village.

For freezing temperatures the mean number of log entries is 6,2%, or the equivalent of ten days. From the official climate records the proportion of freezing days is 19,82% or 34 days. We suggest this discrepancy partly because of the explanations noted above because of the difference between water and land locations where the temperatures are recorded.

A quantitative analysis of the impacts of weather elements on shipping

While visibility, wind and freezing temperatures represent elements of weather that are particularly constraining on shipping operations in the coastal waters of Nunavik, there is a need to assess quantitatively their impacts. Average vessel turnaround time (ATT) is presented as a particularly relevant metric of shipping operations, because in the case of poor weather, shipping operations at best are curtailed and at worse cancelled. In the academic literature on shipping ATTs are seen as a critical factor, especially in container shipping because supply chains demand on-time performance, and port delays have been examined as key causes of service unreliability (Saldanha, Russell, & Tyworth, 2006; Ducruet, Itoh, & Merk, 2014; Slack, Comtois, Wiegmans, & Witte, 2017). Coastal shipping in Nunavik is completely different in scale, scope and character, but here weather-induced delays in port can add greatly to the overall service time and operating costs. The shipping lines sailing in Arctic waters are even more dependent on weather than all others sailing across non-polar seas.

Pearson product-moment correlations between the dependent variable, ATT and the village mean scores of three weather conditions are revealed in Tables 1.2 and 1.3.

Visibility and temperatures present the strongest correlations, but none are statistically significant at 0,05. One factor is that the number of cases (11) is small. We undertook a multiple regression analysis using ATTs as dependent variable and the four weather conditions as independent variables. While the multiple R^2 is 0,627, the adjusted R square coefficient is 0,012 indicating that there are problems with some of the independent variables. Examination of the p values of the independent variables revealed that all are greater than p=0,15, and therefore none are significant statistically.

Table 1.2 Average turnaround times at the villages 1993–2016 (in hours)

Villages	ATTs
Akulivik	47,14
Aupaluk	66,33
Inukjuak	101,81
Kangiqsualujjuaq	33,82
Kangiqsujuaq	100,88
Kangirsuk	79,71
Kuujjuarapik	269,89
Puvirnituq	88,19
Quaqtaq	75,5
Tasiujaq	65,92
Umiujaq	35,22

Table 1.3 Correlation and regression coefficients between ATTs and climate variables

	r with ATT
Visibility ≤ 2	0,50
Wind Force ≥ 5	0,20
Wind Force ≥ 7	−0,12
Temperature ≥ 0c	−0,42
Multiple regression of all four climate variables	R^2 = 0,627 Adjusted R^2 = 0,012

Discussion

Weather conditions at 11 villages in Nunavik have been shown to vary from year to year, but overall it is difficult to identify any significant trends over the period 1993 to 2016. Differences in the occurrence of weather conditions between individual villages are more pronounced. The variability in weather presents particular challenges to the shipping lines. Each year their operations have to confront weather patterns that are different in varying degrees to those of the preceding years. This uncertainty has to be factored into their service schedules and timetables. The differences in weather conditions experienced at the villages offer an even greater challenge. Although experience has provided the companies and the ships captains with a deep knowledge of the weather particularities of each village, when it comes to the actual conditions they encounter on arrival, they confront uncertainty. Day-to-day weather forecasting in Nunavik is often unreliable. Ships captains told of the frustrations of receiving a forecast of favourable weather at a village only to find on arrival that conditions prevented operations.

The variability and unpredictability of weather represents a particularly acute challenge for shipping in Nunavik because there are no port infrastructures at the villages. If there were wharves alongside which vessels could berth, cargo transfers could take place during all but the most extreme weather conditions. At the same time safety would be greatly enhanced. The reasons why port infrastructures have not been built at any of the villages are largely economic: the cost of construction and maintenance; and, the small amount of traffic generated by each village with only a few ship calls over the shipping season. Another factor, however, is political, with a historic lack of interest by Transport Canada in investing in port infrastructures in the Arctic despite it having a specific mandate to serve isolated communities. This is different from Greenland where the coastal villages possess port infrastructures (Brooks & Frost, 2012).

There have been increasing pressures on the federal government to invest in port infrastructures in Nunavut, and there is now a project to build a terminal to serve Iqaluit, the Territory capital. It is expected to be completed by 2020 (Streiger, 2016). The government of Quebec is committed to improve the transport infrastructure of Nunavik through its ambitious 'Plan Nord'. No specific projects have been drawn up as yet, but the results of this study suggest that the weather conditions examined in this study should be an element in the site selection process. For example, a comparison between the 11 villages provides a rank order of suitability based on the weather elements (see Table 1.4). The ranks of each village are scored on a scale of 1 to 11, with 1 being the most favourable. The results indicate that Aupaluk and Kangiqsualujjuaq are tied with the best scores, while Quaqtaq is indicated as the village exhibiting the most challenging conditions.

Other factors would have to be considered as well. Site conditions and bathymetry represent important considerations. Perhaps the most important factors would have to be locational and economic. If one port was to be developed it would have

Table 1.4 Ranking of villages based on weather scores

	Visibility ≤2	Wind ≥5	Temp ≤0c	SUM	Overall rank
Akulivik	2	6	7	15	Tie 4
Aupaluk	3	3	5	11	Tie 1
Inukjuak	11	11	3	24	9
Kangiqsualujjuaq	4	1	6	11	Tie 1
Kangiqsujuaq	7	8	11	26	10
Kangirsuk	6	2	9	17	7
Kuujjuarapik	10	4	1	15	Tie 4
Puvirnituq	5	9	8	21	8
Quaqtaq	9	10	10	29	11
Tasiujaq	1	7	4	12	3
Umiujaq	8	5	2	15	Tie 4

to possess centrality to all the other settlements to reduce distribution costs and time, but it would also have to represent a large market and a potential for future economic development, including mining or other resource activity in order to justify the investments.

Conclusion

Much of the literature on Arctic shipping is based on the challenges of sea ice. This chapter reveals that three weather conditions have the potential to interrupt ship operations and affect safety in the Inuit coastal settlements in Nunavik. These villages are extremely dependent on shipping for basic supplies. Delays and disruptions affect the abilities of the supply shipping lines to operate commercially. Poor visibility and high winds result in stoppages of normal ship operations, and along with the incidence of freezing temperatures during the shipping season represent safety issues.

The paper goes on to establish that the variability in occurrence of these weather conditions represent an additional challenge to shipping. Conditions vary year to year, and there are marked differences in the exposure of the different villages to these weather conditions. Using means and standard deviations, the settlements providing the highest and lowest incidences are identified. The findings indicate that it is not useful to make broad generalisations about Arctic weather since there is so much diversity between sites, and that local conditions must be taken into account.

An attempt was made to quantify the relationships between the weather variables and the length of times ships spend in port. The results of correlation and regression analysis reveals that the associations are not statistically significant. This is due in part to the small sample size. An effort is being made to use the ships' log data for the three ports not included in the study to increase the sample size.

Our ongoing research is pushing the analysis forward in time. We are examining how climate change and the different weather conditions that are predicted to take place will impact on shipping in Nunavik. A detailed risk assessment is underway, and our goal is to identify possible mitigation responses.

References

Brooks, M., & Frost, J. (2012). Providing freight services to remote Arctic communities: Are there lessons for practitioners from services to Greenland and Canada's northeast? *Research in Transportation Business & Management, 4,* 69–78. doi:10.1016/j. rtbm.2012.06.005

Ducruet, C., Itoh, H., & Merk, O. (2014). *Time efficiency at world container ports.* International Transport Forum/OECD. Paris. 30 pp. doi:10.1787/2223439X

Dunlop, S. (2008). *A dictionary of weather.* Oxford: Oxford University Press. doi:10.1093/ acref/9780199541447.001.0001

Dunn, B. (2015, October 26). The challenges that everyday shipping faces in the north. *Canadian Sailings,* 11–13. Retrieved from https://canadiansailings.ca/

First Air. (2017). *Cargo rates.* Retrieved March 27, 2017, from https://firstsair.ca/cargo/ rates

Giguère, M. A., Comtois, C., & Slack, B. (2017). Constraints on Canadian Arctic maritime connections. *Case Studies on Transport Policy, 5*(2), 355–366.

Lasserre, F., & Pelletier, S. (2011). Polar super seaways? Maritime transport in the Arctic: An analysis of shipowners' intentions. *Journal of Transport Geography, 19*(6), 1465–1473. doi:10.1016/j.jtrangeo.2011.08.006

Melia, N., Haines, K., & Hawkins, E. (2016). Sea ice decline and 21st century trans-Arctic shipping routes. *Geophysical Research Letters, 43*(18), 9720–9728. doi:10.1002/2016GL069315

NEAS. (2017). *Cargo rates.* Retrieved March 27, 2017, from https//neas.ca/rates

Pizzolato, L., Howell, S. E. L., Derksen, C., Dawson, J., & Copland, L. (2014). Changing sea ice conditions and marine transportation activity in Canadian Arctic waters between 1990 and 2012. *Climatic Change, 123,* 161–173. doi:10.1007/s10584-013-1038-3

Prowse, P. D., Furgal, C., Chouinard, R., Melling, H., Milburn, D., & Smith, S. L. (2009). Implications of climate change for economic development in northern Canada: Energy, resource, and transportation sectors. *Ambio, 38*(5), 272–281. doi:10.1579/00044-7447-38.5.272

Saldanha, J. P., Russell, D. M., & Tyworth, J. E. (2006). A disaggregate analysis of ocean carriers' transit time performance. *Transportation Journal, 45*(1), 39–60. Retrieved from www.jstor.org/stable/20713633

Slack, B., Comtois, C., Wiegmans, B., & Witte, P. (2018). Ships time in port. *International Journal of Shipping and Transport Logistics, 10*(1), 45–62.

Smith, L. C., & Stephenson, S. R. (2013). New trans-Arctic shipping routes navigable by midcentury. *Proceedings of the National Academy of Sciences, 110*(13), E1191–E1195. doi:10.1073/pnas.1214212110

Spears, K. J. (2016). Summer 2016: An assessment of Canada's Arctic critical marine infrastructure. *Canada Sailings.* Retrieved November from https://canadiansailings.ca/

Streiger, R. B. (2016). Government of Nunavut moves forward with northern port development. *Canada Sailings.* Retrieved November from https://canadiansailings.ca/

2 Approaches of the profitability of Arctic shipping in the literature[1]

Dimitrios Theocharis

Introduction

The future use of the so-called Arctic routes could reshape maritime transport geography. This includes development of new trade routes for bulk and specialised shipping as well as possible reconfigurations of liner shipping networks or the launch of new ones, between origin-destinations (OD) in Northwest Europe, the Baltic and the Arctic to Northeast Asia and North America. Recent studies project future accessibility of both the Northern Sea Route (NSR) and the Northwest Passage (NWP) by 2050 for non-ice-class vessels. Polar class 6 type (PC6) vessels will also be able to operate through the Transpolar Sea Route (TSR) (Smith & Stephenson, 2013; Melia, Haines, & Hawkins, 2016), whilst there is also a high possibility for non-ice-class vessels to use the TSR (Melia et al., 2016) by that time. Opportunities for more frequent use of polar routes could be facilitated by the gradual change in Arctic sea-ice conditions. The implications could be lower fuel costs, greenhouse gas (GHG) and non-GHG emissions, shorter transit times, improved network connectivity and lower overall transport costs.

Comparative studies between Arctic and traditional routes have grown considerably during the last ten years. Lasserre (2014, 2015) and Meng, Zhang and Xu (2016) reviewed 26 and 25 studies respectively, whilst Theocharis, Rodrigues, Pettit and Haider (2018) systematically reviewed 33 peer-reviewed studies concerning both research and methodological considerations. This chapter offers an updated review of the literature based on Theocharis et al. (2018) with a particular focus at the micro-economic level. The economic feasibility (costs, profits) and environmental assessment (emissions, environmental costs) of Arctic routes are reviewed by including studies that were published during 2018.[2]

Review methodology

A systematic review of the literature is based on comprehensive and unbiased searches of relevant studies by explicitly formulating review questions and using specific search terms and inclusion criteria for that purpose.

Various approaches are used to synthesise findings in order to identify emerging themes, key results or any links to theory or concepts (Tranfield, Denyer, & Smart, 2003). Traditional routes and oceanic canals dominate bulk shipping and determine connectivity in global liner networks. However, the emergence of new hubs, future canal development or expansion (Rodrigue & Ashar, 2016; Yip & Wong, 2016; Martinez, Steven & Dresner, 2016) and the potential opening of polar routes (Notteboom, 2012) could redefine the maritime transport geography landscape and increase network diversity (Ducruet, 2013). Generally, economic and environmental sustainability in shipping is achieved by employing vessels on traditional maritime routes and shipping canals. Different approaches to make shipping more cost-effective and greener include: slow steaming (e.g. Corbett, Wang, & Winebrake, 2009; Notteboom & Vernimmen, 2009), scheduling optimisation (Lam, 2010), expansion of existing canals (De Marucci, 2012) or new ship designs, technologies and fuels (Lindstad, Jullumstrø, & Sandaas, 2013; Lindstad & Bø, 2018). On the other hand, Arctic routes could potentially become a viable alternative option to the classical shipping routes and canals so as to address both the economic and environmental sustainability in shipping, possibly by reducing the extent of the trade-offs involved between the latter two (Mansouri, Lee, & Aluko, 2015). All else being equal, the comparative advantage of Arctic routes stems from the fact that shorter geographical distances could mean shorter transit times and lower transport costs, higher service frequency and potentially lower fuel consumption, which in turn means lower GHG and non-GHG emissions.

Search strategy

According to the research scope of this review, only papers reporting original results on cost and emissions assessments of Arctic routes at the micro-economic level were included. Quality control is increased only by restricting the searches to journal papers (David & Han, 2004). Studies dealing with shifts in global trade flows or other macro-economic variables and future emissions inventories in the Arctic based on traffic assessments are beyond the scope of this review and therefore excluded. Major shipping canals and maritime routes were used as keywords in Scopus and Web of Science, as well as variations of terms that have similar meanings. A total of 35 unique papers were retrieved and analysed based on their research and methodological considerations regarding only cost and emissions assessments.

Results

General statistics

Only a small number of papers assessed the potential of Arctic routes during the 1980s and, most importantly, from 1991 to 2000. Nevertheless, the lack of research interest during that period could be attributed to the underutilisation of Arctic routes and the lack of interest from the shipping industry in general. Of the 35 papers reviewed, two were published in the 1990s, seven between 2001 and 2010 and 26 between 2011 and 2018. This increasing trend in publications appears to be consistent with the view that scholarly research followed developments in narratives about the potential use of Arctic routes, and regarding the actual utilisation of Arctic routes. For instance, it was only from 2011 onwards that an increasing number of non-Russian flagged vessels started to use the NSR (CHNL, 2018). The 35 papers selected for this review were published in 22 journals. *Maritime Policy & Management* and *Transportation Research Part A: Policy and Practice* have the most frequent publications followed by the *Journal of Transport Geography*, whereas the remaining journals each published one paper between 1992 and 2018 (Table 2.1).

Thirteen countries have contributed to Arctic shipping research concerning cost and emissions assessments of Arctic routes. The selection of countries was based on the country of affiliation of the first author of each paper. China and Canada have the biggest contributions whereas South Korea, Germany, Singapore, Australia and Finland have the lowest rate of contribution with one paper each.

Table 2.1 Number of articles published per academic journal

Name of Journal	No. of Articles
Maritime Policy & Management	5
Transportation Research Part A: Policy and Practice	5
Journal of Transport Geography	4
Maritime Economics & Logistics	2
International Journal or Production Economics	1
Transportation Research Part E: Logistics and Transportation Review	1
Climatic Change	1
International Journal of e-Navigation and Maritime Economy	1
International Journal of Geographical Information Science	1
Journal of Ship Production and Design	1
Journal of Maritime Research	1
Transport Policy	1
Polar Record	1
Journal of Navigation	1
International Challenges	1
Journal of Ocean Technology	1
Applied Mechanics and Materials	1
Advanced Science Letters	1
Transportation Research Board	1
Ambio	1
Izvestiya, Atmospheric and Oceanic Physics	1
Journal of Nuclear Science and Technology	1
Sustainability	1

Methodological considerations

The categorisation extended to include the methodological characteristics of the reviewed papers. Only research methods and data analysis techniques employed on cost and emissions assessments are reported.

Research methods

The categorisation scheme of research methods was adopted from Wacker (1998). In empirical research, data from the 'real world' are used in order to verify the relationships under investigation by using an inductive approach to theory, whereas in analytical research, logic, mathematics and/or statistics are primarily employed by using a deductive approach to theory to reach a conclusion (Wacker, 1998). Analytical mathematical methods (modelling or simulation) were reported in 29 papers, whereas empirical statistical and case studies were found in four and two papers respectively (Table 2.2).

Analytical modelling and simulation are used with the aim of developing mathematical relationships to explain the behaviour of real-world systems by investigating the performance of dependent variables or models under different conditions (Meredith, Raturi, Amoako-Gyampah, & Kapplan, 1989). Papers that used transport cost models, optimisation or mathematical simulation techniques through case examples belong to the category of analytical mathematical methods.

Empirical statistical research aims at verifying theoretical relationships by analysing large samples of data from real business processes (Wacker, 1998). Studies that employed regression analysis fall under this research methodology. Case studies focus on a specific phenomenon with the aim of revealing empirical relationships and usually serve for exploration in the early stages of research. They are also used to examine dependent variables under different scenarios or to provide counter-arguments to prior hypotheses or even to

Table 2.2 Methodological considerations of the reviewed articles

Methodological characteristics	Categories	No. of articles
Research methods	Analytical mathematical	29
	Empirical statistical	4
	Empirical case study	2
	Transport cost model	26
	Optimisation model	4
	Regression analysis	3
Data analysis techniques	Monte Carlo simulation	2
	GIS simulation	1
	None	2
	Other	3

come up with new insights in debatable areas (Meredith et al., 1989). Papers classified under this research method have not made use of data analysis techniques.

Data analysis techniques

Optimisation models were reported in four papers. Regression, Monte Carlo simulation and GIS simulation are reported in three, two and one papers respectively. On the other hand, 26 studies report general scenario-based transport cost models. The preference for general cost models and optimisation techniques, to a lesser extent, could be attributed to the fact that researchers focus on route-specific economic characteristics and their overall competitiveness from a shipowner/charterer's perspective. At the same time researchers from various disciplinary backgrounds have been trying to address their research questions through more sophisticated techniques. Nevertheless, Arctic shipping is an emerging topic within maritime transport research and it is expected that new techniques will emerge in the future to address specific research inquiries.

Research considerations

Routes, transport systems and OD pairs

The majority of reviewed papers assessed the NSR (23), four studies chose the NWP, three assessed both routes and one addressed the feasibility of both the NSR and the TSR. Ten studies included emissions assessments or environmental costs. Most of them juxtaposed Arctic routes with the Suez Canal Route (30), four of them chose the route via the Panama Canal and two considered the route via the Cape of Good Hope amongst others. Two papers reported all-rail routes, two an all-air route, one paper included intermodal routes (sea-air) as alternatives, whereas five studies examined a combined schedule (summer season in the NSR and winter season in the Suez Canal Route).

Liner shipping is the dominant transport system studied (21 studies), six studies selected dry bulk segments, four studies examined oil tanker segments, three studies dealt with liquefied natural gas (LNG) tanker shipping and two studies investigated both liner and bulk shipping. The OD pairs vary widely in terms of the ports chosen by the identified studies. The majority of the reviewed papers focus on origins in Northwest Europe and destinations in East Asia, whilst some others opted for ports in Russia, USA, Mexico and Canada.

Cost and emissions assessments

Overall, Arctic routes were found to be either cost-competitive or profitable in 13 of 35 studies, and unprofitable or not cost-competitive in eight. Ten studies

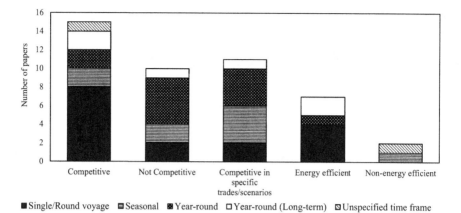

Figure 2.1 Cost and emissions assessment results based on the time frame of operations

suggest that they are competitive under specific scenarios and certain trade routes. The remaining two papers project that Arctic routes would become cost-effective in the long term. Of the ten studies that appraised emissions, two concluded that Arctic routes are either less energy efficient than the traditional ones or incur increased environmental costs when using region-specific Global Warming Potential (GWP) factors. Figure 2.1 shows that Arctic routes tend to be either uncompetitive or demonstrate mixed results in most of the studies which assume an annual operating period, especially for liner shipping (e.g. Verny & Grigentin, 2009; Liu & Kronbak, 2010; Lasserre, 2015; Zhao, Hua, & Lin, 2016; Xu, Yang, & Weng, 2018). The picture is similar regarding seasonal sailings, where four studies report mixed results (Lasserre, 2014, 2015; Shibasaki, Usami, Furuichi, Teranishi, & Kato, 2018; Wan, Ge, & Chen, 2018). In contrast, they were found competitive in most of the studies that assumed round or single voyages mainly for bulk or specialised shipping (e.g. Wergeland, 1992; Schøyen & Bråthen, 2011; Raza & Schøyen, 2014; Lu, Park, Choi, & Oh, 2014; Cariou & Faury, 2015). Finally, the competitiveness of these routes increases for year-round liner shipping operations only in the long term (Khon & Mokhov, 2010; Khon, Mokhov, Latif, Semenov, & Park, 2010).

Discussion and future directions

Research insights

The number of influential factors, which determine route choice, extend to include navigational, revenue, operational and cost factors amongst others. Important variables are discussed below in order to understand how they affect route choice at the operational and tactical level, as well as the interrelations between them.

Route selection

The NSR is identified as the most preferable route in the literature, probably due to currently more favourable sea-ice conditions compared to the other Arctic routes, and recent infrastructure and project developments. However, studies investigating the future accessibility of Arctic routes indicate extended navigation seasons for several vessel types and for all the routes (NSR, NWP and TSR) throughout the 21st century. Khon et al. (2010) estimated the navigation season to be 3–6 (2–4) months for the NSR and NWP respectively, whilst in Khon, Mokhov and Semenov (2017) the season for NSR is 4–6,5 months regarding low ice-class ships by late century. Stephenson, Smith, Brigham and Agnew (2013) projected the NSR navigation season to be approximately 103, 113 and 120 days for non-ice class, PC6 and PC3 ships respectively by the end of the 21st century.

Stephenson, Brigham and Smith (2014) found high inter-annual variability of the NSR navigation season taking into account sea ice and bathymetry from 2013–2027. Further, Stephenson and Smith (2015) identified a gradual increase in the number of voyages through the TSR for PC6 vessels by mid-century whilst the possibilities of utilising the NWP rise by 2060. In contrast, Laliberté, Howell and Kushner (2016) found both the NWP and TSR to be ice covered beyond mid-century, whilst Pizzolato, Howell, Dawson, Laliberté and Copland (2016) and Liu, Ma, Wang, Wang and Wang (2017) also concluded that multi-year ice in the NWP poses significant obstacles for shipping activities in the medium term. According to Melia et al. (2016), the TSR is projected to become available for non-ice-class ships by mid-century whilst voyages from Europe to the Far East will take 17 days by late century. Aksenov et al. (2017) identified sea-ice extent and thickness as the most determining factors for shipping in the Arctic until 2030–50, whereas other ice properties (e.g. ice ridging, drift ice and internal pressure), ocean circulation, winds, currents and waves will mostly affect navigation beyond that period.

Taking into account these findings, future research should also pay attention to the TSR as an alternative route. In addition, more focus is needed in simulating the NWP, and alternative sub-routes of the NSR, as these could enable the employment of larger vessels. Moreover, the possible opening of the Nicaragua and Kra Canals, the expansion of both Panama and Suez Canals as well as alternative land-based (e.g. Tran-Siberian Railway, New Eurasian Land Bridges) and other established trade routes will also have an impact to their northern rivals (Figure 2.2) (Notteboom, 2012; Yip & Wong, 2016; Martinez et al., 2016; Zeng, Wang, Qu, & Li, 2017; Shibasaki et al., 2018).

Cost, operational and navigational variables

A wide variety of navigational, operational and cost factors were identified. The assumed period of operations was identified to be a crucial factor across all reviewed papers. Under the current winter navigational and climatic conditions, Arctic routes could serve as seasonal alternatives during the summer/autumn

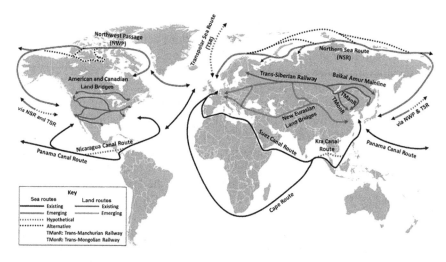

Figure 2.2 Alternative sea and land routes between Eurasia and North America
Source: Theocharis et al. (2018)

season, mainly for bulkers and tankers rather than offering regular access to ships on an annual basis. An extended navigation season with low icebreaking fees and high fuel prices increases significantly the competitiveness of Arctic routes (Liu & Kronbak, 2010; Lasserre, 2014, 2015; Zhao et al., 2016; Lin & Chang, 2018; Xu et al., 2018; Wan et al., 2018) and even when assuming the use of larger vessels on the traditional routes (Furuichi & Otsuka, 2015). However, any fuel cost savings could be offset by the need to deploy additional ships on a NSR/SCR combined liner network when assuming very high fuel prices (Xu et al., 2018). Further, increased load factors and high average speeds, which implies high frequencies, could improve profitability, especially for liner shipping (Wergeland, 1992; Guy, 2006; Lasserre, 2014, 2015; Zhu, Fu, Ng, Luo, & Ge, 2018; Wan et al., 2018).

The capital cost premium is in the order of 20–30% in most cases and was identified as an important cost factor amongst others (Somanathan, Flynn, & Szymanski, 2007, 2009; Liu & Kronbak, 2010; Xu et al., 2018; Wan et al., 2018). The importance of an extended sailing season is crucial in order to exploit the advantages of operating on shorter routes by utilising ice-class vessels, which entail increased capital costs. According to Somanathan et al. (2007), a well-trained crew is required for Arctic operations whilst additional costs occur when ice navigators or additional crew are included as well.

Insurance costs are usually high for ice-class vessels operating in the Arctic. Generally, a common denominator is difficult to find since each voyage in Arctic waters is evaluated individually. Sarrabezoles, Lasserre and Hagouagn'rin

(2016) report H&M and cargo insurance premiums up to 50%, and P&I premiums up to 25% in most of the cases. Yet, safety factors are considered very important from the shipping industry as well as from the underwriters' point of view. This implies that insurance premiums are still assessed on a case-by-case basis regardless of the fact that the Polar Code aimed at addressing these issues amongst others (Shyu & Ding, 2016; Tseng & Cullinane, 2018; Fedi, Faury, & Gritsenko, 2018).

The icebreaking fees assumed in the reviewed papers either refer to the official NSRA fees or to discounts offered in particular cases from time to time. This discrepancy stems from the fact that transit fees have been subject to the practice of negotiated tariffs (Gritsenko & Kiiski, 2016). Yet, independent navigation is allowed depending on certain conditions since 2012, and the official NSRA 2014 tariffs have improved the fees structure, especially with respect to economies of scale (Gritsenko & Kiiski, 2016). It was found that substantially reduced fees lower the optimal range of fuel prices for a competitive NSR/SCR liner network (Xu et al., 2018), whilst the sensitivity of icebreaking fees becomes more pronounced than that of fuel prices when taking into account the ruble/US dollar exchange rates (Shibasaki et al., 2018).

The average speed used in the models also differs widely. The operating speed depends on the speed realised on ice waters since the speed in open waters will be the same as in classical routes. According to transit data, the average speed recorded in 2010–13 is around 10 kts (CHNL, 2018), which is in line with the operating speeds realised in first-year sea ice in the Bay of Bothnia during the ice season. However, it can be easily reduced to 5–6 kts or even to zero depending on the ice and local climatic conditions.

Increased fuel consumption is also assumed in some studies due to greater engine power required on ice water and the additional weight of an ice-class vessel. Whilst the use of Arctic routes imply lower fuel costs, this largely depends on transit times and possible delays due to deviation of a vessel from its predefined navigational route in order to avoid difficult ice conditions. Solakivi, Kiiski and Ojala (2017, 2018) estimate on average 10% and 30% additional fuel consumption for the current fleet of ice-class containerships, and dry bulk and tankers respectively.

The fuel types to be used in the Arctic or elsewhere may also affect the economics of alternative routes in the future due to either future environmental regulations or the use of special fuels in the Arctic or the possibility of fuel taxation globally (Lasserre, 2014, 2015; Schøyen & Bråthen, 2014; Cariou & Faury, 2015; Wan et al., 2018). Moreover, alternative approaches of estimating the environmental impact of maritime operations on different regions may give different results (Lindstad, Bright, & Strømman, 2016; Zhu et al., 2018).

Revenue and market factors

Optimal operating speeds are adjusted depending on the prevailing market conditions and fuel prices amongst others. Low freight rates and/or high fuel prices impose speed reductions which favour slow steaming and vice versa (Notteboom & Vernimmen, 2009; Devanney, 2010). Various combinations of freight rates and fuel prices may favour one route over the others and this largely depends on other cost factors, such as insurance premiums, and more importantly, transit fees. Route choice also depends on the transport system in question, fleet supply and geopolitics amongst others. Generally, shorter routes are preferred in a high fuel price environment, which is also confirmed by the literature. Low freight rates may favour longer routes, but scheduled services require short transit times due to capacity requirements that have to be met at certain periods of time.

Low load factors, high icebreaking fees, potential delays and uncertainty when it comes to liner shipping favour the classical routes, even under high fuel prices (Liu & Kronbak, 2010; Lasserre, 2014, 2015; Zhang et al., 2016; Xu et al., 2018; Zhu et al., 2018). Low dwt utilisation and small ship sizes were also found to favour traditional routes for bulk shipping even under high fuel prices (Zhang et al., 2016). Other factors, such as cargo value, in-transit inventory and operating cost premiums also affect the relationship between speed, freight rates and fuel prices. The net effect of these factors upon the route choice depends critically on the logistical context of the calculations. Commodity prices and proximity to the markets play an important role too. In addition, alternative ship sizes and ice-class designs are also important factors, which could be further investigated in the future.

Maritime transport systems

Liner shipping is mostly investigated in the literature, although this transport system does not seem to be feasible in the short to medium term. A number of factors contributing to this are: potential delays and schedule unreliability due to prevailing sea-ice conditions, limited navigation season, remoteness of Arctic ports, lack of proximity to markets and access to hinterlands, regional bottlenecks and poor port infrastructure and services amongst others (Lasserre & Pelletier, 2011; Lasserre, Beveridge, Fournier, Têtu, & Huang, 2016; Beveridge, Fournier, Lasserre, Huang, & Têtu, 2016). Some of the reviewed papers partly tackle these issues by incorporating either lower load factors or smaller vessels on Arctic routes. Some studies report a network structure in the literature (Xu, Yin, Jia, Jin, & Ouyang, 2011; Zhao et al., 2016; Lin & Chang, 2018; Xu et al., 2018; Wan et al., 2018). Further research could shed light on network structure and the feasibility of liner operations from this perspective.

On the other hand, both bulk and specialised shipping are less studied, although these systems are the most feasible for Arctic operations due to their nature. Besides, bulk shipping (e.g. oil products, LNG, iron ore, coal and other minerals, frozen fish) dominated transit records during 2011–16 (CHNL, 2018). Recent surveys also report that bulk and specialised shipping fit better with the Arctic environment than liner shipping (Lasserre & Pelletier, 2011; Lee & Kim, 2015; Beveridge et al., 2016; Lasserre et al., 2016).

Methodological characteristics

Operational research and cost models

Most of the papers reviewed in this systematic review consider the assignment of one vessel in single or annual voyages. Operational research methods could increase the number of parameters by considering several alternative options related to fleet size, route choice, the number of voyages and networks. Examples are the comparative studies of Zhao et al. (2016) and Lin and Chang (2018). Speed adjustments to minimise fuel consumption and/or costs or to maximise profits in both liner and tramp shipping are very relevant (Psaraftis & Kontovas, 2013). Environmental sustainability is also addressed through multi-objective optimisation techniques (Mansouri et al., 2015). Thus, modelling could be informed from all the aforementioned techniques to address operational, economic and environmental aspects.

Scenario-based transport cost models could be developed further to include more assumptions considering not only operational and cost factors but also environmental factors. Studies evaluating future accessibility in the Arctic could also aid the modelling approaches with respect to navigation season, sea-ice conditions and transit times so as to better quantify these factors. Global climate models projecting ice and weather conditions under different emissions scenarios could be used as inputs to simulations (Schröder, Reimer, & Jochmann, 2017). On the other hand, more diversity is needed in terms of scenarios and assumptions so as to provide fruitful insights and counter-arguments.

Empirical case studies

Lasserre (2014, 2015) mentions the discrepancies in hypotheses and assumptions made in the literature regarding operational and cost factors as well as market conditions. This is a result of the infancy of Arctic maritime operations, which in turn leads to the lack of relevant data and statistics. Empirical case studies and interviews with key stakeholders can complement the data reported in databases and other publicly available sources to further refine any modelling approach where there is no insufficient or inaccurate statistical data. The identified case studies report empirical data obtained through interviews and records from real voyages occurred in the NSR (Raza & Schøyen, 2014; Zhao & Hu, 2016). This type of research could help increase the understanding of Arctic maritime operations.

Regression analysis and other techniques

Lu et al. (2014) use regression analysis in order to investigate the cost determinants on both the NSR and the Suez Canal Route. Other techniques such as discrete choice and Multi-Criteria Decision-Making (MCDM) models could aid model-based research by investigating stakeholders' perspectives regarding influential decision-making factors and the potential of Arctic shipping amongst others (e.g. Moon, Kim, & Lee, 2015; Shyu & Ding, 2016; Benedyk & Peeta, 2016; Wang, Zhang, & Meng, 2018; Tseng & Cullinane, 2018).

Conclusion

The results of this updated review generally confirm those of Theocharis et al. (2018) regarding the economic potential of Arctic routes. These are considered more competitive than traditional routes in 13 of the 35 papers that evaluated their economic potential, less competitive in eight papers whereas ten report mixed results. Two papers project that they will become competitive in the long term, especially for liner shipping. Whilst eight out of ten studies find the Arctic routes more energy efficient than their traditional rivals, two conclude that the use of the former could increase GHG and non-GHG emissions and environmental costs. The competitiveness of these routes decreases as we move towards year-round operations. This means that under the current winter navigational and climatic conditions they could serve mainly as seasonal alternatives rather than offering regular access to ships on an annual basis. Consequently, Arctic routes appear to be more suitable for bulk rather than liner shipping in the short to medium term.

Further research is required to investigate the potential of all Arctic routes. Attention should be paid to revenue attributes, commodity and fuel prices, and how these factors along with Arctic sea-ice conditions determine the competitiveness of Arctic routes. Ice conditions as well as other physical constraints are critical factors that affect the operating speed or the size of the vessels used in Arctic waters, which in turn affect the revenue, transit time, operating and voyage costs. More model-based research with robust sensitivity analyses is needed in order to overcome discrepancies in the assumptions regarding operational and cost factors as well as to shed light on interrelations between various variables. Future research could also take into account insights from studies assessing the future accessibility of Arctic routes. As regards the environmental aspects of Arctic shipping, future research could focus on alternative fuels and new technologies. The study of future Arctic sea-ice regimes along with trade and traffic flows could further improve our understanding regarding the environmental impact of shipping activities in the Arctic.

The literature focuses mainly on liner shipping and to a lesser extent on bulk shipping. However, bulk and specialised shipping will mostly benefit from Arctic routes in the short to medium term. As a relatively new topic in maritime transport area, Arctic shipping could be addressed by many methodologies and techniques used in social sciences, namely, operational research, case studies, regression analysis as well as discrete choice and MCDM techniques amongst others. Finally, this review limited its scope to studies reporting on cost and emissions assessment of Arctic routes at the micro level. A broader review of the literature could include conceptual and descriptive studies, surveys and studies focusing on time/distance effects, shifts in trade flows, ice-class ship evaluation or on the environmental impact and other economic factors at a macro level.

Acknowledgements

This work was supported by the Economic and Social Research Council (ESRC Wales Doctoral Training Partnership).

Notes

1 This is a modified version of the paper: Theocharis, D., Pettit, S., Rodrigues, V. S., & Haider, J. (2018). Arctic shipping: A systematic literature review of comparative studies. *Journal of Transport Geography, 69*, 112–128.
2 As of September 2018.

References

Aksenov, Y., Popova, E. E., Yool, A., Nurser, A. J. G., Williams, T. D., Bertino, L., & Bergh, J. (2017). On the future navigability of Arctic sea routes: High-resolution projections of the Arctic Ocean and sea ice. *Marine Policy, 75*, 300–317.

Benedyk, I. V., & Peeta, S. (2016). A binary probit model to analyze freight transportation decision-maker perspectives for container shipping on the Northern Sea Route. *Maritime Economics and Logistics, 20*(3), 1–17.

Beveridge, L., Fournier, M., Lasserre, F. Huang, L., & Têtu, P. L. (2016). Interest of Asian shipping companies in navigating the Arctic. *Polar Science, 10*(3), 404–414.

Cariou, P., & Faury, O. (2015). Relevance of the Northern Sea Route (NSR) for bulk shipping. *Transportation Research Part A: Policy and Practice, 78*, 337–346.

CHNL (Center for High North Logistics). (2018). *Transit statistics: Data from NSR*. Retrieved from www.arctic-lio.com/nsr_transits

Corbett, J. J., Wang, H., & Winebrake, J. J. (2009). The effectiveness and costs of speed reductions on emissions from international shipping. *Transportation Research Part D: Transport and Environment, 14*(8), 593–598.

David, R. J., & Han, S. K. (2004). A systematic assessment of the empirical support for transaction cost economics. *Strategic Management Journal, 25*(1), 39–58.

De Marucci, S. (2012). The expansion of the Panama Canal and its impact on global CO_2 emissions from ships. *Maritime Policy & Management, 39*(6), 603–620.

Devanney, J. (2010). The impact of bunker price on VLCC spot rates. *Proceedings of the 3rd International Symposium on Ship Operations, Management and Economics*. Retrieved from www.c4tx.org/pub/vlcc_rates.pdf

Ducruet, C. (2013). Network diversity and maritime flows. *Journal of Transport Geography, 30*, 77–88.

Fedi, L., Faury, O., & Gritsenko, D. (2018). The impact of the Polar Code on risk mitigation in Arctic waters: a "toolbox" for underwriters? *Maritime Policy & Management, 45*(4), 478–494.

Furuichi, M., & Otsuka, N. (2015). Proposing a common platform of shipping cost analysis of the Northern Sea Route and the Suez Canal Route. *Maritime Economics and Logistics, 17*(1), 9–31.

Gritsenko, D., & Kiiski, T. (2016). A review of Russian ice-breaking tariff policy on the Northern Sea Route 1991–2014. *Polar Record, 52*(2), 144–158.

Guy, E. (2006). Evaluating the viability of commercial shipping in the Northwest Passage. *Journal of Ocean Technology, 1*(1), 9–15.

Khon, V. C., & Mokhov, I. I. (2010). Arctic climate changes and possible conditions of Arctic navigation in the 21st century. *Izvestiya, Atmospheric and Oceanic Physics*, *46*(1), 19–25.

Khon, V. C., Mokhov, I. I., Latif, M., Semenov, V. A., & Park, W. (2010). Perspectives of Northern Sea Route and Northwest Passage in the twenty-first century. *Climatic Change*, *100*(3–4), 757–768.

Khon, V. C., Mokhov, I. I., & Semenov, V. A. (2017). Transit navigation through Northern Sea Route from satellite data and CMIP5 simulations. *Environmental Research Letters*, *12*(20), 1–7.

Laliberté, F., Howell, S. E. L., & Kushner, P. J. (2016). Regional variability of a projected sea ice-free Arctic during the summer months. *Geophysical Research Letters*, *43*(1), 256–263.

Lam, J. S. L. (2010). An integrated approach for port selection, ship scheduling and financial analysis. *NETNOMICS: Economic Research and Electronic Networking*, *11*(1), 33–46.

Lasserre, F. (2014). Case studies of shipping along Arctic routes. Analysis and profitability perspectives for the container sector. *Transportation Research Part A: Policy and Practice*, *66*, 144–161.

Lasserre, F. (2015). Simulations of shipping along Arctic routes: Comparison, analysis and economic perspectives. *Polar Record*, *51*(3), 239–259.

Lasserre, F., Beveridge, L., Fournier, M., Têtu, P. L., & Huang, L. (2016). Polar super seaways? Maritime transport in the Arctic: An analysis of shipowners' intentions II. *Journal of Transport Geography*, *57*, 105–114.

Lasserre, F., & Pelletier, S. (2011). Polar super seaways? Maritime transport in the Arctic: An analysis of shipowners' intentions. *Journal of Transport Geography*, *19*(6), 1465–1473.

Lee, T., & Kim, H. J. (2015). Barriers of voyaging on the Northern Sea Route: A perspective from shipping companies. *Marine Policy*, *62*, 264–270.

Lin, D. Y., & Chang, Y. T. (2018). Ship routing and freight assignment problem for liner shipping: Application to the Northern Sea Route planning problem. *Transportation Research Part E: Logistics and Transportation Review*, *110*, 47–70.

Lindstad, E., & Bø, T. I. (2018). Potential power setups, fuels and hull designs capable of satisfying future EEDI requirements. *Transportation Research Part D: Transport and Environment*, *63*, 276–290.

Lindstad, H., Bright, R. M., & Strømman, A. H. (2016). Economic savings linked to future Arctic shipping trade are at odds with climate change mitigation. *Transport Policy*, *45*, 24–30.

Lindstad, H., Jullumstrø, E., & Sandaas, I. (2013). Reductions in cost and greenhouse gas emissions with new bulk ship designs enabled by the Panama Canal expansion. *Energy Policy*, *59*, 341–349.

Liu, M., & Kronbak, J. (2010). The potential economic viability of using the Northern Sea Route (NSR) as an alternative route between Asia and Europe. *Journal of Transport Geography*, *18*(3), 434–444.

Liu, X., Ma, L., Wang, J., Wang, Y., & Wang, L. (2017). Navigable windows of the Northwest Passage. *Polar Science*, *13*, 91–99.

Lu, D., Park, G. K., Choi, K., & Oh, K. (2014). An economic analysis of container shipping through Canadian Northwest Passage. *International Journal of e-Navigation and Maritime Economy*, *1*, 60–72.

Mansouri, S. A., Lee, H., & Aluko, O. (2015). Multi-objective decision support to enhance environmental sustainability in maritime shipping: A review and future directions. *Transportation Research Part E: Logistics and Transportation Review*, 78, 3–18.

Martinez, C., Steven, A. B., & Dresner, M. (2016). East coast vs. west coast: The impact of the Panama Canal's expansion on the routing of Asian imports into the United States. *Transportation Research Part E: Logistics and Transportation Review*, 91, 274–289.

Melia, N., Haines, K., & Hawkins, E. (2016). Sea ice decline and 21st century trans-Arctic shipping routes. *Geophysical Research Letters*, 43(18), 9720–9728.

Meng, Q., Zhang, Y., & Xu, M. (2016). Viability of transarctic shipping routes: a literature review from the navigational and commercial perspectives. *Maritime Policy & Management*, 44(1), 1–26.

Meredith, J. R., Raturi, A., Amoako-Gyampah, K., & Kapplan, B. (1989). Alternative research paradigms in operations. *Journal of Operations Management*, 8(4), 297–326.

Moon, D. S., Kim, D. J., & Lee, E. K. (2015). A study on competitiveness of sea transport by comparing international transport routes between Korea and EU. *The Asian Journal of Shipping and Logistics*, 31(1), 1–20.

Notteboom, T. E. (2012). Towards a new intermediate hub region in container shipping? Relay and interlining via the Cape route vs. the Suez route. *Journal of Transport Geography*, 22, 164–178.

Notteboom, T. E., & Vernimmen, B. (2009). The effect of high fuel costs on liner service configuration in container shipping. *Journal of Transport Geography*, 17(5), 325–337.

Pizzolato, L., Howell, S. E. L., Dawson, J., Laliberté, F., & Copland, L. (2016). The influence of declining sea ice on shipping activity in the Canadian Arctic. *Geophysical Research Letters*, 43(23), 12146–12154.

Psaraftis, H. N., & Kontovas, C. A. (2013). Speed models for energy-efficient maritime transportation: A taxonomy and survey. *Transportation Research Part C*, 26, 331–351.

Raza, Z., & Schøyen, H. (2014). The commercial potential for LNG shipping between Europe and Asia via the Northern Sea Route. *Journal of Maritime Research*, XI(II), 6779.

Rodrigue, J. P., & Ashar, A. (2016). Transshipment hubs in the New Panamax Era: The role of the Caribbean. *Journal of Transport Geography*, 51, 270–279.

Sarrabezoles, A., Lasserre, F., & Hagouagn'rin, Z. (2016). Arctic shipping insurance: Towards a harmonisation of practices and costs? *Polar Record*, 52(265), 393–398.

Schøyen, H., & Bråthen, S. (2011). The Northern Sea Route versus the Suez Canal: Cases from bulk shipping. *Journal of Transport Geography*, 19(4), 977–983.

Schröder, C., Reimer, N., & Jochmann, P. (2017). Environmental impact of exhaust emissions by Arctic shipping. *Ambio*, 46(3), 400–409.

Shibasaki, R., Usami, T., Furuichi, M., Teranishi, H., & Kato, H. (2018). How do the new shipping routes affect Asian liquefied natural gas markets and economy? Case of the Northern Sea Route and Panama Canal expansion. *Maritime Policy & Management*, 45(4), 543–566.

Shyu, W. H, & Ding, J. F. (2016). Key factors influencing the building of Arctic shipping routes. *The Journal of Navigation*, 69(6), 1261–1277.

Smith, L. C., & Stephenson, S. R. (2013). New Trans-Arctic shipping routes navigable by midcentury. *Proceedings of the National Academy of Sciences of the United States of America*, 110(13), 4871–4872.

Solakivi, T., Kiiski, T., & Ojala, L. (2017). On the cost of ice: estimating the premium of ice class container vessels. *Maritime Economics & Logistics*, 1–16. doi:10.1057/s41278-017-0077-5

Solakivi, T., Kiiski, T., & Ojala, L. (2018). The impact of ice class on the economics of wet and dry bulk shipping in the Arctic waters. *Maritime Policy & Management*, *45*(4), 530–542.

Somanathan, S., Flynn, P. C., & Szymanski, J. F. (2007). Feasibility of a sea route through the Canadian Arctic. *Maritime Economics & Logistics*, *9*(4), 324–334.

Somanathan, S., Flynn, P., & Szymanski, J. (2009). The Northwest Passage: A simulation. *Transportation Research Part A: Policy and Practice*, *43*(2), 127–135.

Stephenson, S. R., Brigham, L. W., & Smith, L. C. (2014). Marine accessibility along Russia's Northern Sea Route. *Polar Geography*, *37*(2), 111–133.

Stephenson, S. R., & Smith, L. C. (2015). Influence of climate model variability on projected Arctic shipping futures. *Earth's Future*, *3*(11), 331–343.

Stephenson, S. R., Smith, L. C., Brigham, L. W., & Agnew, J. A. (2013). Projected 21st-century changes to Arctic marine access. *Climatic Change*, *118*(3–4), 885–899.

Theocharis, D., Rodrigues, V. S., Pettit, S., & Haider, J. (2018). Arctic shipping: A systematic literature review of comparative studies. *Journal of Transport Geography*, *69*, 112–128.

Tranfield, D., Denyer, D., & Smart, P. (2003). Towards a methodology for developing evidence-informed management knowledge by means of systematic review. *British Journal of Management*, *14*(3), 207–222.

Tseng, P. H., & Cullinane, K. (2018). Key criteria influencing the choice of Arctic shipping: A fuzzy analytic hierarchy process model, *Maritime Policy & Management*, *45*(4), 422–438.

Verny, J., & Grigentin, C. (2009). Container shipping on the Northern Sea Route. *International Journal of Production Economics*, *122*(1), 107–117.

Wacker, J. G. (1998). A definition of theory: Research guidelines for different theory building research methods in operations management. *Journal of Operations Management*, *16*(4), 361–385.

Wan, Z., Ge, J., & Chen, J. (2018). Energy-saving potential and an economic feasibility analysis for an Arctic route between Shanghai and Rotterdam: Case study from China's largest container sea freight operator. *Sustainability*, *10*(4), 1–13.

Wang, H, Zhang, Y., & Meng, Q. (2018). How will the opening of the Northern Sea Route influence the Suez Canal Route? An empirical analysis with discrete choice models. *Transportation Research Part A: Policy and Practice*, *107*, 75–89.

Wergeland, T. (1992). The Northern Sea Route – rosy prospects for commercial shipping? *International Challenges*, *12*(1), 43–57.

Xu, H., Yang, D., & Weng, J. (2018). Economic feasibility of an NSR/SCR-combined container service on the Asia-Europe lane: A new approach dynamically considering sea ice extent. *Maritime Policy & Management*, *45*(4), 514–529.

Xu, H., Yin, Z., Jia, D., Jin, F., & Ouyang, H. (2011). The potential seasonal alternative of Asia-Europe container service via Northern Sea Route under the Arctic sea ice retreat. *Maritime Policy & Management*, *38*(5), 541–560.

Yip, T. Z., & Wong, M. C. (2016). The Nicaragua Canal: Scenarios of its future roles. *Journal of Transport Geography*, *43*, 1–13.

Zeng, Q., Wang, G. W. Y., Qu, C., & Li, K. X. (2017). Impact of the Carat Canal on the evolution of hub ports under China's belt and road initiative. *Transportation Research Part E: Logistics and Transportation Review*, *117*, 96–107.

Zhang, Y., Meng, Q., & Ng, S. H. (2016). Shipping efficiency comparison between northern sea route and the conventional Asia-Europe shipping route via Suez Canal. *Journal of Transport Geography*, *57*, 241–249.

Zhao, H., & Hu, H. (2016). Study on economic evaluation of the Northern Sea Route: Taking the voyage of Yong Sheng as an example. *Transportation Research Board, 2549,* 78–85.

Zhao, H., Hua, H., & Lin, Y. (2016). Study on China-EU container shipping network in the context of Northern Sea Route. *Journal of Transport Geography, 53,* 50–60.

Zhu, S., Fu, X., Ng, A. K. Y., Luo, M., & Ge, Y. E. (2018). The environmental costs and economic implications of container shipping on the Northern Sea Route. *Maritime Policy & Management, 45*(4), 456–477.

3 Modeling the profitability of liner Arctic shipping

Frédéric Lasserre

As detailed in Chapter 2, several models and simulations have been designed to assess the profitability of commercial shipping along Arctic routes. Most of these scenarios are based on NSR simulations, but not all. A significant share also analyze costs based on a single transit, which is consistent with the ad hoc service that is taking shape along the NSR, but that does not picture adequately a possible regular service that could be set up during a whole shipping season for instance, and that would imply a loop service.

These simulations also display a significant variability from one another. Their different conclusions on economic feasibility mainly result from case variability, as these different models do not take into account the same variables, and when they do, there may be differences between the values of the parameters. Different cost models produce different results as they rest on different assumptions, variables and parameters.

This case study compares the cost of exploitation per carried TEU of a regular container ship along the Suez route, with an ice-class container ship plying the Northern Sea Route. The scenario is based on the initial parameters in Table 3.1.

Several simulations consider a cost analysis for a single journey. This analysis is rather based on a cost analysis per transported TEU, over a whole summer shipping season, thus taking into account some market and performance parameters such as speed and load factor. The ships, depending on their speed, will be able to make several rotations and will carry a different volume of containers depending on the number of rotations and the load factor: the cost per TEU will thus be a function of speed, load factor and cost per trip. Table 3.2 details the sources we used to set up the values of the included parameters.

Two initial ports of origin are considered: Shanghai and Yokohama. Although they are not that distant (1750 km), they do impact the simulation inasmuch as the sailing time between Yokohama and Rotterdam is much shorter along the NSR as well as the proportion of the route with slower steaming on the NSR (13 kts). The two cases underline the fact that, over six months of shuttle service, a modest distance between the origin points does make a difference.

This research is a model and thus, like all models, simplifies reality to try and assess the profitability of Arctic container shipping over a whole season along the NSR.

Table 3.1 General initial parameters

	NSR route	Suez route
Ship		4 500 TEU, 70 000 GRT, 54 000 dwt Less than 5 years old Ice class on NSR route: 1AS
Origin		Asia – with a comparison between Shanghai and Yokohama as departure points
Destination		Rotterdam
Shipping season		May 1st–Nov. 1st = 180 days
Suez Canal delay		2 days
Intermediate ports called at	0	3

Table 3.2 Commercial, operating and fixed costs parameters

	Values in the literature	*Set value*
Distance		Shanghai-Rotterdam: Along the NSR: 15 793 Through Suez: 19 550 Yokohama-Rotterdam: Along the NSR: 13 400 Through Suez: 21 200 Source: MapInfo GIS
Load factor	Suez route 2012: 85% (Alphaliner, 2012) 2015: 86% in 2015, 90% in 2014 (World Maritime News, 2015) 2017: about 90% (LoadStar, 2017). Strong differential between eastbound and westbound; eastbound around 60% (Informa, 2017). Significant load factor differential between routes (eastbound/ westbound, but also expected differential Suez/Arctic) according to several shipping companies (Lasserre & Pelletier, 2011; Lasserre et al., 2016).	Suez route: westbound 92% eastbound 62% NSR: westbound 70% eastbound 50%
Maintenance days per year	Stopford (1997): 10 d Greiner (2013): 18 d Somanathan, Flynn, & Szymanski (2009): 14 d for PC4 Correspondence with executive at Desgagnés Transarctik, June 26, 2018: ice-class vessels require longer maintenance.	Regular container vessel: 12 Ice-class vessel: 15

(Continued)

Table 3.2 (Continued)

	Values in the literature	Set value
Speed	Used to be around 22 kts With slow steaming, around 17–18 kts.	Along the NSR: 13 kts Outside NSR: 20 kts
Maintenance cost	Somanathan et al. (2009): 320 K$/yr Wergeland (1992): 1100$/d = 401 500 S/yr, or 657 K$/yr in 2018 inflation-corrected. Stopford (1997): 234 K$/yr worth 47 K$/yr inflation-corrected Greiner (2013): 450 K$/yr for container ship.	Regular container vessel: 450 K$/yr Ice-class vessel: +20% premium, thus 540 K$/yr
Insurance: H&M, P&I	Srinath (2010): 1,4 M$/yr Premium for ice journey: DNV (2010); Srinath (2010); Somanathan et al. (2009): +50% Sarrabezoles et al. (2016): premiums between +25% and +50%	Annual fare: 1,5 M$ Premium for Arctic shipping: +30%
Capital cost and depreciation	Conventional 4 500 TEU container ship: 60 M$ (Liu & Kronbak, 2010), 4 300 TEU 47 M$ (Murray, 2016), 4 500 TEU 47 M$ (Furuichi & Otsuka, 2014) for 4 000 TEU 64 M$ for Panamax 70 000 t tanker in 2007 (Polo, 2012). Financed at 8% over 20 years, straight-line depreciation method; consistent with Počuča (2006); Gkonis and Psaraftis (2010); Kemene (2018). Premium for an ice-class vessel 1AS: see Table 3.3.	Cost of ship: Regular 4 500 TEU: 50 M$ 1AS: 60 M$ Premium for an ice-class vessel 1AS: +20%
Crew	4 500 TEU container ship: 23 people – www.fairship.com.ph 120 K$/month in 2012 for 21 Indian crew (Galanis, 2018) NSR: requires experimented crew, Lasserre and Pelletier (2011); Lasserre et al. (2016); Doyon et al. (2016); Polar Code, chapter 12, Part I-A.	130 000 $/month, regular route NSR crew: +15%
Transit fees/ pilot fee	NSR icebreaker assistance: for Arc7 ship in transit in summertime, 28 464 150 Rb = 455 K$/transit (www.nsra.ru, August 31, 2018).	NSR icebreaker assistance: will be considered to be required 65% of the time: 35% of the transits do not require icebreaking assistance.

	Values in the literature	Set value
	Pilot fee: Furuichi and Otsuka (2014): 673 $/d between Kara and Bering straits. Grandinetti (2017): 1000 $/d + travel Suez: 265 000$/transit, www.suezcanal.gov.eg, August 31, 2018 Suez Canal Authority may enforce rebates for tankers (JOC, 2017) as it already does for tankers (Drewry, 2006) and dry bulk (Wilhelmsen, 2018).	We also consider the NSRA may offer a 40% rebate: transit costs 273 K$. Pilot fee assumed to be 1000 $/d in 2018, travel included. Suez: a 20% rebate is considered. Transit cost: 212 K$.
Fuel consumption rate	Guy (2006): 170 t/d at 22 kts; Počuča (2006): 108 t/d at 22 kts Somanathan et al. (2009): 83 t/d at 20 kts Notteboom and Vernimmen (2009): 90 t/d at 20 kts for 5000 TEU Notteboom and Cariou (2009): 75 t/d at 20 kts for 4500 TEU; about 40 t/d at 14 kts Kiiski (2017): 25 t/d at 13 kts Fednav *Arctic* cargo ship (PC4, 27 000 dwt) burns 34 t/d at 13 kts; the *Nunavik* ship (PC4, 31 754 dwt) burns 35 t/d (Fednav, 2018). Wegerland uses formula as a function of cube of speed; Furuichi and Otsuka (2015) as a function of square of speed. Notteboom and Vernimmen (2009) underline that consumption rate stabilizes at low speeds.	Fuel consumption rate in open water for standard vessel: at 20 kts: 85 t/d at 13 kts: 37 t/d.
Specific fuel consumption for ice class and navigation in ice	Ice-class ships definitely consume more; friction in the ice as well incurs higher fuel consumption, but it is difficult to assess (Lasserre & Pelletier, 2011; Lasserre et al., 2016; personal communications with shipping companies Desgagnés Transarctik & Fednav, 2018). **Ice-class ship-specific fuel consumption:** Same fuel consumption as regular ship (World Gas Intelligence, 2013)	Consumption increased by 8% because of ice class. Overconsumption for friction with ice: +10%.

Table 3.2 (Continued)

Values in the literature	Set value
+0,5 % for 1A (Dvorak, 2009) +5 to 15% depending on class (Erikstad & Ehlers, 2012): +10% for 1A (Furuichi & Otsuka, 2015). +40% at 13 kts for 1A (Kiiski, 2017).	
Ice friction Real impact of ice friction on fuel consumption (Rolls Royce, 2015; Grandinetti, 2017). Icebreaking escort is expensive but reduces ice friction (Grandinetti, 2017): friction is thus acknowledged to be significant. +67% Liu and Kronbak (2010); Pastusiak (2016). +50% Somanathan et al. (2009) +10% Solakivi, Kiiski and Ojala (2017). For "water containing ice", consumption = 0,5 tons/nm at v = 10 kts, and for ice-free water, cons. = 0,3 tons/nm at v = 18 kts (Way, Khan, & Veitch, 2015), which implies a substantial consumption differential.	
Fuel cost	Prices August 31, 2018 HFO: 321 $/t (EnergyMarket Price, www.energymarketprice.com/). Most widely fuel used at the time. IFO 380: 450 $/t (Ship&Bunker Prices, https://shipandbunker.com/prices) NDF: 605 $/t (Desgagnés Transarctik manager, personal communication, Sept. 5, 2018)	We tested the sensitivity of a likely ban of HFO in the Arctic.

It does not claim to take into account all variables, and simplifications were introduced. The model thus works with a set of assumptions:

1 The Arctic area is not considered profitable for container shipping during the winter time, thus the model works with a six-month sailing season.
2 Revenue per TEU is assumed to be the same for both routes without considering customer preferences for saved transportation time (Lasserre et al., 2016),

nor customer risk aversion for the risk of delay when using the NSR route in early spring or late fall, so cost is the determinant for route selection.

3   Penalties for delayed delivery due to ice were not considered, whereas this is a major concern for shipping companies when considering liner Arctic services (Lasserre & Pelletier, 2011; Lasserre et al., 2016).

4   The load factor is set as higher along the Suez route, considered safer and with more stopovers where the ship can load/unload containers and tap into different markets (Lasserre & Pelletier, 2011; Beveridge, Fournier, Lasserre, Huang, & Têtu, 2016; Lasserre et al., 2016).

5   Port charges were not considered in this simulation. Besides, the ships stop for two days at every port.

6   Sailing speed of Arctic routes is slower than that of conventional routes, and an average within the Arctic area is considered, although this of course is a simplification between the likely ice-free end of summertime, and the possibly ice-choked spring and early winter.

Table 3.3 Estimates of capital cost premium for a commercial ice-class ship depending on the class, from the selected simulations

Author (s)	Ice-class category considered	Capital cost premium versus open water (OW) ship
Griffiths, 2005; Mejlaender-Larsen, 2009; Wergeland, 2013	"Ice class"	+10 to 35%
Liu & Kronbak, 2010	1B	+20%
Mulherin et al., 1996; Kamesaki, Kishi, & Yamauchi, 1999; Kitagawa, 2001	PC7 (1A)	+20 to 36%
Mulherin et al., 1996; Schøyen & Bråthen, 2011	PC7 (1A) to PC4	+20%
Mulherin et al., 1996; Dvorak, 2009	PC6 (1AS)	+1 to +20%
DNV, 2010	PC4	+30%
DNV, 2010	PC4 and DAS	+120%
Dvorak, 2009	PC3	+6%
Somanathan, Flynn, & Szymanski, 2007, Somanathan et al., 2009	PC2	+30%
Srinath, 2010	PC2	+40%
Chernova & Volkov, 2010	DAS with "high ice class":	+30 to 40%
Erikstad & Ehlers, 2012	1A	+9,5%
	1AS	+12%
Grandinetti, 2017	PC4 versus 1A	+30%
ShipTechnology, nd; ICIS, 2006; Baudu, 2018	PC3/ARC7 YamalMax LNG carrier (*Chr. De Margerie*) versus QMax OW	+33%

7   Both the Suez Authorities and the Northern Sea Route Administration are likely to offer rebates on their official fees.
8   The average speed for the NSR route is the arithmetic average of speed along the NSR segment (5635 km at 13 kts) and of speed along non-NSR segments, at 20 kts.

First case study: Shanghai-Rotterdam

This scenario compares the traditional route between Shanghai and Rotterdam along the Suez route, with a route along the NSR. In this benchmark scenario, ships are assumed to use HFO. See Table 3.4.

Table 3.4 Matrix of cost calculation, route Shanghai-Rotterdam

		NSR	*Suez*
Distance (MapInfo GIS) in nm		15 793	19 550
Load factor			
Westbound		70%	92%
Eastbound		50%	62%
Number of TEUs per trip			
Westbound		3 150	4 140
Eastbound		2 250	2 790
Maintenance, days		15	12
	Suez Canal delay		2
	Ports called at	1	4
Stop days total		2	10
Average speed (in kts)		17,11	20
Loop time			
Sailing time (days)		21,4	22,6
Total segment time (in days)		23,4	32,6
Total possible rotations			
Calculated		7,06	5,15
Rounded at		7	5
Total TEUs transported		19 350	18 000
Cost analysis		(for 6 months)	
OPEX and CAPEX (in USD)		NSR	Suez
Crew		897 000	780 000
Insurance: H&M, P&I		975 000	750 000
Capital cost		3 136 650	2 509 333
Maintenance		540 000	450 000
Transit fees		1 312 387	1 060 000
Proportion of transits requiring icebreaking assistance		0,65	
Average transit fee per trip		187 483,83	212 000
Fuel consumption surcharge for ice-strengthened ship		8%	
Fuel consumption surcharge for friction with ice along the NSR		10%	

	NSR	*Suez*
Average fuel consumption rate, t/d	69,33	85
Sailing days per segment	21,4	22,6
Fuel consumed per trip	1 480,92	1 923,32
Bunker price, HFO, $/t	321	321
Fuel cost per trip	475 373,99	617 386,28
Fuel cost, total (in USD)	3 327 617,95	3 086 931,42
Total cost, 6 months	10 188 654,77	8 636 264,42
Cost per TEU (in USD)	**526,55**	**479,79**

Several observations can be inferred from these results:

- Even with a lower load factor, the service along the NSR route carries more containers because of the faster rotation rate, 7 trips against 5 because of the shorter route and despite the slower pace along the NSR.
- Fuel consumption is much lower along the NSR, 1480,92 tons per trip, as opposed to 1923,32 tons per trip with the Suez route.
- Despite this commercial and operational advantage, higher costs burden the cost efficiency of the service along the Arctic route, making the cost per container less competitive at 526,55 $ against 479,79 $ for the Suez route.

Second case study: Yokohama-Rotterdam

The second scenario (Table 3.5) compares the traditional route between Yokohama and Rotterdam along the Suez route with the NSR route.

In this scenario:

- Starting from a more northerly port, the ice-class ship is able to perform one more trip for a total of 8 instead of 7 in the Shanghai case. The ship is thus able to carry 21 600 TEUs against 18 000 along the Suez route.
- Fuel consumption is much lower along the NSR, 1266,08 tons per trip, as opposed to 2085,65 tons per trip with the Suez route.
- In this case study, the shipping service is cheaper along the NSR route, with a 476,84 $/container cost as against 494,27 $/container along the Suez route.

The different starting point thus accounts for a competitive advantage for the Arctic route in this scenario: a shorter route that enables the ship to make more rotations and a better fuel consumption per trip. The more northerly the origin and destination points are, the shorter the route can be along the NSR versus along the Suez route; the better the reduced fuel consumption can bring costs down, the more rotations the ship can make over a whole shipping season. So as to underline this,

Table 3.5 Matrix of cost calculation, route Yokohama-Rotterdam

	NSR	Suez
Distance (MapInfo GIS)	13 400	21 200
Load factor		
Westbound	70%	92%
Eastbound	50%	62%
Number of TEUs		
Westbound	3 150	4 140
Eastbound	2 250	2 790
Maintenance, days	15	12
Suez Canal delay		2
Ports called at	1	4
Stop days total	2	10
Average speed	16,31	20
Loop time		
Sailing time (days)	19	24,5
Total segment time (days)	21	34,5
Total possible segments		
Calculation	7,85	4,86
Rounded at	8	5
Total TEUs transported	21 600	18 000
Cost analysis	(for 6 months)	
	NSR	Suez
Crew	897 000	780 000
Insurance: H&M, P&I	975 000	750 000
Capital cost	3 136 650	2 509 333
Maintenance	540 000	450 000
Transit fees	1 499 871	1 060 000
Proportion of transits requiring icebreaking assistance	0,65	
Average transit fee per trip	187 483,83	212 000
Fuel consumption surcharge for ice-strengthened ship	8%	
Fuel consumption surcharge for friction with ice along the NSR	10%	
Average Fuel consumption rate, t/d	66,56	85
Sailing days per segment	19,0	24,5
Fuel consumed	1 266,08	2 085,65
Bunker price, HFO, $/t	321	321
Fuel cost per trip	406 411,16	669 493,06
Fuel cost, total	3 251 289,24	3 347 465,28
Total cost, 6 months	10 299 809,90	8 896 798,28
Cost per TEU	**476,84**	**494,27**

we also ran the simulation from Manila; the distance to Rotterdam with the NSR is 17 393 km, and distance through Suez is 17 950 km. In this scenario, the costs per container amount to 612,2 $ and 465,8 $ respectively, underlining the very poor performance of the NSR for southern ports.

Making hypotheses: tuning the parameters

Fuel cost: an important parameter if fuel consumption rates are significant

The literature readily underlines that Arctic routes, being shorter, could imply a significant cost advantage because of a reduced fuel consumption, stemming both from a shorter distance and from a reduced speed. This is underlined by the model, as a single trip consumes less for the NSR route. However, when the fuel cost parameter is modified and higher fuel costs are introduced, the cost differential (hereafter, the cost for a container carried along the NSR versus the cost of a container carried through Suez) does not display a significant advantage for the NSR. This is verified for the Yokohama case but, quite the contrary, the differential diminishes when the fuel cost increases in the Shanghai case (Table 3.6).

This can be explained by the fact the study is not based on a single trip cost analysis, but on a whole season. The ship along the NSR route may consume less than along the Suez road, but it makes more shuttles, with less containers on board, thus eroding the cost advantage of a reduced fuel consumption per trip.

This is illustrated when the fuel consumption rate parameter is modified (see Table 3.7).

These figures underline the fact that the real cost advantage of a reduced fuel consumption per trip converts into a significant cost differential over a whole season only when the fuel consumption rate is substantially different. If this fuel

Table 3.6 Cost differential given variations in fuel cost

Hypothetic fuel cost, $/t	Cost differential	
	Shanghai case	Yokohama case
100	46,43	6,98
321 (benchmark)	46,75	−17,42
500	47,02	−37,19
900	47,61	−81,36

Table 3.7 Cost differential given variations in fuel cost and consumption rate

Shanghai case	Standard ship fuel consumption rate				
Hypothetic fuel cost, $/t	80	85 (benchmark)	95	105	115
100	47,36	46,43	44,57	42,71	40,85
321 (benchmark)	49,74	46,75	40,78	34,81	28,84
500	51,67	47,02	37,72	28,42	19,12
900	55,98	47,61	30,87	14,13	−2,6

consumption rate is reduced, then the fuel consumption advantages is seriously eroded for the NSR route.

The likely ban of heavy fuel in the Arctic

Another important point is the fact the benchmark scenario rests on the assumption both ships, through Suez and along the NSR, use the same type of fuel, here HFO. This is increasingly unrealistic, as the industry increasingly orders ice-class ships to work with IFO 380; and as there is a mounting pressure on the IMO to enforce a ban on heavy fuel in the Arctic for pollution-control purposes (George, 2018, 2019; Kaltenstein, 2018; Sevunst, 2018), that is gaining momentum despite the opposition of Russia for instance (*Over the Circle*, 2018). When making the scenarios with different fuels, i.e. HFO through Suez and IFO 380 along the NSR, then the cost differential plunges and no route is profitable along the NSR (Table 3.8).

Icebreaking assistance

This analysis rests on the idea, documented in the literature, that shipping companies negotiate discounts with the Northern Sea Route Authority or the Suez Canal Authority. Besides, the melt trends in successive summers hints there may be an increasing occurrence of transits where icebreaking assistance is not required for a 1AS cargo ship. If this did not materialize, what impact would it have? See Table 3.9.

Table 3.8 Cost differential when IFO 380 is considered along the NSR

	NSR with IFO 380 (450 $/t)	Suez with HFO (321 $/t)	Cost differential
Shanghai case	595,65	479,79	115,86
Yokohama case	537,33	494,27	43,07

Table 3.9 Cost differential given the probabilistic share of transit with icebreaking assistance. IFO 380 used along the NSR

	IFO 380 along the NSR		HFO along the NSR	
	Shanghai	Yokohama	Shanghai	Yokohama
100 %	150,43	78,46	81,32	17,97
85%	135,61	63,29	66,5	2,8
Benchmark: 65%	115,86	43,07	46,75	−17,42
45%	96,11	22,84	27	−37,65
25%	76,36	2,62	7,25	−57,87

It appears the impact of sea-ice presence, thus the necessity to use icebreaking assistance and thus pay the transit fees, does affect significantly the cost differential. In particular, for the Yokohama route, the concentration of ice, and thus the need to request icebreaking assistance, can make the difference between no profit and near profitability when IFO 380 is used (at 25%), or profitability below 65% if HFO is used.

Speed along the NSR

This study rests on an average speed along the NSR set at 13 kts. If the average speed were improved in Arctic waters, how would that impact the cost differential? With an increased average speed, then of course fuel consumption rate increases as well. For the sake of the simulation, we tried with another average speed of 16 kts and a fuel consumption rate of 60 t/d at that speed (Table 3.10).

With this parameter, it is apparent the cost differential can be significantly improved along the Yokohama route, a faster speed enabling the ice-class ship to perform one more rotation without incurring a significant increase in cost per trip, thus improving its cost differential per container. Along the Shanghai route however, the higher fuel cost per trip can be offset in the HFO scenario but not if the ship has to use IFO 380.

The load factor: a critical parameter

Operational and fixed costs determine the cost differential per trip. In both scenarios, Shanghai and Yokohama, the direct costs are lower per trip, even when considering mandatory IFO 380 along the NSR route. As it can make more rotations, the ice-class ship can spread the fixed costs (crew, capital, insurance, maintenance) over more trips and thus reduce the impact of higher costs (Table 3.11).

These figures underline why so many simulations, based on the cost per trip approach, underline Arctic shipping is profitable: indeed, on this basis, the NSR appears to have an advantage and ad hoc transits could therefore develop in the future, as costs are lower. But costs are not all as the commercial dimension must

Table 3.10 Cost differential with speed at 16 kts along the NSR, with two fuel scenarios

	If HFO used along NSR	If IFO 380 used along NSR
Shanghai case	38,55	115,99
(benchmark at 13 kts)	46,76	115,86
Yokohama case	−38,45	27,51
(benchmark at 13 kts)	−17,42	43,07

Table 3.11 Cost per trip when considering the use of IFO 380 in the Arctic

	NSR	Suez
Shanghai case	1 646,6 K$ (7 trips)	1 727,3 K$ (5 trips)
Yokohama case	1 450,8 K$ (8 trips)	1 779,36 K$ (5 trips)

Table 3.12 Cost differential per container depending on the load factor along the NSR

Load factor along the NSR	With IFO 380 along the NSR		With HFO along the NSR	
	Shanghai case	Yokohama case	Shanghai case	Yokohama case
70/50 (benchmark)	115,86	43,07	46,75	−17,42
75/53	78,23	9,48	13,49	−47,23
80/57	41,86	−23,61	−18,66	−76,59
85/60	12,77	−49,58	−44,38	−99,64
92/62 (same value as Suez)	−17,46	−75,57	−71,10	−122,70

be taken into account. Table 3.12 presents the form of the load factor, especially if a regular service is to be developed.

It becomes apparent here that if a regular market can be developed so as to ensure a significant load factor along the Arctic route, then even with a higher fuel price for Arctic waters, in the Yokohama case the Arctic service becomes profitable even with a moderate load factor, less so in the Shanghai case. Reaching a high load factor on a regular basis on a route without intermediate ports is for now a major uncertainty.

Conclusion

As opposed to many simulations and case studies in the literature, this case here does not focus on a single journey, nor only on cost variables. It rather integrates operational and market variables such as the variability of sea ice demanding icebreaking assistance, speed that determines the number of rotations, and the load factor, thus presenting an analysis more suitable for the question of profitability of Arctic shipping for a regular service, rather than for a single, ad hoc transit.

The analysis underlines that:

• The impact of the location of the origin/destination port is clear: the more northerly the pair is, the more competitive a shuttle service along the NSR is going to be.
• When the likelihood of a ban on heavy fuel is considered, then Arctic shipping profitability is damaged, but not radically altered, especially in the Yokohama

case. The fact is that despite higher fixed costs, possibly lower transit costs and reduced fuel costs even with IFO380 make room for profitability if other parameters display favorable values.

• Operational and market parameters such as average speed and load factor present a very significant impact on the cost differential per container. The higher the speed along the NSR, despite increased fuel consumption, the more transits the ship can perform and thus the more containers can be carried, reducing the impact of higher fixed costs; the same applies with a higher load factor that entails a larger volume of transported containers.

Commercial Arctic shipping could therefore be profitable for liner services in the Arctic, but uncertainty remains as to which lines could be profitable, especially given the variability of several parameters such as speed, the need for icebreaking assistance or the possible ban of heavy fuel in the years to come. This research also underlines that market parameters such as the load factor (included in this model), or the risk aversion for the uncertainty of transit time (not included), may tilt the balance in favor of the development of liner service in the Arctic or not.

References

Alphaliner (2012, October 17). Container shipping 2013 market outlook. *TPM Asia Conference*, Shenzhen.

Baudu, H. (2018, September 14). *Professor, naval technology and piloting, école nationale superieure maritime* (Marseille, France). Personal communication.

Beveridge, L. M. Fournier, F. Lasserre, L. Huang, P., & Têtu, L. (2016). Interest of Asian shipping companies in navigating the Arctic. *Polar Science*, *10*(3), 404–414.

Chernova, S., & Volkov, A. (2010). *Economic feasibility of the Northern Sea Route container shipping development*. MSc Business and Transportation, Bodø Graduate School of Business.

Det Norske Veritas (DNV) (2010). *Shipping across the Arctic Ocean*. Høvik: DNV Research and Innovation, Position Paper 4.

Doyon, J. F. F., Lasserre. P., Pic, P. L., Têtu, M., Fournier, L., Huang, L., & Beveridge, W. (2016). Perceptions et stratégies de l'industrie maritime de vrac relativement à l'ouverture des passages arctiques. *Géotransports*, *8*, 5–22.

Drewry (2006). *Annual LNG shipping market review & forecast*. London: Maritime Research.

Dvorak, R. (2009). *Engineering and economic implications of ice-classed containerships* (MSc Dissertation). Massachusetts Institute of Technology, Cambridge.

Erikstad, S. O., & Ehlers, S. (2012). Decision support framework for exploiting Northern Sea Route transport opportunities. *Ship Technology Research*, *59*(2), 34–42.

Fednav (2018, September 12). Fleet. *Arctic*. Retrieved from www.fednav.com/en/fleet/arctic; *Nunavik*, www.fednav.com/en/nunavik

Furuichi, M., & Otsuka, N. (2014). Economic feasibility of finished vehicle and container transport by NSR/SCR-combined shipping between East Asia and Northwest Europe. In *Proceedings of the IAME 2014 Conference. Norfolk, USA*.

Furuichi, M., & Otsuka, N. (2015). Proposing a common platform of shipping cost analysis of the Northern Sea Route and the Suez Canal Route. *Maritime Economics & Logistics, 17*(1), 9–31.

Galanis, K. (2018). *Costs and accounting: Institute of chartered shipbrokers.* Greek branch.

George, J. (2018, April 12). Pressure's on UN shipping agency to embrace heavy fuel oil ban. *Nunatsiaq News.* Retrieved September 17, 2018, from http://nunatsiaq.com/stories/article/65674pressures_on_un_shipping_agency_to_embrace_heavy_fuel_oil_ban/

George, J. (2019, February 25). Push continues to phase out heavy fuel oil in the Arctic. *Nunatsiaq News.* Retrieved February 26, 2019, from https://nunatsiaq.com/stories/article/push-to-phase-out-heavy-fuel-oil-in-the-arctic-continues/

Gkonis, K. G., & Psaraftis, H. N. (2010). *Some key variables affecting liner shipping costs.* Working Paper, Laboratory for Maritime Transport, National Technical University of Athens.

Grandinetti, S. (2017). *Development of a cost-benefit model for shipping in the Arctic* (Master's thesis). In Naval Architecture & Ocean Engineering, Chalmers University of Technology, Gothenburg, Sweden.

Greiner, R. (2013). *Ship operating costs: Current and future trends.* Public presentation, Moore Stephens.

Griffiths, F. (2005). New illusions of a Northwest Passage. In M. Nordquist, J. N. Moore, & A. S. Skaridov (Eds.), *International energy policy, the Arctic and the Law of the Sea* (pp. 303–309). Leiden: Martinus Nijhoff Publishers.

Guy, E. (2006). Evaluating the viability of commercial shipping in the Northwest Passage. *Journal of Ocean Technology, 1*(1), 9–15.

ICIS. (2006). QFlex and QMax to make the most of bettering boil-off losses. *ICIS.* Retrieved September 20, 2018, from www.icis.com/resources/news/2006/11/03/9291538/qflex-and-qmax-to-make-the-most-of-bettering-boil-off-losses/

Informa. (2017). Europe-Asia eastbound ocean prices approach westbound levels. April 10. *Lloyds Loading List.* Retrieved September 8, 2018, from www.lloydsloadinglist.com/freight-directory/news/Europe-Asia-eastbound-ocean-prices-approach-westbound-levels/69072.htm#.W5Ka7OhKiUk

JOC. (2017). Discounts help stabilize Suez Canal traffic. *Journal of Commerce JOC.* Retrieved September 12, 2018, from www.joc.com/maritime-news/container-lines/discounts-help-stabilize-suez-canal-traffic_20170606.html

Kaltenstein, J. (2018, May 25). The foreseeable end of vessel heavy fuel oil use in the Arctic. *Friends of the Earth.* Retrieved September 12, 2018, from https://foe.org/foreseeable-end-vessel-heavy-fuel-oil-use-arctic/

Kamesaki, K., Kishi, S., & Yamauchi, Y. (1999). *Simulation of NSR navigation based on year round and seasonal operation scenarios* (INSROP Working Paper 8). Oslo: INSROP.

Kemene, A. (2018). Newbuildings & Yards 2018. (Head of Market Analysis, Optima Shipping services). *Marine Money Week,* June 18–20, New York.

Kiiski, T. (2017). *Feasibility of commercial cargo shipping along the Northern Sea Route* (Doctoral Thesis). Turku School of Economics, University of Turku.

Kitagawa, H. (2001). *The Northern Sea Route. The shortest sea route linking East Asia and Europe.* The Ocean Foundation, Tokyo.

Lasserre, F. L., Beveridge, M., Fournier, P. L., Têtu, L., & Huang, R. (2016). Polar seaways? Maritime transport in the Arctic: An analysis of shipowners' intentions II. *Journal of Transport Geography, 57*(2016), 105–114.

Lasserre, F., & Pelletier, S. (2011). Polar super seaways? Maritime transport in the Arctic: An analysis of shipowners' intentions. *Journal of Transport Geography*, *19*(6), 1465–1473.

Liu, M., & Kronbak, J. (2010). The potential economic viability of using the Northern Sea Route (NSR) as an alternative route between Asia and Europe. *Journal of Transport Geography*, *18*, 434–444.

LoadStar. (2017). Container lines praised for finally finding capacity management skills. *Load Star*. Retrieved September 3, 2018, from https://theloadstar.co.uk/container-lines-praised-finally-finding-capacity-management-skills/

Mejlaender-Larsen, M. (2009). ARCON – Arctic container. *DNV Container Ship Update*, *2*, 9–11.

Mulherin, N., Eppler, D., Proshutinsky, T., Proshutinsy, A., Farmer, L. D., & Smith, O. (1996). *Development and results of a Northern Sea Route transit model* (CRREL Research Report 96–5). US Army Corps of Engineers, Hanover, NH.

Murray, W. (2016). *Economies of scale in container ship costs*. United States Merchant Marine Academy.

Notteboom, T., & Carriou, P. (2009). Fuel surcharge practices of container shipping lines: Is it about cost recovery or revenue making? *Proceedings of the 2009 International Association of Maritime Economists* (IAME) Conference. June 24–26, Copenhagen.

Notteboom, T., & Vernimmen, B. (2009). The effect of high fuel costs on liner service configuration in container shipping. *Journal of Transport Geography*, *17*, 325–337.

Over the Circle. (2018, April 18). A burning question: Governments agree to an Arctic heavy fuel oil ban. *Over the Circle. Arctic Politics and Foreign Policy*. Retrieved September 17, 2018, from https://overthecircle.com/2018/04/14/a-burning-question-governments-agree-to-an-arctic-heavy-fuel-oil-ban/

Pastusiak, T. (2016). *The Northern Sea Route as a shipping lane: Expectations and reality*. Hamburg: Springer.

Počuča, M. (2006). Methodology of day-to-day ship costs assessment. *Transportation Economics Review, Traffic and Transportation*, *18*(5), 337–345.

Polo, G. (2012). On maritime transport costs, evolution, and forecast. *Ship Science & Technology*, *5*(10), 19–31.

Rolls-Royce. (2015). Polar push. *Indepth Magazine*, *26*, 30–31.

Sarrabezoles, A., Lasserre, F., & Hagouagn'rin, Z. (2016). Arctic shipping insurance: Towards a harmonisation of practices and costs? *Polar Record*, *52*(4), 393–398.

Schøyen, H., & Bråthen, S. (2011). The Northern Sea Route versus the Suez Canal: Cases from bulk shipping. *Journal of Transport Geography*, *19*, 977–983.

Sevunst, L. (2018 April 11). Inuit activist blasts Canada's foot-dragging on dirty fuels ban in the Arctic. *RCInet*. Retrieved September 17, 2018, from www.rcinet.ca/en/2018/04/11/inuit-activist-blasts-canadas-foot-dragging-ban-dirty-fuels-hfo-arctic/

Ship Technology (nd). Christophe de Margerie class icebreaking LNG carriers. *Ship Technology*. Retrieved September 20, 2018, from www.ship-technology.com/projects/christophe-de-margerie-class-icebreaking-lng-carriers/

Solakivi, T., Kiiski, T., & Ojala, L. (2017). On the cost of ice: Estimating the premium of ice class container vessels. *Maritime Economics & Logistics*. doi:10.1057/s41278-017-0077-51-16

Somanathan, S., Flynn, P., & Szymanski, J. (2007). Feasibility of a sea route through the Canadian Arctic. *Maritime Economics & Logistics*, *9*, 324–334.

Somanathan, S., Flynn, P., & Szymanski, J. (2009). The Northwest Passage: A simulation. *Transportation Research Part A*, *43*, 127–135.

Srinath, B. N. (2010). *Arctic shipping: Commercial viability of the Arctic sea routes* (MSc Dissertation). City University, London.

Stopford, M. (1997). *Maritime economics*, 2nd ed. London: Routledge.

Way, B., Khan, F., & Veitch, B. (2015). The Northern Sea Route vs the Suez Canal Route: An economic analysis incorporating probabilistic simulation optimization of vessel speed. *Proceedings of the ASME 2015 34th International Conference on Ocean, Offshore and Arctic Engineering.* Paper No. OMAE2015–42054, 10 p., doi:10.1115/OMAE2015–42054. American Society of Mechanical Engineers.

Wergeland, T. (1992). The Northern Sea Route – rosy prospects for commercial shipping? *International Challenges, 12*(1), 43–57.

Wergeland, T. (2013). Northeast, Northwest and transpolar passages in comparison. In W. Østreng, (Ed.), *Shipping in Arctic waters: A comparison of the Northeast, Northwest and Trans Polar Passages* (pp. 299–352). Berlin: Springer Verlag and Praxis.

Wilhelmsen. (2018). Suez Canal: Frequently used toll rebate schemes. *Wilhelmsen.* Retrieved September 18, 2018 from www.wilhelmsen.com/ships-agency/suez-canal/suez-canal-latest-rebates/

World Gas Intelligence. (2013 October 30). Horizon: Ice class LNG vessel orders mount as Arctic sea ice shrinks. *Energy Intelligence.* Retrieved September 3, 2018, from http://www3.energyintel.com/WebUploads/gei-moscow/media-files/iod-story-30-10-2.html

World Maritime News. (2015 July 13). Drewry: Ship utilisation hit by overcapacity. *World Maritime News.* Retrieved September 5, 2018, from https://worldmaritimenews.com/archives/166371/drewry-ship-utilisation-hit-by-overcapacity/

4 An economic analysis on the NSR viability of an ice-class 1A oil tanker vessel

Pierre Cariou and Olivier Faury

Introduction

The profitability of the Arctic navigation depends on numerous economic parameters that are impacted by climatic conditions. Some of these parameters are related to the vessel. The reason is that in order to limit the risk represented by ice extent and thickness or by sailing in the fragile Arctic ecosystem, underwriters may for instance impose the use of ice-class vessel and icebreakers in polar waters (Fedi et al., 2018). This leads to higher capital (CAPEX), operating (OPEX) and voyage costs that directly affect the profitability of vessels. Ice conditions (thickness, extent . . .) are also having a direct impact on the economic NSR viability as additional insurance and icebreakers costs may be incurred. The impact of all these different costs remains relative, as according to the month of the year, the freight rates and the bunker prices are fluctuating and may limit the effect from higher bunker costs or icebreaker costs on the total profitability. If these elements remain mostly exogenous for shipowners, they are also likely to influence the choice on the sailing speed inside and outside the NSR. The aim of this chapter is to analyse the way an ice-class 1A reacts to change in climatic and market conditions and to determine the monthly NSR viability when sailing through the Arctic. To do so, the chapter first presents a literature review on the main factor affecting the NSR viability. The next section develops a model to show how economic and climatic conditions affect the shipowners' profitability and how speed has to adapt to the ice conditions in order to maintain a safe navigation. Then, Section 4 applies the model to a business case relative to the voyage of a 1A Ice-Class Panamax oil product tanker sailing from Murmansk (Russia) to Daesan (South Korea). The "Sensitivity Analysis" section shows how the changes in two economic parameters (fuel prices and freight rates) and in one climatic parameter (ice thickness) affect the NSR competitiveness and the last section provides some conclusions.

Literature review

The factors influencing the decision to sail through the Arctic has been intensively discussed in former years (Theocharis, Pettit, Rodrigues, & Haider, 2018; Lasserre, 2014; Meng, Zhang, & Xu, 2017). The choice is mostly influenced by sailing conditions (Comiso, 2012) as well as by some technical (Mulherin et al., 1996) and economic parameters (Lasserre, 2014; Cariou & Faury, 2015). These three elements are highly interrelated. For instance, sailing conditions impact profits but the impact differs with the type of vessels (ice class) and with prevailing market conditions such as fuel prices, freight rate or the NSR transit fee (Ragner, 2000a, 2000b; Farré et al., 2014; Ng et al., 2018; Zhang, Meng, & Ng, 2016; Pastusiak, 2016; Marchenko, 2014b; Meng et al., 2017).

Regarding the sailing conditions related to climatic parameters, most scholars agreed on a global year-to-year downward trend in ice extent and thickness, despite a high level of unpredictability in the short term (Comiso, 2012; Stephenson & Pincus, 2018; Comiso, Parkinson, Gersten, & Stock, 2008; Aksenov et al., 2017; Lindsay & Schweiger, 2015; Kwok & Rothrock, 2009; Maslanik et al., 2007; Meng et al., 2017). Stephenson, Brigham, Smith and Agnew (2013) and Marchenko (2014a) provide more detailed analysis on the capacity of a polar-class vessel to sail along the NSR, knowing that ice conditions are changing according to the area and to the seasons (Pastusiak, 2016; Lensu, Heale, Riska, & Kujala, 1996), without assessing, however, the economic viability of sailing through the Arctic.

Technical elements to ensure safe navigation within the Arctic (Pastusiak, 2016; Fedi et al., 2018) also impact Capital (CAPEX) and Operational (OPEX) expenditures as well as voyage costs (Erikstad & Ehlers, 2012; Lasserre, 2014; Theocharis et al., 2018; Cariou & Faury, 2015; Pruyn, 2016; Ragner, 2008; Xu, Yang, & Weng, 2018). This has led many scholars to investigate the structure of costs for various types of vessels sailing through the Arctic, and in particular for containerships (Verny & Grigentin, 2009; Lasserre, 2014; Liu & Kronbak, 2010; Furuichi & Otsuka, 2018; Xu et al., 2018), car carriers (Erikstad & Ehlers, 2012) or for bulk carriers (Schøyen & Bråthen, 2011; Faury & Cariou; 2016; Pruyn, 2016; Mulherin et al., 1996).

In order to face the challenges represented by Arctic navigation, vessels are grouped into ice classes, each class with specific conditions with regards to the hull (ability to resist to ice pressure), to the engine (enough power to crash the ice) and to the ability to resist to extreme low temperature (Pastusiak, 2016; Marchenko, 2014b; Fedi et al., 2018). All these elements impact CAPEX and OPEX up to 20–120% according to the vessel class and compared to ships who are sailing in open waters (Lasserre, 2014; Erikstad & Ehlers, 2012; Theocharis, 2018; Mulherin et al., 1996; Furuichi & Otsuka, 2012; Lasserre, 2014; Xu et al., 2018). Besides, they also have a direct impact on voyage cost (Erikstad & Ehlers, 2012; Schøyen & Brathen, 2011; Koskinen & Hilmola, 2005; Faury & Givry, 2017).

Economic conditions are also important when assessing the viability of the NSR (Cariou & Faury, 2015). Koskinen and Hilmola (2005) and Stopford (2009) shed light on the importance of the relation between the freight rate market and investment decision. Lasserre (2014) highlights that fuel is one of the main components for Arctic navigation profitability and attractiveness Furuichi and Otsuka (2012). Gritsenko and Kiiski (2016) and Faury (2015) stress the importance of the

NSR fees (NSRA, 2017), while Lin et al. (2018) mention seafarers' skills, bunker price and transit time.

The NSR attractiveness changes with the type of cargo and shipping operational features. Regarding bulk transportation, the focus of this chapter, the guarantee to arrive on time (speed) and to provide a safe navigation compared to the conventional shipping lane are key factors. Due to the sailing conditions, reliability at the port of destination is hardly reachable for some months (Lasserre & Pelletier, 2011). Yet, the use of a higher ice class and the increase of speed outside the NSR may reduce the transit time. However, as stressed by Marchenko (2014b) and Lasserre and Pelletier (2011), speed plays a key role as a cause of incident within the Arctic, as a non-adapted speed can affect safety.

If speed impacts the safety of the navigation, it is also a paramount factor to understand the costs which are largely impacted by ice thickness, ice extent and concentration (Stoddard, Etienne, Fournier, Pelot, & Beveridge, 2016; Kitagawa, 2001; Furuichi & Otsuka, 2018; Löptien & Axell, 2014; Xu et al., 2018). Fuel consumption being one of the most important expenditure (Stopford, 2009), the type of fuel used has a strong impact on the potential attractiveness of the NSR (Lasserre, 2014). For now heavy fuel oil (HFO) is not banned, yet, but requirements for an alternative fuel type (Nilsen, 2017) could negatively impact the NSR attractiveness.

Yet, the 40% potential shortcut represented by the NSR (Ragner, 2008) is an opportunity to decrease fuel consumption (Pastusiak, 2016) and thus to save money (Falck, 2012). Although Cariou and Faury (2015) define the potential savings represented by sailing through the NSR as a function of the speed, they do not analyse what is the optimal speed in order to maximize earnings, and how this optimal speed may be affected by weather conditions along the NSR route. This study aims at filling this gap in providing a simple model and application to determine the optimal speed of a vessel to maximize the Time Charter Equivalent (TCE) of a vessel sailing through the Arctic and to assess if the TCE is sufficient to cover operating expenses.

Model

In bulk shipping, and without considering port time or demurrage, a shipowner that aims at maximizing its profit considers the Time Charter Equivalent per day (Evans & Marlow, 1990):

$$TCE = \frac{R.W}{\dfrac{d}{24.s}} - p\left(k.\left(24.s\right)^{\beta} + F_A\right) \tag{4.1}$$

where TCE is the Daily Time Charter Equivalent (in USD/day), R the freight rate (in USD/ton of cargo), W the deadweight available for cargo (in tons), p the price of fuel (in USD per ton), d the distance travelled (in nautical miles), s the speed (in nautical miles/hour), k a ship-specific constant of proportionality and F_A the fuel consumption per day for the auxiliary engine. In most studies (Psaraftis & Konto-vas, 2013, 2014), the beta-value is equal to 3 and k is estimated using information on the design speed (S_{ds}) and on the fuel consumption at design speed (FC_{ds}) so that $k = \dfrac{F_{ds}}{\left(24.s_{ds}\right)^{3}}$.

In the short run and in a pure and perfect competition market such as for the tramping market (Stopford, 2009), freight rate and fuel prices are exogeneous and therefore outside the shipowners' control. Therefore, the only adjustable param-eter in order to maximise profit is the speed along the route. The optimal speed is then a function of distance to travel, freight rate and fuel price and is obtained when $\dfrac{dTCE}{ds} = 0,$ equivalent to:

$$s^{*} = \frac{1}{24}\sqrt{\frac{R.W}{3.p.k.d}} \tag{4.2}$$

In open water (OW), the speed (S_{OW}) can be continuously adjusted within a lower S_{min} (for safe navigation) and a higher S_{max} (for maximum speed) bound. When a vessel sails within a restricted area, such as through the NSR, weather conditions, related for instance to ice thickness, restrict the maximum allowable speed (S_{NSR}) to a limit lower than the maximum speed (S_{max}). Furthermore, as vessels need icebreaker assistance, the vessel bears additional costs, related to the NSR fee for icebreaker assistance (Fee_{NSR}). Therefore, the new TCE when a vessel sails along the NSR and when a speed limit (S_{NSR}) exists inside the NSR due to climatic condi-tions is now equal to:

$$TCE = \frac{RW - Fee_{NSR}}{\left(\dfrac{d_1}{24.s_{OW}} + \dfrac{d_{NSR}}{24.s_{NSR}}\right)} - \frac{pk\left(s_{OW}^{3}\dfrac{d_1}{24.s_{OW}} + s_{NSR}^{3}\dfrac{d_{NSR}}{24.s_{NSR}}\right)}{\left(\dfrac{d_1}{24.s_{OW}} + \dfrac{d_{NSR}}{24.s_{NSR}}\right)} - p.F_A \cdot \tag{4.3}$$

Under such conditions, the speed can only be adjusted when the vessel is sailing outside the NSR, in open water for $S_{OW}\left(\dfrac{dTCE}{ds_{OW}} = 0\right)$ and as S_{OW} appears on both side of the equation, the optimal speed can only be found by iterations, i.e. in estimating the TCE for various speeds. The next section presents a business case corresponding to two different voyages.

Business case

We applied the model in considering the information gathered in Faury and Car-iou (2016) relative to the voyage of a 1A Ice-Class Panamax oil product tanker (the MV Mari Ugland) sailing from Murmansk (Russia) to Daesan (South Korea).

Vessel-specific parameters are as follows: design speed (S_{ds}) is 16 kts and the fuel consumption for the main engine at design speed (FC_{ds}) is 44,9 tons/day (Table 4.1). The auxiliary engine fuel consumption is 3,5 tons/day and the deadweight tons available for cargo W is 73 434 tons. For route-specific characteristics, the distance to travel is 5 320 nautical miles (nm), with 2 630 nm on the NSR.

Vessels speed within the ice is impacted by ice thickness, concentration, typology and the friction of the ice against the hull. If our model did not integrate the concentration and the friction of the ice, we defined the speed according to the ice

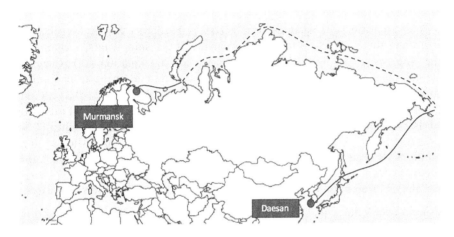

Figure 4.1 Shipping lane

Source: Authors (2019)

Table 4.1 Vessel characteristics

Ice class	1A
DWT (W)[1]	73 434
Design speed (kts) (S_{ds})[1]	16
Speed at the vessel ice limit (kts) (S_{min})[2]	3
Main engine daily fuel consumption at design speed (ton/day) (FC_{ds})[1]	44,9
Auxiliary engine daily fuel consumption at design speed (ton/day) (F_A)[1]	3,5
Bunker cost (USD/ton)[2]	530
Operational expenditure (USD/day)	8 500
Freight rate (USD/ton) (R)[1]	12
Total distance (nm)[3]	5 320
Distance ice free (nm)[3]	2 510
Distance of the NSR/Pechora Sea (nm)[3]	2 630 / 180

Sources: [1]Clarkson database (2018); [2]Clarkson database (2018), with a 33% premium (Lasserre, 2014); [3]Faury and Cariou (2016)

thickness and using the typology of Konygin et al. (2015). October is the month with the lower ice thickness (Lensu et al., 1996) whereas September is the month with the lower ice extent.[1]

In order to estimate the average speed (S_{OW}) along the NSR, we considered the average speed per month along the seven NSR zones (Table 4.2), as reported in Faury and Cariou (2016) for 2013 (Table 4.3), and in the case of ice thickness lower bounds. We also integrated the ice thickness encounter within the Pechora Sea, as despite the fact that this sea is not part of the NSR (NSRA, 2017; Faury & Cariou, 2016), constraint on maximum speed can also apply on this sea. The ice-class vessel is able to sail from June to February and the corresponding values for the average speed as well as the NSR fees (Fee_{NSR}) are reported in Table 4.3.

A first question to consider is whether the speed limits imposed when sailing along the NSR (S_{NSR}) represent a constraint for shipowners, meaning if the NSR speed is lower than the optimal speed S^* (equation 4.2) when no sailing speed constraints apply. To estimate the optimal speed to maximize TCE (equation 4.1), additional information on the spot freight rate (R) and on the fuel price (p) is needed. The 2018 average bunker price (six first months) of 400 USD/ton of fuel (Clarkson, 2018) was considered, to which a 33% premium applies when vessels are using a more expensive fuel when sailing on the NSR (Faury & Cariou, 2016) or p=530 USD/ton. For the Panamax oil product tanker freight rate, we consider the average freight rate for 177 transactions reported during the six first months of 2018 or 12 USD/ton. Therefore, using a beta-value equal to 3 and $k = \dfrac{F_{ds}}{\left(24.s_{ds}\right)^3} = 7,93^{-7}$, the optimal speed is equivalent to (from equation 4.2):

$$s^* = \frac{1}{24}\sqrt{\frac{12*73434}{3*530*7,93^{-7}*5320}} = 15,1\,kts. \tag{4.4}$$

When comparing S^* with the average values reported in Table 4.3, it appears that sailing through the NSR always brings a constraint compared to the optimal speed of 15,1 kts that would bring (equation 4.1) a TCE of 38 170 USD/day. Figure 4.2 presents the TCE per month as a function of the speed outside the NSR (in open water), considering that the speed inside the NSR is fixed and that assistance fees apply, except during the September-November period (Table 4.3).

Assuming that daily Operating Expenses (OPEX) are set at around 8 500–10 000 USD/day for a 1A Ice-Class Panamax oil product tanker, there are three months when a vessel can generate sufficient earnings when sailing through the Arctic, i.e. from August to October. From November to February, as well as in June, transiting through the Arctic does not bring enough earnings to cover OPEX. October is the month of the year when the highest TCE can be achieved (would be September if ice extent was used to assess speed limit), at 37 456 USD/day, a

Table 4.2 Ice thickness and speed per month along the Pechora Sea and the seven NSR zones

Month	Pechora Sea		Zone 1 Kara Sea west		Zone 2 Kara Sea east		Zone 3 Laptev Sea		Zone 4	Zone 5 East Siberian Sea west		Zone 6 East Siberian Sea east		Zone 7 Chuckhi Sea	
	Ice thickness (cm)	Speed (kts)	Ice thickness (cm)	Speed (Kts)	Ice thickness (cm)	Speed (kts)	Ice thickness (cm)	Speed (kts)	Speed (kts)	Ice thickness (cm)	Speed (kts)	Ice thickness (cm)	Speed (kts)	Ice thickness (cm)	Speed (kts)
January	29	6,5	36	5,5	49	4,3	51	4,3	4,2	60	3,7	56	3,9	40	5,1
February	36	5,5	45	4,7	56	3,9	60	3,9	3,7	69	3,4	65	3,5	49	4,3
March	45	4,7	51	4,2	65	3,5	71	3,5	–	76	–	71	–	56	3,9
April	49	4,3	56	3,9	69	3,4	76	3,4	–	80	–	80	–	65	3,5
May	49	4,3	60	3,7	71	–	80	–	–	85	–	80	–	65	3,5
June	31	6,1	49	4,3	60	3,7	69	3,7	3,4	69	3,4	65	3,5	53	4,1
July	16	10,5	36	5,8	49	4,6	56	4,6	4,2	51	4,5	51	4,5	45	5
August	0	14,5	25	7,6	36	5,8	45	5,8	5	40	5,4	40	5,4	36	5,8
September	0	14,5	11	13,4	29	6,8	29	6,8	6,8	29	6,8	29	6,8	29	6,8
October	0	14,5	4	14,5	11	13,4	9	13,4	14,5	16	10,5	16	10,5	9	14,5
November	11	13,4	16	10,5	25	7,6	29	7,6	6,8	31	6,4	29	6,8	20	8,8
December	20	8,6	25	7,3	36	5,5	40	5,5	5,1	45	4,7	45	4,7	31	6,1

Source: Faury and Cariou (2016)

Table 4.3 Average speed along the NSR (S_{NSR}) and NSR fee (Fee_{NSR})

Month	(S_{NSR}) (in kt)	(Fee_{NSR}) (in USD)	Month	(S_{NSR}) (in kt)	(Fee_{NSR}) (in USD)
January	4,3	1 566 607	August	5,7	462 919
February	3,8	1 602 558	September	7,7	0
. . .	. . .	. . .	October	12,9	0
June	3,6	1 498 467	November	7,5	0
July	4,6	580 394	December	5,4	1 154 931

Source: Faury and Cariou (2016)

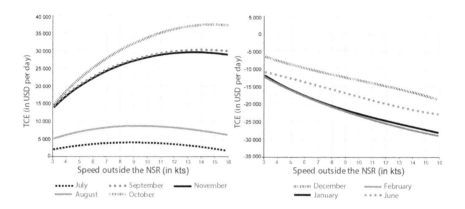

Figure 4.2 Time Charter Equivalent in USD/day as a function of speed outside the NSR (Monthly speed inside the NSR is reported in Table 4.3)

value close to the TCE of 38 170 USD/day that would be the maximum profit if the vessel was in open water. To reach this result in October, the speed is 15 kts in open water, meaning during the (5 320–2 630 nm) nm outside the NSR and then limited to 12,9 kts (Table 4.1) when inside the NSR. The situation is different when a vessel has to sail at a lower speed such as for instance in August (5,7 kts max). Under such condition, the optimal solution is then not to speed up on open water, as this will bring too much additional fuel costs. The optimal solution is to sail at around 10 kts (Figure 4.1), at the expense of a longer transit time of 30 days (against 16 days in October).

Sensitivity analysis

In this last section, we investigate how our findings on the monthly economic viability of the NSR can be affected by changes in the various parameters, assuming that the vessel does not change fuel to alternative fuel such as MDO.

We focused our attention on three elements that could be subject to change in the near future.

1 The HFO fuel price, assuming an increase in the short/medium run of 50% compared to the initial business case, equivalent to 800 USD/ton of fuel (Figure 4.2).

2 Ice thickness, assuming that its evolution could result into a simultaneous 50% increase in the average speed along the NSR (S_{NSR}) and to lower icebreaker assistance fees (less zones where assistance is needed and without increase in the cost per icebreaker assistance) by 50% compared to the previous period (Figure 4.3).

3 Freight rates, assuming that the reduction in transit time and better sailing conditions would not be enough for non-ice class vessels to be competitive but could give rise to a 50% increase in freight rate for ice-class vessels deployed on the NSR (Figure 4.4).

When keeping a limit for the OPEX at approximatively 10 000 USD/day as a minimum, a rise of 50% in fuel prices (Figure 4.3) has various implications for the NSR competitiveness. For instance, in October, the optimal speed without speed limit is at around 12 kts against 15 kts. Finally, the global effect is a reduction in TCE from 38 000 USD/day to less than 30 000 USD/day in October, a reduction that could be underestimated owing the increase in transit time due to a lower open water optimal speed.

Assuming a decrease in ice thickness and extent that would give the possibility to increase the NSR sailing speed by 50% and to decrease the icebreaker fees by 50% (Figure 4.4), it would then have a large impact on the NSR attractiveness. For all months between July and November, sailing through the NSR is now

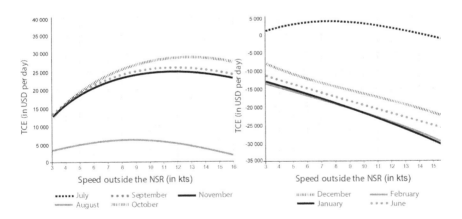

Figure 4.3 Time Charter Equivalent in USD/day as a function of speed outside the NSR Fuel price (+50% or 800 USD/ton)

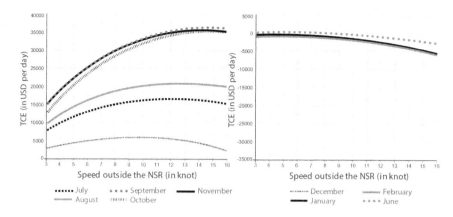

Figure 4.4 Time Charter Equivalent in USD/day as a function of speed outside the NSR. Assuming NSR speed (+50%) and icebreakers fees (−50%) in Table 4.3.

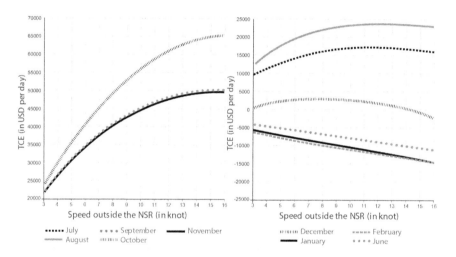

Figure 4.5 Time Charter Equivalent in USD/day as a function of speed outside the NSR. Freight rate (+50% or 18 USD/ton)

becoming a viable/profitable option. Furthermore, sailing in December is now bringing positive earnings, but however not enough to cover OPEX.

Finally (Figure 4.5), when assuming a freight rate at 18 USD/ton (+50% compared to the initial case of 12 USD/ton), there is a large increase in TCE for all months. Despite this increase, December–July earnings are still, however, too limited to pay for OPEX.

Conclusion

The objective of this chapter was, when assessing the bulk shipping NSR competitiveness, to shed light on the relationship between climatic and economic conditions. Our findings only hold for specific assumptions on the relationship between climatic and sailing conditions. In particular, sailing speed is only affected in our model by ice thickness, while other factors should be considered for a more comprehensive assessment to include, for instance, ice extent, concentration, fastened ice or floes that are also playing on the maximum allowable speed along the NSR.

Based on empirical data and on our assumptions, and using the standard Time Charter Equivalent formula to assess the shipowner profitability, we discuss how ice conditions have a direct impact on the Arctic shipping profitability, and in particular though its impact on sailing speed and icebreakers fees. The paper shows, as expected, that if the summer months are those that generate the highest profitability, sailing during this period is not enough to guarantee a high profitability as the sailing speed has a strong influence on profit, as illustrated for August. Among the many parameters that can impact such a relationship, we investigate the likely effect from an increase in the NSR sailing speed, in fuel price and in freight rate. Findings from a sensitivity analysis lead to conclude that an improvement in sailing conditions and an increase in bunker prices would have a limited impact on the NSR competitiveness, contrary to an increase in freight rate that could lead to a large increase in TCE.

Note

1 https://nsidc.org/

References

Aksenov, Y., Popova, E. E., Yool, A., Nurser, A. J. G., Williams, T. D., Bertino, L., & Bergh, J. (2017). On the future navigability of Arctic sea routes: High-resolution projections of the Arctic Ocean and sea ice. *Marine Policy, 75*, 300–317.

Cariou, P., & Faury, O. (2015). Relevance of the Northern Sea Route (NSR) for bulk shipping. *Transportation and Research Part A, 78*, 337–346.

Clarksons. (2018). *Clarksons database*. Retrieved from www.clarksons.net/portal

Comiso, J. C. (2012). Large decadal decline of the Arctic multiyear ice cover. *Journal of Climate, 25*(4), 1176–1193.

Comiso, J. C., Parkinson, C. L, Gersten, R., & Stock, L. (2008). Accelerated decline in the Arctic sea ice cover. *Geophysical Research Letters, 35*, L01703.

Erikstad, S. O., & Ehlers, S. (2012). Decision support framework for exploiting Northern Sea Route transport opportunities. *Ship Technology Research, 59*(2), 34–43.

Evans, J. J., & Marlow, P. (1990). *Quantitative methods in maritime economics*, 2nd ed. Coulsdon: Fairplay Publications.

Falck, H. (2012). *Shipping in Arctic waters: The Northern Sea Route*. Tschudi Shipping Company: Presentation to the Marine Insurance Seminar 2012. Mariehamn (Finland), April 26.

Farré, A. B., Stephenson, S., Chen, L., Czub, M., Da, Y., Demchev, D., . . . Kivekäs, N. & Wighting, J. (2014). Commercial Arctic shipping through the Northeast Passage: Routes, resources, governance, technology, and infrastructure. *Polar Geography*, *37*(4), 298–324.

Faury, O. (2015). *Risk management in the Arctic from an underwriter's perspective*. Proceedings of the International Association Maritime Economics Conference, 2015, Kuala Lumpur, Malaysia, August 23–27. Paper ID 59.

Faury, O., & Cariou, P. (2016). The Northern Sea Route competitiveness for oil tankers. *Transportation Research Part A: Policy and Practice*, *94*, 461–469.

Faury, O., & Givry, P. (2017). Evolution of ice class investment attractiveness depending on climatic and economic conditions. *Proceedings of the International Association Maritime Economics Conference*, Kyoto, Japan, June 27–30. Paper ID 83.

Fedi, L., Faury, O., & Gritensko, D. (2018). The impact of the Polar Code on risk mitigation in Arctic waters: A 'toolbox' for underwriters? *Maritime Policy and Management*, *45*(4), 478–494. doi:10.1080/03088839.2018.1443227

Furuichi, M., & Otsuka, N. (2012, May 21). Effect of the Arctic sea routes (NSR and NWP) navigability on port industry. *International Association of Port and Harbour, Presentation, Port Planning and Development Committee (PPDC) Project*, Jerusalem.

Furuichi, M., & Otsuka, N. (2018). Examining quick delivery at an affordable cost by the NSR/SCR-combined shipping in the age of Mega-ships. *Maritime Policy & Management*, *45*(8), 1057–1077.

Gritsenko, D., & Kiiski, T. (2016). A review of Russian ice-breaking tariff policy on the Northern Sea Route 1991–2014. *Polar Record*, *52*(2), 144–158.

Kitagawa, H. (2001). *The Northern Sea Route – The Shortest Sea Route linking East Asia and Europe*. Tokyo: Ship Ocean Foundation.

Konygin, A., Nekhaev, S., Dmitruk, D., Sevastyanova, K., Kovalev, D., & Cherenkov, V. (2015). Oil tanker transportation in the Russian Arctic. *International Journal of Scientific Technology Research*, *4*(3), 27–33.

Koskinen, M. M., & Hilmola, O. P. (2005). Investment cycles in newbuilding market of ice- strengthened oil tankers. *Maritime Economics & Logistics*, *7*(2), 173–188.

Kwok, R., & Rothrock, D. A. (2009). Decline in Arctic sea ice thickness from submarine and ICES at records: 1958–2008. *Geophysical Research Letter*, *36*, doi:10.1029/2009GL039035

Lasserre, F. (2014). Case studies of shipping along Arctic routes: Analysis and profitability perspectives for the container sector. *Transportation Research Part A*, *66*, 144–161.

Lasserre, F., & Pelletier, S. (2011). Polar super seaways? Maritime transport in the Arctic: An analysis of shipowners' intentions. *Journal of Transport Geography*, *19*, 1465–1473.

Lensu, M., Heale, S., Riska, K., & Kujala, P. (1996). *Ice environment and ship hull loading along the NSR*. (INSROP Working paper no 66).

Lindsay, R., & Schweiger, A. (2015). Arctic sea ice thickness loss determined using subsurface, aircraft, and satellite observations. *The Cryosphere*, *9*, 269–283.

Löptien, U., & Axell, L. (2014). Ice and AIS: Ship speed data and sea ice forecast in the Baltic Sea. *The Cryosphere*, *8*, 2409–2418.

Lin, D. Y., & Chang, Y. T. (2018). Ship routing and freight assignment problem for liner shipping: Application to the Northern Sea Route planning problem. *Transportation Research Part E*, *110*, 47–70.

Liu, M., & Kronbak, J. (2010). The potential economic viability of using the Northern Sea Route (NSR) as an alternative route between Asia and Europe. *Journal of Transport Geography*, *18*(3), 434–444.

Marchenko, N. (2014a). *Northern Sea Route: Modern state and challenges.* Proceedings of the 33rd international conference on ocean, offshore and arctic engineering. OMAE2014. June 8–13, San Francisco, CA.

Marchenko, N. (2014b). *Floating ice induced ship casualties. 22nd IAHR International Symposium on Ice.* Singapore, August 11–15.

Maslanik, J. A., Fowler, C., Strove, J., Drobot, S., Zwally, J., Yi, D. & Emery, W. (2007). A younger, thinner Arctic ice cover: Increased potential for rapid extensive sea ice loss. *Geophysical Research Letter*, vol. 34, L24501.

Meng, Q., Zhang, Y., & Xu, M. (2017). Viability of transarctic shipping routes: A literature review from the navigational and commercial perspective. *Maritime Policy and Management, 441,* 16–41.

Mulherin, N., Eppler, D., Proshutinsky, T., Proshutinsky, A., Farmer, L. D., & Smith, O. (1996). *Development and results of a Northern Sea Route transit model* (CRREL Research Report 96–3). US Army Corp. of Engineers, Hanover, NH.

Ng, A. K. Y., Andrews, J., Babb, D., Lin, Y., & Becker, A. (2018). Implications of climate change for shipping: Opening the Arctic seas. *Climate Change, 9*(2), e507.

Nilsen, T. (2017). EU wants ban on heavy fuel in Arctic. *The Barents Observer.* Retrieved February 1, 2017, from https://thebarentsobserver.com/en/arctic/2017/02/eu-wants-ban-heavy-fuel-arctic

NSRA (2017). Tariffs for the icebreaker escorting of ships rendered by FSUE "Atomflot" in the water area of the Northern Sea Route. Retrieved December 2017, http://www.nsra.ru/en/ofitsialnaya_informatsiya/tarrifs_for_icebreaker_escort_atomflot/f79.html

Pastusiak, T. (2016). Principles of vessel route planning in ice on the Northern Sea Route. *Transnav, 10*(4), www.transnav.eu/Article_Principles_of_Vessel_Route_Planning_Pastusiak,40,682.html

Pruyn, J. F. J. (2016). Will the Northern Sea Route ever be a viable alternative? *Maritime Policy & Management, 43*(6), 661–675.

Psaraftis, H. N., & Kontovas, C. A. (2013). Speed models for energy-efficient maritime transportation: A taxonomy and survey, *Transportation Research Part C, 26,* 331–351.

Psaraftis, H. N., & Kontovas, C. A. (2014). Ship speed optimization: Concepts, models and combined speed-routing scenarios, *Transportation Research Part C, 44,* 52–69.

Ragner, C. L. (2000a). *Northern Sea Route cargo flows and infrastructure – Present state and Future potential. The Fridtjof Nansen Institute* (Fridtjof Nansen Institute [FNI] Report 13/2000).

Ragner, C. L. (2000b). The Northern Sea Route – commercial potential, economic significance, and infrastructure requirements. *Post-Soviet Geography and Economics Journal, 41*(8), 541–580.

Ragner, C. L. (2008). Den norra sjövägen. In H. Torsten, (Ed.), *Barents – ett gränsland I Norden* (pp. 114–127). Stockholm: Arena Norden.

Schøyen, H., & Brathen, S. (2011). The Northern Sea Route versus the Suez Canal Route: Cases from bulk shipping. *Journal of Transport Geography, 19,* 977–983.

Stephenson, S. R., Brigham, L. W., Smith, L. C., & Agnew, J. A. (2013). Projected 21st century changes to Arctic marine access. *Climate Change, 118*(3–4), 885–899.

Stephenson, S. R., & Pincus, R. (2018). Challenges of sea-ice prediction for Arctic marine policy and planning. *Journal of Borderlands Studies, 33*(2), 255–272.

Stoddard, M. A, Etienne, L., Fournier, M., Pelot, R. & Beveridge, L. (2016). Making sense of Arctic maritime traffic using the Polar Operational Limits Assessment Risk Indexing System (POLARIS). *9th Symposium of the International Society for Digital Earth*

(ISDE) IOP Publishing IOP Conf. Series: Earth and Environmental Science, 34 (2016) 012034.

Stopford, M. (2009). *Maritime economics* (3rd ed.). London: Routledge.

Theocharis, D., Pettit, S., Rodrigues, V. S., & Haider, J. (2018). Arctic shipping: A systematic literature review of comparative studies. *Journal of Transport Geography, 69,* 112–128.

Verny, J., & Grigentin, C. (2009). Container shipping on the Northern Sea Route. *International Journal Production Economics, 122,* 107–117.

Xu, H., Yang, D., & Weng, J. (2018). Economic feasibility of an NSR/SCR-combined container service on the Asia-Europe lane: A new approach dynamically considering sea ice extent. *Maritime Policy & Management, 45*(4), 514–529.

Yiru Zhang, Y., Meng, Q., & Ng, S. H. (2016). Shipping efficiency comparison between Northern Sea Route and the conventional Asia-Europe shipping route via Suez Canal. *Journal of Transport Geography, 57,* 241–249.

5 Compared transit traffic analysis along the NSR and the NWP

Frédéric Lasserre, Qiang Meng, Chuanbei Zhou, Pierre-Louis Têtu and Olga Alexeeva

Introduction

The melting of sea ice in the Arctic in recent decades and the reduction in the extent and thickness of sea ice has resulted in an increase in both industrial and private sector shipping and maritime transportation opportunities in the region (Melia, Haines, & Hawkins, 2016). For instance, quantitative assessments of Arctic shipping from 2011 to 2014 shows increasing activity, particularly for the Norwegian and Barents Seas (Eguíluz et al., 2016). The opening of polar sea routes renewed the idea that both the Northern Sea Route (NSR)[1] and the Northwest Passage (NWP) could become busy transit shipping routes through the frozen north and support global trade, a narrative so common that some analysts take it for granted (Borgerson, 2008; Abdul Rahman, Saharuddin, & Rasdi, 2014; Zhang, Meng, & Zhang, 2016). Today, more than 90% of global trade takes place by sea (IMO, 2019). Some observers still consider the NSR and the NWP as potentially viable and economically advantageous routes connecting the Atlantic and Pacific Oceans in the frame of climate change.

Several studies of Arctic transit routes (see, among others: Guy, 2006; Arpiainen and Kiili, 2006; Borgerson, 2008; Somanathan et al., 2009; Mejlaender-Larsen, 2009; Verny & Grigentin, 2009; Liu & Kronbak, 2010; DNV, 2010; Lasserre, 2014, 2015; Stephenson & Smith, 2015; Zhang et al., 2016) were carried out to determine their potential cost or operational advantages. Notwithstanding highly variable operational conditions during shipping seasons over the years, important and limiting challenges are affecting commercial shipping activities in the Arctic (Lasserre & Pelletier, 2011). Despite a limited interest due to various logistical and physical barriers through both the NWP and the NSR (Beveridge et al., 2016; Lasserre, Beveridge, Fournier, Têtu, & Huang, 2016; Lasserre & Alexeeva, 2015), Arctic shipping appears attractive for some shipping companies such as COSCO (Wan, Ge, & Chen, 2018), or for destinational traffic like Fednav, Sovcomflit, Nordic Bulk, Teekay or MOL. The potential savings on fuel consumption, bunker and operating costs, GES emissions and journey time are among the reasons for the interest (Abdul Rahman et al., 2014; Hong, 2012). The polar sea routes are also attractive for China, heavily dependent on seaborne trade for exports and raw material imports, and for which a large share of maritime traffic goes through the busy Strait of Malacca.

The potential opening up of shipping routes through the Northwest Passage across the Canadian archipelago as well as along the Northeast Passage raised security concerns as it implies a potential surge in navigation of all sorts of ships (Lasserre & Pelletier, 2011). The development of commercial shipping through newly accessible routes will thus raise a number of difficult issues such as establishing an effective response capability in the event of accidents, monitoring the exploitation of natural resources and curbing illegal trafficking in all of its forms. An increase in maritime transit traffic could also underline disagreements about the legal status of the new sea lanes and the right to exercise authority over them. After two decades of media forecasting a fast expansion of transit traffic, to what extent is it expanding along these two Arctic passages? What picture can be drawn of its unfolding? While all of these questions warrant careful analysis and consideration, this chapter focuses on the present state of commercial transit shipping in the Arctic by distinguishing main trends, similitudes and particularities of the Northwest Passage and the Northern Sea Route. First, we introduce the data source and categorization methods as well as the limits these data sets present. Analyses are carried out from four perspectives: 1) cargo type and volume, 2) transit volumes by transit and cargo types and ship flag, 3) origin and destination of transits and 4) ships size type.

Methodology

Data sources

The analysis of transit traffic whether Russian/Canadian, domestic, international through the Northwest Passage and the Northern Sea Route in this chapter is based on data collected by various institutions of Canada and Norway/Russia.

The Canadian government collects information on vessel traffic across Canada's navigable waterways through the Vessel Traffic Management Information System (VTMIS-INNAV) initially developed by XST Solutions based in Quebec City. In the Canadian Arctic, sometimes referred as the Northern Canada Vessel Traffic Services Zone (NORDREG) from a shipping point of view, the Canadian Coast Guard's Marine Communications and Traffic Services (MCTS), located in Iqaluit, monitors marine traffic. According to the Canada Shipping Act (2001), vessels entering the NORDREG Zone[2] have to carry an Automatic Identification System (AIS) transmitter that enhances traceability. They must also provide extensive information on various technical information, including the vessel's name, the call signal and IMO numbers, the flag and type of vessel, the dimensions, engine power, tonnage and ice class, the number of people on board, the cargo volume, date and place of entry and exit of the NORDREG zone, etc. Depending on the vessel's speed, their positions are broadcast frequently, approximately every 2–10 seconds or every 3 minutes if at anchor (Chénier et al., 2017). Because there is no active ground AIS station to collect data at a higher precision in the Canadian

Arctic, the position cannot be acquired at this frequency and the INNAV system relies mainly on satellite AIS (SAT-AIS) (ibid.), allowing for the georeferencing of the ship location.

For the Northwest Passage, multiple analyses of partial and full NWP transits were conducted on a vessel traffic dataset (1990–2017) provided by MCTS Iqaluit. The sum of partial and full NWP transits were calculated based on existing statistics (see Table 5.1). On the other side of the Arctic basin and at a lesser precision than data originating from Canada for the NWP, the Centre for High North Logistics (CHNL) established the online database ARCTIS (Arctic Resources and Transportation Information System), an international knowledge hub providing information on non-living resources, shipping and logistics in the Euro-Russian Arctic. The development of this database is a joint initiative between CHNL and Rosatomflot (Russia) with additional financial support coming from the Norwegian Barents Secretariat. CHNL, with its main office located in Kirkenes (Norway) with another office in Murmansk (Russia), publishes data gathered by the Northern Sea Route Administration (NSRA), a Russian federal state institution that controls traffic through the NSR. In this study, the CHNL database (2011–2016) is the main data source, cross checked and supplemented by NSRA data (2013–2015) when possible. Table 5.1 summarizes the number of records reported by CHNL from 2011 to 2016, those provided by the NSRA (2013–2015), and the number of transits recorded by the MCTS in Iqaluit. The major difference between the two datasets is that CHNL reports partial transits between 2011 and 2014, while the NSRA does not. Table 5.1 summarizes the number of records the datasets of the various institutions provide.

NORDREG's dataset covering Canada and the NWP distinguishes ten vessel categories[3] and CHNL's dataset displays seven[4] for Russia and the NSR. The number of pleasure craft and adventurers is a piece of information collected and

Table 5.1 Traffic data from CHNL, the NSRA and NORDREG (MCTS-Iqaluit system)

	2011	*2012*	*2013*	*2014*	*2015*	*2016*
CHNL – transits	41	46	71	53	18	18
NSRA – transits	N/A	N/A	37	23	17	N/A
Transits along the Northwest Passage 1903–2016, Official Version, NORDREG	40	41	34	28	43	47
NORDREG Voyages	317	314	349	301	315	347
	Voyages of every type of vessel (Canadian Coast Guard vessels, general cargo vessels, tankers, tugs/barges, passenger vessels, research vessels, bulk carriers, grain ships, fishing vessels, pleasure craft and adventurers) recorded under SOLAS Convention and Canadian Legislation in the NORDREG maritime area.					

Table 5.2 Summaries of the information fields reported by CHNL and NORDREG

Year	Information fields	
	CHNL	*NORDREG System*
2011	Vessel's name, type, flag, cargo, port of loading and port of destination	Vessel's name, call sign, IMO numbers, flag, type of vessel, dimensions, engines, tonnage, ice class, number of people on board, GRT of cargo carrying, date of entry/exit of NORDREG zone, latitude & longitude, # days in zone, locations, sub-locations, remarks, information on transit
2012	Vessel and flag, ice class, shipowner/operator, cargo, destination, port and date of sail, entry to NSR, exit from NSR, time on NSR and average speed	
2013	Vessel and flag, ice class, GRT (gross registered tonnage), vessel owner/operator, cargo, port of destination, port and date of departure, entry to NSR, exit from NSR, days spent at NSR and average speed	
2014	Name of vessel, flag, type, GRT, date and place of entering the NSR water area, date and place of leaving the NSR water area and days spent at NSR	
2015	Vessel name, flag, shipowner, ice class, type, cargo owner, cargo, passengers, max draught, departure, destination, icebreaking assistance, entry and exit points at NSR and NSR passage time	
2016	Vessel name, flag, shipowner, ice class, type, cargo owner, cargo, passengers, dwt, max draught, departure, destination, i/b assistance, entry and exit points at NSR and NSR passage time	

available for Canada but not for the NSR even if pleasure crafts are known to navigate Russian waters (Nikiforov, 2010; Arktika, 2016).

Categories of voyages via the NSR and NWP: towards a harmonized typology

The Northern Sea Route refers to a long coastline segment of Russia in the Arctic region, regulated by Russian authorities. The Russian legislation defines the NSR boundaries from Novaya Zemlya in the west to the Bering Strait in the east. Typically, the Kara Gate or Cape Zhelaniya are the entry points to NSR from the west, and the Bering Strait at Cape Dezhnev is the entry point from the east. The first successful voyage along the NSR dates back to 1878, and trade shipping began in the Kara Sea in the second half of the 19th century (Belyi, 2014). With the developments of icebreakers technology and improvements to ice forecasting, more and more shipping activities took place for trades, natural resources exploration and research purposes in the Arctic. The NSR officially opened as an international shipping route on January 1, 1991 (Moe, 2014).

The Northwest Passage is the name given to the five marine routes based on the Arctic Marine Shipping Assessment 2009 Report from the Arctic Council. It refers to the passage between the Atlantic and Pacific Oceans along the northern coast of North America that span the Canadian Arctic Archipelago (Yu, 2016). Roald Amundsen (1872–1928) when aboard his vessel *Gjöa*, entered the passage through Baffin Bay in 1903 and completed the passage in 1906, beginning the first to successfully navigate the NWP (ibid.).

There are different ways to define *transit* along the NSR or the NWP, and the authors in this study categorize the voyages in two ways. The recorded voyages are categorized according to two typologies depending first on the origin and destination (OD) of the voyage and, second, on whether it transited along the entire NSR/NWP or only part of these routes. The analysis thus articulates a two-tiered typology, with first data on OD, then with data on the voyage along the NSR or the NWP.

Sub-categories detail the voyages originating from and/or to the Arctic region from those that do not. Non-Arctic NSR/NWP voyages happen when the voyage is between two international countries beyond the Arctic region (like European and Asian countries), or when the ship arrives at a Russian port beyond the Arctic region, like Nakhodka.

The term "Arctic region" is here defined based on the Arctic Council's Arctic Monitoring and Assessment Programme (AMAP) report in 1997 and the Norwegian Insurance Plan. A voyage originating from or ending at a point within the Arctic region is categorized as an "Arctic voyage". Figure 5.1 shows the limits of the Arctic region used in this research, more general than the definition used in the Polar Code for instance, that did not include parts of the Barents Sea. For example, "Arctic domestic" refers to shipping activity within Russian or Canadian internal waters or territorial seas or EEZ and with at least one origin or destination (OD) in the Arctic. By introducing the notion of the Arctic in spatial typology, sub-categories are proposed to highlight voyages with origin and/or destination in the Arctic region.

The data about OD distinguishes the following categories.

1a   Domestic transits or voyages: shipping activities with both OD within Russian or Canadian territory.

1b   Arctic domestic: shipping activity within Russian/Canadian territory and with at least one OD in the Arctic (i.e. Murmansk-Nakhodka, or Iqaluit-Vancouver).

2a   Russian/Canadian transits: those with one of the OD in Russia/Canada, and the other in a foreign country.

2b   Arctic Russian/Canadian: voyages with one OD in Arctic Russia/Canada, and the other in a foreign country (i.e. Murmansk-Shanghai, or Milne Inlet-Shanghai).

3a   International transits: voyages with both OD in foreign countries.

3b   International Arctic transits: those with both OD in foreign countries and at least one OD in the Arctic region (i.e. Kirkenes-Shanghai, or Nuuk-Shanghai).

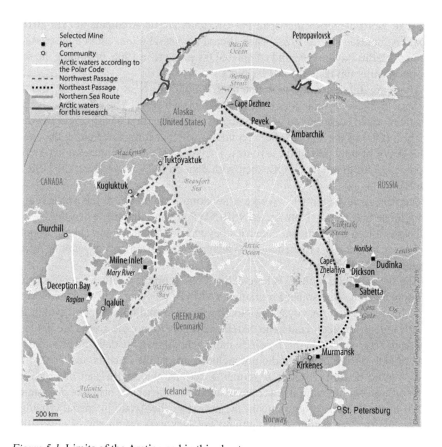

Figure 5.1 Limits of the Arctic used in this chapter

The data about transit distinguishes between:

1   Full transits: voyages traveling the full length of NSR by crossing the Bering Strait/the Cape Dezhnev and the Kara Gate or Cape Zhelaniya; voyages traveling the full length of the NWP between Baffin Bay and the Beaufort Sea in Canada.
2   Partial transits (from the west): voyages crossing the Kara Gate but not as far to the Bering Strait and plying two-thirds of the NSR: past the Kolyma River mouth and the village of Ambarchik; voyages coming from the Beaufort Sea but not as far as Baffin Bay and plying two-thirds of the NWP.
3   Partial transits (from the east): voyages crossing the Bering Strait but not as far as the Kara Gate and plying two-thirds of the NSR: past the Vilkitsky Strait/Northern Territories Islands; voyages entering the NWP from Baffin Bay but not as far the Beaufort Sea and plying two-thirds of the NWP.

4   Voyages (in-between): voyages that remained within the NSR or the NWP, which did not ship beyond any of the two points: Kara Gate/Bering Strait or Baffin Bay/Beaufort Sea; or ships entering the NSR/NWP without making a long journey within the Arctic passage (less than 2/3).

For example, one voyage originated from Asia and docked in Russia sailing through the NSR, thus, it is categorized as Russian/Canadian transit; another voyage shipped goods from Russia and traveled from Cape Zhelaniya to the Kolyma River mouth, thus, it is under the categories of domestic transit and partial transit of the west. For the Northwest Passage in the Canadian Arctic, a voyage originated from Asia and arrived at Resolute Bay in Canada through the NWP, and therefore is described as an Arctic Russian/Canadian partial transit and a voyage from one Canadian port to another one falls under the category of domestic transit or partial transit.

Issues with data consistency

There are inconsistencies between datasets describing shipping along the NWP and the NSR because of unreliable or inconstant quality of the data, especially for the Russian part. Before going into deeper analysis, inconsistencies in the CHNL reports must be outlined. First, the records from 2011 to 2014 include both full transits and partial transits, and the data for 2015 and 2016 are only for full transits whereas these full and partial transits as well as routes followed by vessels are available in NORDREG's database from 1956 to 2017 for the NWP.

Based on CHNL reports, these inconsistencies mean that the numbers of partial transits of 2015 and 2016 through the NSR are zero, and partial transits are only reported from 2011 to 2014. Second, 15 records of the 2011 CHNL report (36%) do not provide information on loading or destination ports, but only indicate "west" or "east". Since most of these ships are Russian and traveled on ballast for repositioning, we assume this description refers to the west part or east part of Russia and that these transits are domestic transits. It is not known either if these voyages are full or partial transits, so we cannot specify how long and which segment these ships traveled along the NSR. Because of this vague information, the count of domestic and partial transits/voyages in 2011 is not accurate. Third, the 2014 CHNL report does not display data about the port of loading (POL) nor the port of destination (POD). Though the NSRA report could supplement such information, it is incomplete, as 31 CHNL records are not found in the NSRA report, without explanation for this discrepancy. Thus, when we discuss the count of international/Russian-Canadian/domestic transits, the reader must note that the count for 2014 is incomplete.

Moreover, if NORDREG's records are more consistent over time, they display data that is different from CHNL: a major difference is that NORDREG figures include pleasure crafts, whereas this category is not reported in CHNL data.

Transit traffic: are Arctic passages witnessing more transit?

How many ships transit the Arctic passages?
A largely Arctic-fed transit traffic

Based on the CHNL and NORDREG reports for the period 2011–2016, we examined the POL and POD and identified if they were within the defined Arctic region. Some transit records do not display a clear POL/POD or at least a clear country of origin and destination. These incomplete records account for 19% (n=47) of all records for the NSR and 10 records for the NWP (3,6%). However, CHNL data are more accurate when describing the length of the transit, as only 15 records do not detail if the transit was full or partial, whereas 124 records (44,4%) of NWP traffic are incomplete regarding the length of the transit. Since most of these incomplete records deal with Arctic domestic transits, it is likely they could be confirmed as partial transits – they are listed as such in NORDREG's database (Table 5.4).

Table 5.3 Transit Numbers by Categories (2011–2016) – NSR

	Arctic inter-national	Inter-national	Arctic Russian/Canadian	Russian/Canadian	Arctic domestic	Domestic	Unknown	Total
Full transit	15	25	35	18	52	21	9	175
Partial transit (from west)	0	0	0	0	20	0	22	42
Partial transit (from east)	0	0	2	0	6	0	0	8
Voyages	0	0	0	0	6	0	1	7
Unknown	0	0	0	0	0	0	15	15
Total	15	25	37	18	84	21	47	247

Table 5.4 Transit Numbers by Categories (2011–2016) – NWP

	Arctic inter-national	Inter-national	Arctic Russian/Canadian	Russian/Canadian	Arctic domestic	Domestic	Unknown	Total
Full transit	78	1	33	2	8	1	8	131
Partial transit (west)	2	0	5	0	5	0	0	12
Partial transit (east)	3	0	8	0	1	0	0	12
Unknown	13	0	9	0	100	0	2	124
Total	96	1	55	2	114	1	10	279

Consequently, only 131 of the 279 (47%) recorded transits along the NWP are full transits, whereas 175 recorded transits along the NSR out of 247 (70,9%) are full transits.

There were 24 partial transits along the NWP and 50 partial transits along the NSR, most of them (42) from the west.

International transits and Arctic international transits account for 40 records along the NSR (16,2%) and for 97 records along the NWP (34,8%). Along the NSR, the majority of these were international (25 out of 40), whereas along the NWP, there was only one international transit and 78 were Arctic international. All the Arctic international voyages were full transits along the entire NSR whereas in the NWP area, 78 (81%) of Arctic International voyages were full transit.

Russian/Canadian and Arctic Russian/Canadian transits were 57 along the NWP (20,4%) and 55 (22,3%) along the NSR. However, the vast majority (55 out of 57) were Arctic Russian/Canadian along the NWP, whereas Arctic Russian/Canadian transits were 37 along the NSR. Through the NSR, almost all Russian/Canadian transits were full transits, with the exception of two of partial transits that completed a round trip between Dudinka, Russia and China without reaching Cape Zhelaniya. Arctic Russian/Canadian transits were mostly full transits along the NWP (33), and 13 partial transits.

There were 105 (42,5%) Arctic domestic and domestic transits along the NSR, and 115 (41,2%) along the NWP. There were only 9 full domestic or Arctic domestic transits through the NWP. The majority (73 voyages, 69,5%) of all domestic transits through the NSR traveled the entire sea route, while 26 (25%) of them were partial transits, and the rest were short voyages only or with unknown ports where ships mainly carried fuel and oil product between Ob Bay and the Kolyma River mouth. Because of the data inconsistency, 47 transits (19% of 247 records) were unknown type of transits due to unknown port of loading (POL)/port of destination (POD). Here again, Arctic domestic transits outnumber other domestic transits 84 to 21.

A few elements must be underlined when analyzing these figures:

- Along the NSR and the NWP, Russian/Canadian/Arctic Russian/Canadian and domestic/Arctic domestic traffic are dominant: 207 records along the NSR (83,8%) and 182 (65,2%) along the NWP; transit traffic is thus largely originating from or heading towards Russia and Canada.
- International transit is more developed along the NSR with 25 transits against only one along the NWP.
- All types of transits, international, Russian/Canadian or domestic, are dominated by Arctic ODs. Arctic OD number 136 along the NSR (55,1%) and 265 (95%) along the NWP. Transit along Arctic routes is thus still largely servicing Arctic areas.

The evolution of traffic along Arctic passages

Tables 5.5 to 5.8 summarize the chronologic evolution of transit numbers, detailing yearly data for types of transit and for OD.

Table 5.5 Transit traffic, type of transit (2011–2016) – NSR

	2011	2012	2013	2014	2015	2016	Total
Full transit	23	43	42	31	18	19	175
Partial transit (from west)	0	1	19	22	0	0	42
Partial transit (east)	3	2	3	0	0	0	8
Voyages	0	0	7	0	0	0	7
Unknown	15	0	0	0	0	0	15
Total	41	46	71	53	18	8	247

Table 5.6 Transit traffic, type of transit (2011–2016) – NWP

	2011	2012	2013	2014	2015	2016	Total
Full transit	21	31	22	17	27	25	143
Partial transit (from west)	9	5	8	6	8	11	47
Partial transit (east)	10	5	8	7	8	11	49
Voyages	0	0	0	0	0	0	0
Unknown	0	0	0	0	0	0	0
Total	40	41	38	30	43	47	239

Table 5.7 Transit traffic, OD (2011–2016) – NSR

	2011	2012	2013	2014	2015	2016	Total
International	1	6	9		4	5	25
Arctic international	1	4	4	3	2	1	15
Russian/Canadian	10	0	3	1		4	18
Arctic Russian/Canadian	5	17	12	1	1	1	37
Domestic	21	2	1	6	3	3	36
Arctic domestic	3	15	41	11	8	4	84
Unknown			1	31			32
Total	41	46	71	53	18	18	247

From these figures, it is apparent that the turning point was in 2014. First, the total number of transits along the NSR dropped to 53 in 2014 from 71 in 2013, a 25% decrease, and then collapsed to 18 in 2015 and 19 in 2016 (27 in 2017). Second, full transits dropped to 31 in 2014 from 42 in 2013, (−26%). Although the number of partial transits remained at a similar level of 22 transits, they lacked information about cargo type and POL/POD, thus we could not tell if they served for commercial purpose. The number of transits continued decreasing from 31 to

Table 5.8 Transit traffic, OD (2011–2016) – NWP

	2011	2012	2013	2014	2015	2016	Total
International						1	1
Arctic international	15	15	17	6	20	22	95
Russian/Canadian		1	1				2
Arctic Russian/Canadian	5	15	5	12	5	10	52
Domestic		1					1
Arctic domestic	26	12	12	17	31	20	118
Unknown	3	2	3		1	1	10
Total	49	45	39	35	57	54	279

18 in 2015 and 19 in 2016. As to the NWP, a turning point also appears to be in 2014, but rather than decreasing, the number of transit numbers increased. The total number of transits was 41 in 2012, 38 in 2013 and dropped to 30 in 2014. It however sharply increased in 2015 (43 transits) and 2016 (47 transits). While the partial transit from west or east remains stable from 2011 to 2016, the increase in the number of full transits is the result of pleasure craft and adventurers growth, not commercial cargo ships.

Along the NSR, domestic and Arctic domestic traffic largely support transit figures, year after year: they account for 24 transits in 2011 (58,5%), 37% in 2012, 42 (59,2%) in 2013, 17 (32%) in 2014, 11 (61%) in 2015 and 7 (38,9%) in 2016. The same phenomenon is observed along the NWP, where traffic is largely sustained by Arctic domestic transits.

Apart from residual traffic due to ballasting, non-commercial purposes and passenger tourism, it is clear that commercial international transits dropped in 2014 along the NSR, and then collapsed in 2015 and 2016 to very low levels, with totally different cargo types and less quantity. Before 2014, the main goods were fuel and oil product and gas products; after 2014, the international transits were for frozen fish and meat, general cargo and bulk cargo like coal, ore and paper pulp. Four out of the total ten international transits in 2015 and 2016 were supported by the Chinese company COSCO Shipping that shipped construction materials for Yamal LNG (Humpert, 2017). The latter two in 2016 was under the "Yongsheng Plus" Arctic Voyage Project. The total number of vessels of this project reached five and it represented the first time that a foreign-flagged operator has sent more than three vessels through the route in a single season (Humpert, 2016). In the meantime, Darliada Ltd started to use the NSR for shipping frozen fish and meat, either from Petropavlovsk-Kamchatsky to St. Petersburg, or from Norway to Japan, an illustration of the potential economic use of the NSR.

The main cargo types of full transits for domestic trade were fuel and oil product and frozen fish and meat. We could see the number of transits dropped for both, but surprisingly the quantity of fuel it shipped surged in 2014, from 52 kt per year (2011–2013) to 94 kt, 87% of which were shipped by a company named as Unicom SPB Ltd. This Russian company appeared only in 2014 and ceased its activity in 2015 and 2016. Another difference is that the fuel and oil product shipped before 2014 could be either eastbound or westbound, but it was only eastbound since 2014.

It is fair to say that full transits declined significantly since 2014. Industry experts suggest the decline in traffic reflects the steep reduction in bunker prices. One reason is that as the cost of fuel decreased sharply, the advantage of saving fuel cost on the shorter NSR route was less significant to vessel operators, in a context where Arctic shipping remains costly and risky (Pettersen, 2016) and freight rates depressed as shipping companies struggle with overcapacity (Doyon et al., 2016). A second reason is the decline of commodity prices, carriage of which requires large-volume shipping to achieve the desired economics. This decline largely triggered the reduced interest of oil and gas companies, except for niche projects such as Yamal LNG (Pettersen, 2016). The decline in commodity prices made several projects unattractive and reduced the need for sea transport; moreover, the number and size of ice-capable ships needed for the route is relatively small (Yu and Bond, 2017). Another opinion is Western sanctions on Russia might have contributed to the decline in foreign shipments at NSR since 2014 (OFC, 2015). The large Yamal LNG project also largely mobilized Russian icebreakers, resulting in a limited availability for transit, a restricted service that may have discouraged several shipping companies (Doyon et al., 2016).

Along the NWP, there is very little cargo transit traffic.

Comparative study of cargo shipments through the NSR and the NWP

What kind of ships were they?

The major ship types transiting the NSR are tanker, general cargo ship and bulk cargo ship, but no containership has crossed the NSR (Zhang et al., 2016) until 2018 with the *Venta Maersk* for a trial transit. Commercial cargo ships were 203 (82%) to transit the NSR between 2011 and 2016 out of 247 vessels, then followed by tugs (19), icebreakers (12), passenger vessels (7) and government ships (7) (see Table 5.9).

In the Canadian Arctic, most full transits are performed by pleasure crafts, followed by passenger ships and Canadian Coast guard (CCG) vessels. Very little cargo traffic transits the entire NWP: from 2011 to 2016, the number of transiting bulk carriers, tankers and general cargo ships represent less than 3% of all transits which are dominated by pleasure crafts (66%), government/icebreaker vessels (13%) and passenger vessels (9,9%) (see Table 5.10). From 2011 to 2016, only two bulk carriers (*Nordic Orion* and *Nunavik*) and two tankers (*Primula* and *Gotland Carolina*) performed a full NWP transit. The *Primula* (Norway) was used as a tank farm for the Hope Bay Mining Project in Robert's

Table 5.9 Transiting ships along the NSR by ship category, CHNL data, 2011–2016

Ship type	2011	2012	2013	2014	2015	2016	Total
Icebreaker	2	3	2	2	1	2	12
Government ship	1	0	1	1	3	1	7
Cruise or passenger ship	1	0	2	3	1	1	7
Tug, supply vessel	4	5	1	1	4	4	19
Commercial cargo ship	31	38	63	45	15	11	203
Research ship	2	0	2	1	0	0	5
Total official transit	41	46	71	53	18	18	247

Bay from January to the end of August; it went from Alaska in 2010 and left the NORDREG zone eastward heading to Göteborg (Sweden) in 2011. In 2012, the *Gotland Carolina* (Bahamas) entered NORDREG Zone from Dutch Harbor, Alaska, to resupply Tuktoyaktuk in Kugmallit Bay in early September. The tanker then exited the NORDREG Zone at the end of September, leaving to Greenland waters. In 2013, the *Nordic Orion* (Liberia) owned by the Norwegian company Nordic Bulk Carriers A/S transited through the Canadian Arctic from Vancouver (Canada) to Pori (Finland), escorted by a Canadian Coast Guard icebreaker in Canadian Arctic Waters, carrying 15 000 metric tons of coal. In 2014, finally, the MV *Nunavik* (Marshall Islands) owned by Canadian-based company Fednav Ltd. entered the NORDREG Zone from Moedijk, Netherlands heading to the Deception Bay mining terminal for loading. The vessel left on September 20th, 2014 through the NWP to Bayuquan (China), where she arrived on October 17th, 2014 after 26 days at sea.

However, when considering partial transits, pleasure crafts account for next to nothing, whereas the largest share is represented by commercial cargo ships, general cargo and tankers. This traffic is largely due to the community resupply, with shipping companies like Desgagnés Transarctik, NEAS, Woodward or NTCL that service villages in the Arctic, delivering fuel, car, construction material, consumer goods that are too bulky to be shipped by air.

When it transited the NSR in 2013, COSCO's *Yongsheng* only had part of its cargo in containerized form, as the *Yongsheng* is a multipurpose vessel and not a containership. Challenges for container shipping via the NSR are huge (Beveridge et al., 2016; Lasserre et al., 2016; Zhang et al., 2016) and few transits involved stopovers. Unlike shipping along traditional routes, container transport demand is very low on both the NSR and the NWP and port-to-port container demand for transits along these polar routes may not be able to cater the capacity of a ship. Second, ice conditions remain challenging for liner shipping. One consideration of the shipping company is the reliability of transportation, and another is related to safety: containerships require high stability due to high stacks of containers on the deck; a slight sway of the ship may result in loss of cargoes and/or danger of shipwreck (Meng et al., 2017). Third, the sailing season of NSR is about five months and almost the same length in the NWP, and the route is definitely

Table 5.10 Type of ships performing full and partial transits along the NWP, 2011–2016

Year	CCG or Canadian gov. ships	Foreign gov. ships	General cargo	Tankers	Bulk carriers	Passenger ships	Tugs	Pleasure crafts and adventurers	Research vessels	Others	Total
Full transits											
2016	3	0	1	0	0	3	0	15	0	1	23
2015	4	2	0	0	0	2	0	19	0	0	27
2014	4	0	0	0	1	2	0	10	0	0	17
2013	2	0	0	0	1	4	0	13	2	0	22
2012	2	0	0	1	0	2	2	23	1	0	31
2011	4	0	0	1	0	1	0	15	0	0	21
Partial transits											
2016	0	0	8	4	0	10	0	0	0	2	24
2015	0	0	6	4	0	6	0	0	0	0	16
2014	2	0	4	4	0	0	1	1	0	0	12
2013	4	0	4	2	0	2	0	0	0	0	12
2012	0	0	4	2	0	4	0	0	0	0	10
2011	0	0	6	6	0	6	0	0	1	0	19

Source: NORDREG (2017)

a seasonal lane. Hence, container companies that run on fixed schedules need to change their timetables twice a year (Lasserre & Pelletier, 2011; Beveridge et al., 2016). Overall, an expansion in container shipping is unlikely in the near future (Zhang et al., 2016). Due to different sea-ice dynamics along the NWP and the NSR, the conditions in the later and the impressive Russian atomic-icebreaker fleet allow more intense commercial activity along the NSR but still not without risks. Just like in the Canadian Arctic, the extreme variability of sea-ice conditions pose serious limitations for full transit of tankers, bulk and cargo vessels.

What volume of goods was carried along the Arctic passages?

Cargo volume is also an important indicator. The cargo volumes in 2012–2013 were stated by CHNL and those in 2014–2015 were counter checked and supplemented by NSRA reports. The trade volumes for various cargo types in 2011 are estimated according to the deadweight tonnage (dwt) for each ship, these proxies being retrieved by searching every vessel name and flag in the World Register of Ships. Dwt indicates the weight a vessel can safely carry, and it is used as the ceiling of cargo volume. NORDREG data provides the dwt value for about 45% of the records, and we similarly completed the data for ships where the value was not provided. Hence, figures for 2011 and 2016 along the NSR using dwt figures, as well as NWP figures, are proxies for the real cargo volume.

Along the NSR, cargo volumes generally grew until 2012–2013 (see Figure 5.2), and dropped sharply later. The liquid and bulk shipments are the most important trades, reflecting the community resupply and, most importantly, the very nature of traffic along the NSR, fueled by the exploitation of natural resources in the Norwegian and the Russian Arctic region. This pattern is similar to that of the number of transits (Zhang et al., 2016; Zhang et al., 2018).

Along the NWP, there are very few full transits completed by cargo ships; they are more numerous to perform partial transits for community resupply as stated above. This translates also in tonnage figures where liquid bulk and general cargo dominate traffic. Cruise vessels account for a larger traffic in full transits than cargo vessels that seldom use the NWP. As noted above, in 2013, the *Nordic Orion* transited a load of coal from Vancouver to Pori (Finland) (Lasserre, 2018); at the time the media hailed the transit as the beginning of a new era of Arctic shipping (National Post, 2013), but it proved to be very short lived. This very limited full transit cargo traffic could develop with natural resources extraction, notably thanks to the Raglan and Jilin Jien nickel mines in Northern Quebec and the Mary River iron mine in Baffin Island. However, two recent voyages by ships from the Danish company that owns the *Nordic Orion*, Nordic Bulk Carriers, hint the NSR may be preferred: in November 2018, two bulk carriers, the *Nordic Olympic* and *Nordic Oshima*, left the Mary River loading port of Milne Inlet and crossed to Asia along the NSR rather than the NWP. More NSR shipments from the Canadian Arctic mine could follow. According to the mining company, about 5,1 million tons of iron ore was, in the course of 2018, shipped from Baffin Island to markets in Europe, Taiwan and Japan, a 20% increase compared with 2017 (Staalesen, 2018).

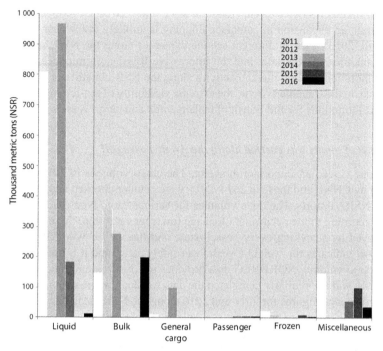

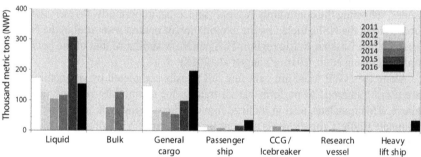

Figure 5.2 Transit trade tonnage by cargo type for the NSR and the NWP

Note: For the NSR the volumes for 2011 reestimated, see Zhang et al. (2016)

Overall transit cargo volume appears larger along the NSR. However, it experienced a severe decline in 2014, still ongoing in 2017 with only 194 364 tons before experiencing a sharp expansion in 2018, whereas it increased along the NWP in 2015. The figures below also underline that if transit tonnage declined along the NSR, overall tonnage experienced a strong expansion, with 3,2 million tons in 2011; 6,1 Mt in 2016; 9,7 Mt in 2017 and 18 Mt in 2018 (see Table 5.11).

Table 5.11 Total transit cargo volume (metric tons) along the NSR and the NWP, 2011–2016

	2011	2012	2013	2014	2015	2016	2017	2018
NWP	331 591	209 400	261 220	299 654	429 461	403 225		
NSR	979 187	1 266 775	1 355 897	201 957	39 723	214 759	194 364	491 000
NSR, total cargo	3 225 000	3 750 000	3 914 000	3 982 000	5 432 000	6 060 000	9 700 000	18 Mt

Through the NSR, cargo vessels are among the most common to transit. They carry fuel and oil product (28% of recorded ships), general cargo (12%) and bulk cargo (8%). The evolution of fuel and oil products is not linear: this segment witnessed a strong growth with a peak of 27 transits in 2013, then a sharp drop to none in 2015 and only one in 2016. The shipped fuel and oil was intended for domestic needs more than international trade – on average during the six years (2011 to 2016), 69 recorded vessel movements were carrying fuel and oil product, 42 (60%) were for domestic trade, 7 (10%) were for international trade, and 4 (5%) were shipped in/out Russian/Canadian. The 16 (23%) records remaining had incomplete information (no O/D).

There were 29 transits for general cargo in the past six years, with a similar increasing trend to a peak of 13 in 2013 and 2014, followed by a dramatic decrease to none in 2015 and one in 2016 respectively. Half of all these 29 general cargo transits traveled the entire NSR as full transits, and the other half traveled segments of the NSR as partial transits. It is difficult to identify whether they were domestic or international transits, since the records for 2014 do not display information on loading ports/destination ports. Despite that, among the other available records (16 transits in 2011, 2013 and 2016), most general cargo journeys (62%) were for domestic trade.

As for bulk cargo, the number of transits remained at a stable level, and the overall average number of transits was around four trips each year, with a slight decrease to one in 2014 and zero in 2015. Most of the transits carrying bulk cargo completed a full transit over NSR, half of which were Russian/Canadian transits and the other half were international trade. Hence, shippers tended to ship fuel and oil products and general cargo for domestic use, and bulk cargo for international and national trade.

Gas condensate and LNG, which contributed 9% of all recorded transits, were exported from Russia and Norway to Asian countries, and the two main importers were South Korea and China. However, this share is expected to increase in the next years, since the first line of the Yamal LNG project was completed in 2017, and two more respectively in August and November 2018. Sovcomflot's *Christophe de Margerie* PC3 LNG carrier that sailed in August 2017 from Norway to South Korea (CHNL, 2017) performed the first voyage that successfully used the NSR with ships designed for the Yamal LNG project. Frozen fish was another important cargo for NSR transits, though there were only ten transits, making up to 4% of all transits mainly for domestic trade. Most of those transits were westbound, from the fishing port of Petropavlosk-Kamchatsky to St. Petersburg. Only two out of the ten transits were eastbound international transits, shipping frozen ship and meat from Norway to Japan for the company Darliada Ltd., one in 2015 and another one in 2016, taking the advantage of the shorter NSR shipping route.

A total of 13 non-commercial ships and five passenger ships were recorded in the CHNL reports since 2014 to 2016. Non-commercial ships in this study refer to rescue ships, ice tugs, and icebreakers and supply vessels. One of the non-commercial ships was to ship cranes for the Ministry of Defense of the Russian Federation. Other miscellaneous cargo types are grouped together taking 3% of all transits, such as chemical tanker, concentrate and equipment. At the same time, it is noteworthy that 28% of all transits were ballasting or repositioning via NSR from 2011 to 2016, and together with fuel and oil products (28%), these became the two largest compositions of cargo types. The number of transits for repositioning or carrying ballast was substantial in all years, with composition of 66% for westbound while 34% for eastbound, which was consistent and reasonable since 64% of laden vessels were heading east and 36% of laden vessels heading west. Such voyages are a natural part of ship movements. However, the high share of ships in ballast may be a cause for concern as it indicates the lack of return cargo (Moe, 2014). This is further confirmed by the fact that dominant proportion of laden vessels traveled eastbound, but empty vessels traveled westbound (Zhang et al., 2016). Another noteworthy point is that passenger ships started from 2014 and maintained one or two transits until 2016 for tourism, crossing the whole NSR. This trend may continue with the global warming effect and possibly expanding the tourism market for the Northern Sea area.

Flag: origin and destination of transits

According to CHNL, in 2011, there was a leading proportion of Russian-flag vessels, followed by Singapore. It became more diverse in 2012, with active participations of ships registered in Panama, Finland and Norway. In 2013, one observes the most diversified flags with a total of 12. However, in 2014, the situation reversed and only five vessels were foreign registered. According to OFC (OFC, 2015), Western sanctions on Russia might be the main reason for the decline in foreign shipments at NSR in 2014. In 2015, the number of transits dropped substantially, and there were eight foreign registered vessels and ten Russian-flag vessels only. Companies interested in the NSR may remain in the waiting or investigating stage (Zhang et al., 2016).

In years from 2011 to 2016, a total of 24 different foreign flags appeared among transiting vessels along the NWP. Twenty-seven vessels used the Canadian flag, the most adopted for domestic transits in 95% of the time.

A Russian-registered vessel once used the Russian flag. International Arctic transits are vessels flagged from France (15%), the United Kingdom (14%), Canada (9%), USA (8%), Bahamas (7%), Cayman Islands (7%) and the Netherlands (4%).

Along the NSR, the Russia flag was the most often used (62%), mainly for domestic transits (90%). The other popular flags were from Panama (7%), Liberia (4%), Finland (4%) and Norway (4%). For international transits, the Finnish flag (15%), Chinese flag (10%), Marshall Island (8%) and Swedish (8%) flags were the most common used. It is interesting to notice that the Finnish, Chinese and Panama flags were the most favored for westbound international transits through the NSR, while eastbound international transits tended to use Marshall Island, St. Kitts and Nevis, and Russia flags more often.

From the perspective of cargo type, a majority of vessels transporting fuel and oil products and general cargo adopted the Russia flag for domestic trade, and favored the Panama flag for shipping dry bulk cargo for destinational and/or international trade. In Canada, the majority of tankers and general cargo vessels are Canadian flagged whereas bulk carriers are mostly registered in the Marshall Islands, Hong Kong, Panama and Canada.

For origin or destination through the NSR, China, South Korea, Norway and Netherlands ports appeared more often. Destinations from all Arctic states appear among the transits. For Asian countries, China and South Korea had the leading number of origin/destination among transit activities; Japan ports appeared in transits in 2013 and 2015; and ports from Singapore, Malaysia, Thailand, Vietnam and North Korea all were serviced once by the route for transportation (Zhang et al., 2016).

NORDREG data does not appear to reliably report OD ports, partly because of the lack of port infrastructure in the Arctic, but also because of reporting accuracy on this point. This is why "Greenland" is mentioned 123 times over the period 2011–2016 as an OD point, the largest figure. "Alaska" is also mentioned 52 times. Several of the transits involved with these ODs are pleasure crafts that may have made a stopover in Greenland or Alaska during their journey.

Montreal appears as the most often mentioned port (77 mentions), followed by "Newfoundland" (53 mentions), Sept-Îles (11 mentions) and St. John's (10 mentions). These ODs are connected to the community resupply as ships from Desgagnés and NEAS, the two general cargo shipping companies servicing the Eastern Arctic, are based in Montreal and often make stopovers in Sept-Îles, whereas Woodward/Coastal Shipping Ltd, the tanker company that delivers fuel to communities, operates from St. John's. A few other ports appear, on the destination side: Chesterfield Inlet (8), Rankin Inlet (7), Kugluktuk (6), Iqaluit (4). The figures do not reflect actual traffic since, for instance, stopovers are much more frequent in Iqaluit, the capital of Nunavut, where traffic is important enough to justify the construction of a real quay to facilitate the unloading of cargo instead of floating barges, the usual loading/unloading technique used in the Canadian Arctic.

Montreal and Quebec City are also used from the Arctic mining ports of Deception Bay and Milne Inlet for nickel and iron ore, but these voyages are not partial transits.

Conclusion

This research endeavored to analyze transit traffic databases produced by CHNL and the NSRA about the NSR, and by NORDREG about the NWP. The limitations and data inconsistency of the two datasets were assessed. It is certainly difficult to directly compare the data from year to year because of inconsistencies, and also difficult to compare traffic along the NWP and the NSR since the databases do not include the same elements. Besides, they do not provide detailed trajectories of actual transits and thus it remains difficult to determine the actual vessel speed on NSR or NWP based on these datasets.

However, a few conclusions could be inferred from this analysis.

Though the length of openness varies from year to year, the sailing season along the NSR lasted for five months in recent years. The number of transits and trade volume both increased from 2011 to 2013 and declined in 2014 until 2016, showing signs of recovery in 2017, indicating an unstable and vulnerable shipping environment thus far. The NSR seems to be more appealing to liquid, bulk and general cargo transportation, while container shipping companies did not carry out any trip until the trial transit by Maersk in 2018.

Most activities were still domestic and destinational in nature. Fuel and oil product and general cargo were shipped more for domestic needs, while bulk cargo was shipped more for international and destinational trade. Almost one-third of the transits were for ballast and repositioning, and the high share of such transits may be a cause for concern as it indicates the lack of return cargo, thus undermining profitability. Almost all the international and Russian transits traveled the entire NSR, but many domestic transits traveled partial NSR due to the nature of the activities. The year 2014 was the turning point, and there were significant differences in cargo types and quantities before and after year 2014, as a result of Western sanctions on Russia and decreases in fuel price and commodity prices. China, South Korea and Japan were active participants in NSR shipping activities, whether through shipping companies or OD.

Commercial activity along the NWP is very different inasmuch as full transits remain very few among a traffic dominated by pleasure crafts. Commercial cargo is more concentrated in partial transits stemming from community resupply. Overall, both in the NSR and the NWP, traffic remains largely destinational: ships come to or go from the Arctic to perform loading or unloading, and full transit of these Arctic routes for commercial cargo is still marginal, when compared with the development of shipping in the Arctic, all the more so when compared with traditional routes through Panama or Suez. This is in line with several studies that underline the very limited interest of the shipping industry for transit traffic given the present market and navigation conditions (Lasserre & Pelletier, 2011; Lee & Kim, 2015; Lasserre et al., 2016; Meng et al., 2017; Tseng & Pilcher, 2017).

Acknowledgments

The authors would like to thank Elsevier that permitted us to reuse our 2016 paper "Is Northern Sea Route Attractive to Shipping Companies? Some Insights from Recent Ship Traffic Data". *Marine Policy, 73*, 53–60 for this chapter.

Notes

1 The Northern Sea Route is administratively specified by the Northern Sea Route Administration (NSRA), based in Moscow, as the sea route between the Kara Gate and the Bering Strait. It is thus a portion of the Northeast Passage that also includes the southern Barents Sea up to the North Cape.
2 NORDREG zone covers the waters of Ungava Bay, Hudson Bay and James Bay and Canada's coastal northern waters within the area enclosed by the 60th parallel of north latitude, the 141st meridian of west longitude and the outer limit of the Exclusive Economic Zone. *Canadian coast guard, notices to mariners*. Retrieved Dec. 12, 2018 from www.notmar.gc.ca/publications/annual-annuel/section-a/a6-en.php.
3 Bulk carriers, fishing vessels, general cargo, tanker ships, government vessels/icebreakers, passenger vessels, pleasure crafts, research vessels and tug/barges. Another category that we created includes others vessels or maritime entity such as offshore supply platform for oil and gas exploration, heavy lift and other uncategorized points. Military vessels are included in government vessels.
4 Liquid, bulk, general cargo, frozen cargo, non-commercial, passenger and ballast. The liquid cargo includes fuel, gas concentrate, LNG and lubricants; the bulk cargo here includes paper pulp, sand, coal and ore, etc.; frozen cargo mainly refers to frozen fish and meat. Non-commercial type refers to supply vessels, tugs, icebreakers, rescue vessels, etc. that are for non-commercial purposes. Another group of other miscellaneous cargo and chemical tanker concentrate and equipment, etc., account for 3% of all shipments.

References

Abdul Rahman, A. N., Saharuddin, A. H., & Rasdi, R. (2014). Effect of the Northern Sea Route opening to the shipping activities at Malacca straits. *International Journal of e-Navigation and Maritime Economy, 1*, 85–98.

Arktika. (2016). Yakhting ne dlya vsekh. Ob osobennostyakh puteshestiy v Arktiku [Яхтинг не для всех. Об особенностях путешествий в Арктику] (Yachting is not for everyone. The particularities of Arctic navigation). *Arktika*. Retrieved July 16, 2019, from https://ru.arctic.ru/analitic/20161115/489835.html

Arpiainen, M. and Kiili, R. (2006). Arctic shuttle container link from Alaska US to Europe. *Report K-63*. Aker Arctic Technology, Helsinki.

Belyi, G. (2014). Metodologiya voprosa osvoeniya Arkticheskogo regiona Rossii v ekonomicheskikh tselyakh [Методология вопроса освоения Арктического региона России в экономических целях] (Methodology of Russian Arctic region developing for economic purposes, Transportnoe delo Rossii [Транспортное дело России]. *Transport Business in Russia, 1*, 228–231.

Beveridge, L., Fournier, M., Lasserre, F., Huang, L., & Têtu, P.-L. (2016). Interest of Asian shipping companies in navigating the Arctic. *Polar Science* 10(3):404–414.

Borgerson, S. (2008). Arctic meltdown: the economic and security implications of global warming. *Foreign Affairs, 87*(2), 63–87.

Chénier, R., Abado, L., Sabourin, O., & Tardif, L. (2017). Northern marine transportation corridors: Creation and analysis of northern marine traffic routes in Canadian waters. *Transactions in GIS, 21*(6), 1085-1097.

CHNL (2017). First of Yamal LNG tankers starts navigation via the NSR. *CHNL Information Office.* Retrieved July 15, 2019, from http://arctic-lio.com/?p=1139

Det Norske Veritas (DNV) (2010). Shipping across the Arctic Ocean. Høvik: DNV Research and Innovation, Position Paper 4.

Doyon, J. F., Lasserre, F., Pic, P., Têtu, P. L., Fournier, M., Huang, L., & Beveridge, L. (2016, June). Perceptions et stratégies de l'industrie maritime de vrac relativement à l'ouverture des passages arctiques. *Géotransports, 8,* 5–22.

Eguíluz, V. M., Fernández-Gracia, J., Irigoien, X., & Duarte, C. M. (2016). A quantitative assessment of Arctic shipping in 2010–2014. *Scientific Reports, 6,* 30682.

Guy, E. (2006). Evaluating the viability of commercial shipping in the Northwest Passage. *Journal of Ocean Technology* 1(1), 9–15.

Hong, N. (2012). The melting Arctic and its impact on China's maritime transport. *Research in Transportation Economics, 35*(1), 50–57.

Humpert, M. (2016, September 30). China's COSCO Shipping Company expands activities on Northern Sea Route. *High North News.* Retrieved October 31, 2018, from www.highnorth news.com/chinas-cosco-shipping-company-expands-activities-on-northern-sea-route/

Humpert, M. (2017, January 23). Shipping traffic on Northern Sea Route grows by 30 percent. *High North News.* Retrieved October 31, 2018, from www.highnorthnews.com/shipping-traffic-on-northern-sea-route-grows-by-30-percent/

IMO (2019). IMO Profile. Retrieved July 15, 2019, from https://business.un.org/en/entities/13.

Lasserre, F. (2014). Case studies of shipping along Arctic routes. Analysis and profitability perspectives for the container sector. *Transportation Research Part A: Policy and Practice, 66,* 144–161.

Lasserre, F. (2015). Simulations of shipping along Arctic routes: Comparison, analysis and economic perspectives. *Polar Record, 51*(3), 239–259.

Lasserre, F. (2018). Arctic shipping: A contrasted expansion of a largely destinational market. In M. Finger, & L. Heininen (Eds.), *The Global Arctic handbook* (pp. 83–100). Cham: Springer.

Lasserre, F., & Alexeeva, O. (2015). Analysis of Maritime Transit Trends in the Arctic Passages. In Lalonde, S. and McDorman, T. (eds.), *International Law and Politics of the Arctic Ocean: Essays in Honour of Donat Pharand.* Leiden: Brill Academic Publishing, p.180-193.

Lasserre, F., Beveridge, L., Fournier, M., Têtu, P. L., & Huang, L. (2016). Polar seaways? Maritime transport in the Arctic: An analysis of shipowners' intentions II. *Journal of Transport Geography, 57*(2016), 105–114.

Lasserre, F., & Pelletier, S. (2011). Polar super seaways? Maritime transport in the Arctic: An analysis of shipowners' intentions. *Journal of Transport Geography, 19*(6), 1465–1473.

Lee, T., & Kim, H. J. (2015). Barriers of voyaging on the Northern Sea Route: A perspective from shipping companies. *Marine Policy, 62,* 264–270.

Liu, M., & Kronbak, J. (2010). The potential economic viability of using the Northern Sea Route (NSR) as an alternative route between Asia and Europe. *Journal of Transport Geography,* 18, 434–444.

Mejlaender-Larsen, M. (2009). ARCON—Arctic container. *DNV Container Ship Update,* 2, 9–11.

Melia, N., Haines, K., & Hawkins, E. (2016). Sea ice decline and 21st century trans-Arctic shipping routes, *Geophysical Research Letters*, *43*, 9720–9728, doi:10.1002/2016GL069315

Meng, Q., Zhang, Y., & Xu, M. (2017). Viability of transarctic shipping routes: A literature review from the navigational and commercial perspectives. *Maritime Policy & Management*, *44*(1), 16–41.

Moe, A. (2014). The Northern Sea Route: Smooth sailing ahead? *Strategic Analysis*, *38*(6), 784–802.

National Post. (2013, September 27). Northwest Passage crossed by first cargo ship, the Nordic Orion, heralding new era of Arctic commercial activity. *National Post*, Retrieved December 20, 2018, from https://nationalpost.com/news/canada/northwest-passage-crossed-by-first-cargo-ship-the-nordic-orion-heralding-new-era-of-arctic-commercial-activity

Nikiforov, M. (2010, June 1). V Arktiku pod parusami [В Арктику под парусами] (Sailing in the Arctic), Nauka I Zhizn [Наука и жизнь] (*Science and Life*). Retrieved December 21, 2018, from www.nkj.ru/news/18069/?%27.$first_url.%27

OFC. (2015). *Western sanctions on Russia affect traffic on Northern Sea Route*. Office of the Federal Coordinator.

Pettersen, T. (2016, March 18). Declining interest in use of Northern Sea Route. *Barents Observer*. Retrieved October 18, 2018, from https://thebarentsobserver.com/en/industry/2016/03/declining-interest-use-northern-sea-route

Somanathan, S.; Flynn, P. and Szymanski, J. (2009). The Northwest Passage: a simulation. *Transportation Research Part A* 43, 127-135.

Staalesen, A. (2018, November 15). Canadian Arctic ore finds way through Northern Sea Route. *The Barents Observer*. Retrieved December 20, 2018, from https://thebarentsobserver.com/en/2018/11/canadian-arctic-ore-finds-way-through-northern-sea-route

Stephenson, S. R., & Smith, L. C. (2015). Influence of climate model variability on projected Arctic shipping futures. *Earth's Future*, *3*, 331–343.

Tseng, P. H., & Pilcher, N. (2017). Assessing the shipping in the Northern Sea Route: A qualitative approach. *Maritime Business Review*, *2*(4), 389–409.

Verny, J., & Grigentin, C. (2009). Container shipping on the Northern Sea Route. *International Journal of Production Economics*, *122*(1), 107–117.

Wan, Z., Ge, J., & Chen, J. (2018). Energy-saving potential and an economic feasibility analysis for an Arctic route between Shanghai and Rotterdam: Case study from China's largest container sea freight operator. *Sustainability*, *10*(4), 921.

Yu, H. and Bond, J. (2017). Future of traffic on the Northern Sea Route. *Frontier Energy*, Winter, 16–17, Retrieved July 21, 2019, from https://ww2.eagle.org/content/dam/eagle/articles/FrontierEnergy_5.18.17.pdf

Yu, Y. (2016). *Research of legal status and navigation regime of Arctic shipping lanes* (Master's Thesis of Arts in Polar Law, Faculty of Law). University of Akureyri, March 2016.

Zhang, Y., Meng, Q., & Zhang, L. (2016). *Is Northern Sea Route attractive to shipping companies? Some insights from recent ship traffic data*. Marine Policy, *73*(12), 53–60.

Zhang, Z., Huisingh, D., & Song, M. (2018). Exploitation of trans-Arctic maritime transportation. *Journal of Cleaner Production*, *212*, 960–973.

6 The evolution and relative competitiveness of global Arctic cruise tourism destinations

Pierre-Louis Têtu, Jackie Dawson and Frédéric Lasserre

Introduction

Traveling and vacationing onboard a cruise ship has become one of the most popular forms of tourism over the past few decades (CLIA, 2018). A 2018 Passenger snapshot prepared by the Cruise Line International Associations (CLIA) outlined the continually increasing number of passengers in the last ten years (CLIA, 2018). For example, the survey found that there were more than 450 cruise ships in 2017 and 2018 that carried more than 27 million passengers and that this number had increased from just 17,8 million passengers in 2009 (ibid.). The increase in cruises internationally reflects global trends in globalization, infrastructure development including deepwater ports that can accommodate larger vessels where the economy of scale enables more affordable cruise options, and overall improvements to global transportation infrastructure related to increasingly well-connected airports, ferries and rail and roadways. Historically speaking, the cruise tourism industry is oriented toward the North American market, but in recent years there has been more and more cruise ship activities in Europe, in the Mediterranean and Baltic Seas, as well as in South America, the Caribbean and in emerging markets such as South East Asia and China.

In recent decades, melting of sea ice in the Arctic region has played an important role in the emergence of a cruise tourism industry in that region. Although the increase in Arctic cruise tourism has certainly been influenced by various forces of change such as global trends, commodity prices, demographics, and globalization (Stewart, Dawson, & Johnston, 2015), the effects of climate change and the melting of summer sea ice in the Arctic has facilitated greater overall accessibility to the region and has thus further enabled new cruising opportunities over the last 25 years (Stewart, Draper, & Dawson, 2010; Tivy et al., 2011; Stewart et al., 2013; Pizzolato, Howell, Derksen, Dawson, & Copland, 2014, 2016; Lasserre & Têtu, 2015; Bystrowska & Dawson, 2017; Dawson et al., 2014, 2018). One of the challenges facing researchers and regulators of this industry is the fact that trends data on cruise ship traffic is difficult to obtain and compare due to a variety of definitional, methodological, and geopolitical factors. What are the present trends in the Arctic cruise market?

The contrasted development of the Arctic cruise market

First, there are many definitions of 'the Arctic' and this in and of itself makes data collection on cruise tourism in the Arctic region challenging. The three types of boundaries most often cited in the literature on polar tourism include: 1) the limit of the continuous permafrost, 2) 10° Celsius isotherm in July, and 3) the treeline. The Arctic is often corresponded to the areas of higher latitude and typically it is outlined as the geographic region that is above the Arctic Circle (66° 34'). This is the boundary utilized by both the Arctic Human Development Report (AHDR) (Nymand & Fondahl, 2014) and the Arctic Monitoring and Assessment Program (AMAP) (Arctic Council, 2019a) and as such is also the delineation we have chosen to use in this chapter.

Second, prior to 1990, there was little information available to describe the evolution of the Arctic cruise tourism sector, which at the time was inconsistent, ad hoc, and limited. Over the past 25 years the Arctic cruise industry has evolved significantly, and more regular and to some extent more consistent statistics are now being kept by relevant authorities, which can be used to compare and contrast national scale development trajectories (Lasserre & Têtu, 2015; Dawson et al., 2018). Data that are now available for Canada typically come from the Canadian Coast Guard. However, this data only includes ships that fall under certain regulatory categories such as those vessels that are over 300 gross tons, and therefore it may not capture all tourism vessels operating in the region. In Greenland, despite the fact that data are freely available through the Statistics Greenland's website, there is only information about the number of passengers landing in Greenlandic harbors for three years (2015 to 2017). A discussion with experts on the website underlined the fact that additional data do exist, but they are not freely available online. Data for Alaska are available for only a few ports. In Alaska and in Norway, data that have been used previously by academics have not typically come from an official government database, but rather are often acquired online from Alaskacruises.com, or in the case of Norway from the Environmental monitoring website for Svalbard and Jan Mayen, which is part of the Norwegian Polar Institute. Data for Svalbard were very difficult to obtain apart for Longyearbyen port, the main settlement in Svalbard. Data for the Russian Arctic are also very limited; they are often obtained from two main publications on cruise tourism in Russian waters and only include reliable information for the Arctic Russian National Park of Franz Josef Land and the Port of Murmansk (Pashkevich & Stjernström, 2014; Shirokiy, 2015).

Third, most regions across the Arctic do not have a homogenous definition of cruise tourism or of a cruise ship. For example, the average size of ships operating in Greenland, Iceland, and Svalbard tend to be large expedition style vessels (i.e. around 700 passengers) and also larger standard-sized cruise vessels that are typically used in more southern locations (i.e. above 2 000 passengers). In comparison, the number of cruise ships, the size of ships, and the total number of passengers visiting the Canadian and Russian Arctic are much smaller. When trying to understand the size of the Arctic cruise tourism sector, and to make comparisons nationally, it is important to consider 1) the number of voyages on offer, and 2) the number of total passengers. For example, if a particular region attracts a high number of small vessels with >200 passengers than the overall impact of the industry may differ greatly from another region that may attract fewer overall vessels but with much greater capacity (i.e. >2 000 in some cases).

Overall, combining all of these definitional inconsistencies with the lack of regular data collection methods or analysis procedures means that it is very difficult to accurately analyze cruise tourism trends across the global Arctic. This data trends challenge is likely to change in the near-term future as the Arctic Council is currently working on a major initiative called the Arctic Ship Traffic Data (ASTD), which aims to collect and share data on all types of Arctic marine vessel trends (Arctic Council, 2019b) based on Automatic Information System (AIS) satellite data. However, this technology is fraught with challenges including the necessity of all vessels to be carrying transponders, which is currently not legally mandated, meaning that only some vessels will be captured via this method. Until it becomes mandatory internationally to carry an AIS transponder on all cruise ships (small and large) the best approach to understanding traffic trends and related implications of the industry is to examine existing national level data that are available.

Based on available data from INNAV (XST, 2019) between the years 2000 and 2017 there was an average of 14 cruise ships visiting Arctic Canada annually with peaks between 2007 and 2010 and again between 2015 and 2017. However, it should be noted that these numbers are lower than those reported by the Canadian Coast Guard and likely slightly underestimate the total number of cruise ships operating in Arctic Canada (Dawson et al., 2018). In Greenland, there was an average of 12 cruise ships annually in the late 1990s, but this number more than doubled in 2004 (29) and 2005 (25), peaked in 2008 (105) and again in 2016 (104). For comparative purposes, the average number of vessels in Greenland between 2000 and 2017 was 57, which is more than four times the number of vessels in Arctic Canada. The numbers of cruise vessels in Iceland's two main ports (Reykjavik and Akureyri) are similar to Greenland with more than 100 in 2017. However, overall, the average number of cruise vessels visiting Iceland is higher than both Canada and Greenland considering that the average number of vessels to Reykjavik between 2011 and 2017 was 96 per year. The Arctic locations that are host to the largest Arctic cruise industry are Svalbard, northern Norway and Alaska. Although their total average annual voyages were lower compared to Greenland and Iceland, the overall size of the cruise industry is bigger in both Svalbard and Alaska because they are able to accommodate large traditional style cruise ships because of the availability of appropriate ports and other infrastructure. The average number of cruise ships visiting these regions annually between 2007 and 2017 was 48 in Svalbard, and 58 in Alaska (Figure 6.1).

Passenger number data is more challenging to obtain compared to voyage data but some information is available from a few of the major Arctic cruise destinations that can be examined. As noted above Svalbard, Norway attracts some of

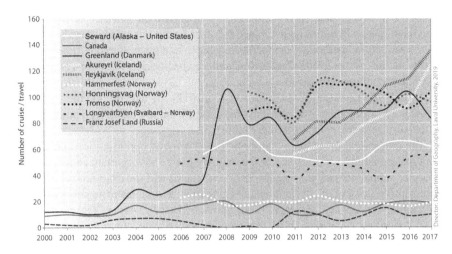

Figure 6.1 Estimated number of cruise ships operating in the Arctic, 2000–2017

Source: AECO (2019); and estimations based on Nunavut Tourism (2011); Government of Nunavut (2013); Dawson et al. (2018)

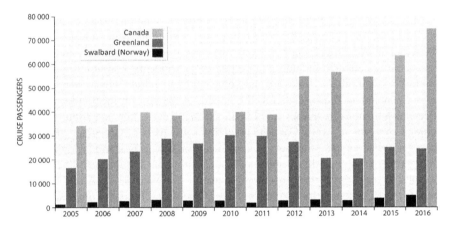

Figure 6.2 Estimated number of annual cruise passengers to Canada, Greenland, and Svalbard (2005–2016)

Sources: AECO (2019); and estimations based on Nunavut Tourism (2011); Government of Nunavut (2013); Dawson et al. (2018)

the largest number of cruise ship passengers internationally, with over 70 000 visitors in 2016 (Figure 6.2). The only other region that rivals Svalbard in terms of passengers numbers is Alaska, which reported more than 1 million cruise passenger visits in 2018 (CIN, 2018). Comparatively, Greenland has attracted around 30 000 cruise passengers annually in 2012 and 2011 but in recent years their numbers have been closer to 25 000 (Dawson et al., 2017; Government of Green-land, 2016). In Canada, cruise passenger numbers are the lowest internationally and have ranged between an estimated 3 500 and 6 000 in recent years. The lack of infrastructure, including port facilities, wharfs, and other tourism infrastructure limits the market in Arctic Canada to smaller expedition-style cruise vessels and the occasional medium-sized vessel such as the *Crystal Serenity* (with visits in 2017 and 2018) and the *World* (with a visit in 2012). By data mining the available sources of information it is also possible to draw a more nuanced picture of the Arctic cruise sector by nation state (Table 6.1).

The cruise tourism industry can bring both risks and opportunities to regional Arctic communities. For example, the industry can be an important source of primary or supplementary income for local settlements and towns, but it can also be a disruptive element of environmental degradation, and can have negative impacts on culture and society (Graeger, 1996; Stewart, Howell, Draper, Yackel, & Tivy, 2007; Marquez & Eagles, 2007; Stewart & Draper, 2008; Lamers & Amelung, 2010; Fay & Karlsdottir, 2011; Stewart & Dawson, 2011; Lenmelin, Johnston, Dawson, Stewart, & Mattina, 2012; Dawson et al., 2014; Johnston, Dawson, De Souza, & Stewart, 2017; Dawson et al., 2018). The effects of a large influx of passengers to Arctic Canada, Svalbard, Greenland, and more recently to the small Franz Josef Island in the Russian Arctic are well known (Hagen, Vistad, Eide, Flyen, & Fangel, 2012; Stewart, & Dawson, 2011). The perceived environmental impacts of Arctic cruise tourism are similar across national regions and often include concerns related to the potential for fuel spills, bilge water release, groundings, and invasive species introduction. Similarly, there are common human safety and security concerns including those related to accidents, human-drug-firearms trafficking, and others. There are also some common cultural concerns across the regions including those related to the impact of tourism on local cultural practices, or intrusions to privacy and livelihoods. However, there are additional and unique concerns in Arctic Canada and across some parts of Greenland and other areas where there are either settled land claims or strong Indigenous populations. Indigenous groups in these regions practice important cultural activities along shorelines and within the marine environment. For example, in Arctic Canada, where there are settled Inuit land claim areas and where Inuit and other northerners regularly travel and hunt in maritime regions there are increasing concerns related to cruise ships disturbing a hunt or disrupting the breeding, feeding, or migration patterns of marine mammals that are an essential part of the diet and cultural practices of local peoples.

The growth in polar travel in recent decades has also been matched by an intensification of scholarly activity related to many aspects of polar tourism (Stewart, Liggett, & Dawson, 2017). Much of the focus of this research body has been on tourism development, management, and experiences. Another way of understanding tourism development is taking a closer examination of the underlying factors that contribute to tourism development and the relative successes of different geographic areas or tourism sectors such as Arctic cruise tourism. There has been limited attention paid to understanding the 'determinants' or factors that have led

Table 6.1 List of data collected on cruise passenger landings and port of calls for seven Arctic destinations inside the AMAP border

Destinations	Canada	Alaska	Greenland	Svalbard	Russia	Norway	Iceland
	By community (n=7) and shore locations (n=152)	By port (n=9)	By harbor (n=19)	Longyearbyen settlement only (n=1)	By shore location (n=1) and by port (n=1)	By port (n=10)	By port (n=9)
Number of passenger landings by community/ town/port/shore locations	1990–2017 (7 communities, 152 shore locations)	2007–2016	2008–2017	2017	2013–2017	2010–2017	2015–2017
Number of cruise ship/port of call	7 communities (2017)	2007–2017	No data	2006–2017	2000–2017	2006–2017	2015–2017
Source of data	Canadian Coast Guard (NORDREG) database	Alaska Cruises website	Statistics Greenland website	Norwegian Polar Institute	Pashkevich and Stjernström (2014); Shirokiy (2015)	Cruise Northern Norway and Svalbard (CNNS) and Cruise Norway websites	Cruise Iceland website

to the successful development of cruise tourism in the global Arctic. Bystrowska and Dawson (2017) examined historical and geographic elements explaining the competitiveness or attractiveness of Svalbard, Iceland and Greenland compared to the less visited Canadian Arctic pointing to major elements related to geography, infrastructure, and government policy. This chapter provides additional attention to this question of how Arctic cruise destinations have evolved and what their relative competitiveness is globally. In this chapter we highlight major historical trends and factors affecting the success or attractiveness of certain Arctic cruise destinations.

Determinants of success: examining factors affecting the historic development of cruise tourism across the global Arctic

The first cruise ship to visit the Polar Regions occurred at the end of the 19th century (1880), when a German chartered ship visited Spitsbergen in Svalbard (Dawson et al., 2014). Experienced by a history of political, geographic, and climatic barriers, the very first cruise ship visiting the Russian Arctic – on Franz Josef Land – took place in 1931 (ibid.). In the Canadian Arctic, the Hudson's Bay Company supplied a ship – *Nascopie* – in the early 1930s and set aside 22 of her 150 passenger berths for 'official tourists'. The very first cruise ship transiting the Northwest Passage did not occur until 1984 (Stewart et al., 2007; Pashkevich et al., 2015) but already, in 1974, the *Lindbald Explorer* visited the Canadian Arctic but did not fully transit the Northwest Passage (Dupré, 2009).

There are a number of determinants or factors that have included this historic development and which will continue to influence the success of certain Arctic regions as polar cruise tourism continues to grow and develop. Based on a review of literature and expert understanding of the sector we outline and overview these potential factors affecting the development, including discussions on drivers and limiters such as climate change and sea-ice reduction, global economic trends, and national policies. Current research needs and challenges are also outlined. Below we discuss 1) the role of assets like icebreakers, 2) the role of geography and sea ice, 3) the role of infrastructure, and 4) the role of governance, policy, and management.

The role of historical assets: ports and icebreakers

Since the collapse of the Soviet Union and the end of the Cold War, the Arctic has experienced a dramatic shift from a sensitive buffer area between the United States and Russia to include a range of initiatives involving transnational cooperation (Young, 2005). During the Cold War, the waters of the Arctic served primarily as a strategic buffer between the two great powers, the United States (US) and the USSR (Dean, Lackenbauer, & Lajeunesse, 2014). While the Arctic's role during the Cold War may have been peripheral, the Cold War did have a profound impact on the North, stimulating its economic and political development but not in a homogenous way. In the Canadian and US Arctic, a network of Arctic air bases and DEW line[1] sites were constructed along the entire Arctic coast. Despite the establishment of this military presence in the North American Arctic during the Cold War, the region had been largely ignored in terms of development of economic infra-structure, which has severely limited maritime capabilities. Conversely, in the Soviet Union, the government established a controlled economic system and deliberately invested large sums to develop the Arctic, building ports and railways to foster the control of the area and exploit natural resources. This political and historical difference resulted in an impressive development of infrastructure (Têtu, Pelletier, & Lasserre, 2015). In this perspective, the Soviet Union developed its Arctic regions very differently from geographi-cally comparable areas such as northern Canada or Alaska. Russia built full-scale industrial facilities especially east of the Urals, near the mining town of Norilsk (Lasserre & Têtu, 2018); large permanent settlements and ports exist along the Northern Sea Route such as Pevek, Tiksi, and Dudinka, and the towns of Arkhangelsk and Murmansk are both equipped with mechanized ports and international airports with multiple international connections. Mur-mansk is host to the Russian North Fleet where nuclear icebreakers such as the *Yamal* (1992–) or *50 Let Pobedy* (2007–) are stationed. The *50 Let Pobedy* (50 Years of Victory) transported cruise passengers from Murmansk to the North Pole in a 14-day voyage with Quark Expedition with an average of $50 000 per passenger (Lasserre & Têtu, 2015). Moreover, Russia has the most impressive fleet of icebreakers in the world with 46 in-service icebreak-ers, 11 under construction, and four planned. Despite an aging fleet, Russia is still the leader, well beyond Canada (seven icebreakers), Finland (ten), Sweden (seven), USA (five), Denmark (four), China (three), or Norway (one) (U.S. Coast Guard, 2017). This icebreaker fleet partly explains the higher densities in shipping traffic along the NSR. Some of these Russian icebreak-ers are indeed chartered by Canadian cruise operators, such as Quark Expedi-tion and One Ocean Expedition, which offer these operators the opportunity to visit remote locations of the Arctic with their passengers. Because there are often high sea-ice concentration areas in some parts of the Arctic, these more robust icebreakers allow passengers to visit some of the most unknown and untouched parts of the northern hemisphere.

Of the vessels coming to the Canadian Arctic there is a large variety of origin, flag state, and strength of ships. For instance, Russian vessels tend to be stronger than vessels from other origins, and there are a large number of weaker vessels sailing in the Canadian Arctic. For instance, the Russian-flagged vessel *Kapitan Khlebnikov* is a strong polar class 3 vessel that since at least 1990 has been operat-ing as a cruise vessel in the Canadian Arctic, but which was requisitioned by its owner, the Far East Shipping Company (FESCO) in 2015 for bulk shipping in the Russian Arctic. In the 1990s and early 2000s sea ice was thicker and it was an asset to have powerful icebreakers that enabled voyages to new areas that had never been explored before by tourist ships.

Yet, despite the heritage from the Soviet planned economy, the presence of a series of Siberian ports and an impressive fleet of icebreakers, it is not the Russian cruise market that is the most flourishing. If the Russian icebreakers were indeed strong assets, they were mostly employed elsewhere when engaged in cruise activities, and only Murmansk seems to develop a significant market base for cruises in the Russian Arctic. Assets are thus not enough to develop a significant cruise shipping market.

The role of geography and sea ice

The development pathway and the success of Arctic cruise operations depend greatly on a number of fundamental factors including: attractiveness of the port of departure/or arrival of the cruise; the itinerary and route; seasonality and weather conditions; and the presence of physical and tourism infrastructure (i.e. ports with passenger terminals, shops, museums, etc.). The presence or absence of these factors has led to the competitive advantage of certain destinations over others. Other important factors that have been identified, which contribute to destination competitiveness include things such as local leadership, political will, tourism operator advocacy investment in tourism-specific facilities, availability of events and programs, accessibility of visitors services, and availability of a local liaison or point of contact to assist external organizations (Bornhorst, Ritchie, & Sheehan, 2010; Bystrowska & Dawson, 2017).

The sea ice in the Arctic and its spatial distribution partly explain the success and cruise ship trends in the region whether it is summer or winter sea ice (Figures 6.3 and 6.4). Generally speaking these past years, the shipping season in the Canadian Arctic has extended from three to five months from June/July to September/October. The shipping season in Greenland, whether it is the east or west coast, also took place during these months, but just like Svalbard, coastal Norway, Iceland, or southern Alaska, these regions are ice free for most of the year. This being said, the number of stopovers and passenger landings in the Canadian Arctic remain low in comparison with other destinations of the Arctic where sea ice is not a significant constraint. In a survey conducted by Lasserre and Têtu (2015) and based on informal discussions with cruise operators operating in the Canadian Arctic, sea-ice conditions remain an important risk associated with marine tourism in the Arctic as well as inexperienced captains and crew when shipping in a sea-ice environment. However, the perceived risks vary from one company to the other where these risks can be managed or represent more or less important challenges, but in the summer shipping season, these seem to be manageable risks. The harsh, unpredictable, and changing weather, the lack of or limited communications in the Canadian Arctic make this area very expensive for the consumer compared to other Arctic regions.

Severely restricted in their movements, vessels without or with a low polar class and carrying more than 1 000 passengers such as the *Crystal Serenity* (1D) in the Canadian Arctic in 2016 and 2017 show the flexibility of Canadian legislation in its Arctic waters – others see the *Crystal Serenity* journey as resulting from

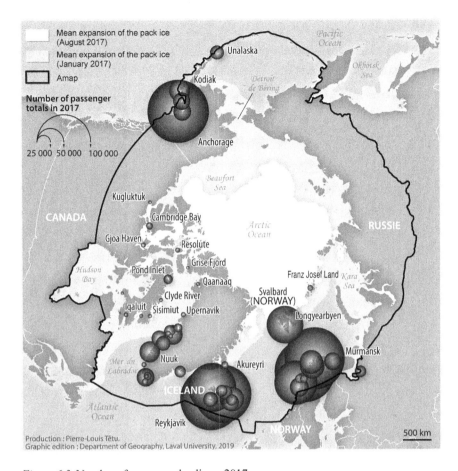

Figure 6.3 Number of passenger landings, 2017

Note: There was no data for Alaska in 2017 so we used 2016 figures. Murmansk and Arkhangelsk are based on data of 2015.

Sources: compiled by the authors, national statistical databases.

loopholes in the regulation. The costs associated with the construction and opera-tion of ice-strengthened ships, the limited availability of such vessels, the cost of fuel as well as the global economic crisis or worldwide economic health are serious challenges for several operators already offering cruises in the Canadian Arctic, but also for those that would like to in the future (Lasserre & Têtu, 2015). There are still significant concerns related to sea ice and these were exemplified with an incident occurring in the 2018 summer cruising season in the Canadian Arctic where the *Akademik Ioffe*, a Russian ice-strengthened vessel, ran aground in the western Gulf of Boothia near Kugaaruk, Nunavut causing the voyage to be canceled and over 200 passengers needing rescue. Heavy ice and poor marine

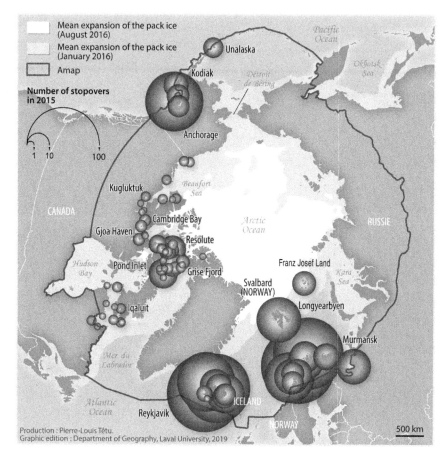

Figure 6.4 Number of Arctic Cruise Ship stopovers, 2015

Note: There was no data available for Greenland at the port level.

charts may have been responsible for the 2018 grounding; the 2010 grounding of the *Clipper Adventurer* was clearly caused by poor marine charts as the ship ventured out of the well-known navigation corridors (Têtu, 2019).

The Canadian government through the Canadian forces and various other agencies and departments are already prepared and trained in case of emergencies such as the grounding of the *Ioffe*, but many observers still agree that a major catastrophe is only a matter of time. Whether the risks associated with Arctic shipping is manageable by cruise operators must differ from one operator or strategy to the other, but the fact that Crystal Cruise gave up Arctic cruises after two years underlines that shipping in the area is not risk free (Coppes, 2017).

The role of infrastructure

Discussions with cruise operators already operating in the Canadian Arctic underline the fact that the lack of limited airstrips constitutes an important challenge for cruise operators in comparison with other Arctic destinations. In the Russian-European Arctic (Greenland, Iceland, Svalbard, and Russia), cruise companies often start their trips from a port that is well connected to air services such as Helsinki, Murmansk, Reykjavik, or Tromsø, for example. Pashkevich and Stjernström (2014) argue that while the tourism industry is dependent on infrastructure, accessibility, transport, hotels, etc., those industries are reliant on a vibrant tourism industry. A survey conducted by Lasserre and Têtu (2015) shows that operators disagree on the impact of poor infrastructure on the Arctic cruise market growth in Canada. The French company Ponant does not see the lack of maritime infrastructure in the Canadian Arctic as a major constraint since part of their broader business strategy is to offer a unique experience to their guests through zodiac excursions (ibid.). On the other hand, Adventure Canada has been quoted as saying that the lack of infrastructure is a limiting factor for the introduction of larger ships. The logistics of transporting 100–200 passengers back and forth to the main cruise vessel by zodiacs is feasible; however, it is not the case with 1 000 passengers or more. Other companies, such as One Ocean Expedition, already present in the region, further see the lack of deepwater ports with refueling and water bunkering facilities as a major limitation to the expansion of their activities. CLIA expressed a similar opinion as well as AECO members Holland America and Silversea. They claim that there is not enough available refueling facilities, and that marine infrastructure in the region is inadequate to berth large passenger vessels, and finally that adequate infrastructure for search and rescue operations is lacking in Arctic Canada. In this regard, once new infrastructure is completed, it is possible that tourism will expand, as has already been witnessed in Greenland and Svalbard (Dawson et al., 2017). Indeed, Greenland, Svalbard, Iceland, Norway, and Alaska can all accommodate large passenger vessels (≥1 000 passengers) as these ships can be more easily accommodated thanks to existing maritime infrastructure.

Many of the cruise operators surveyed signal the lack of maritime infrastructure as a barrier to increasing their activities and organizing the itineraries of large capacity vessels. In order to increase the number of vessels and tourist visitors to the Canadian Arctic to the same level as other Arctic destinations such as Svalbard or Greenland, the region would most certainly need to expand and invest significantly in maritime infrastructure. Indeed, economics tells us that the current cruise prices are limiting the growth of demand for these cruises. The development of maritime infrastructure in the Canadian Arctic could stimulate the interest of companies, which own large capacity vessels that presently operate in the Russian or European Arctic. However, the lack of port infrastructure in Nunavut is blatant, and there are only three ports with berths in the Canadian Arctic, Deception Bay/Raglan, Nanisivik, and Churchill, the first two being industrial ports and the third being remote from classical cruise routes. All other places are serviced with barges and provide no facility for ships to dock. It is expected that the construction of a deepwater port in Iqaluit and Rankin Inlet as well as small craft harbors in the communities are initiatives that, once completed, might increase the attractiveness of certain locations and might promote the development of tourist shipping (Lasserre & Têtu, 2015). In addition, improving maritime infrastructure would facilitate cruise ship calls and stopovers by private yachts in ports of communities that currently receive no ships. A deepwater port in Rankin Inlet would thus increase the potential attractiveness of the Hudson Bay region and neighboring communities and consequently could allow Chesterfield Inlet, Clyde River, Kugaaruk, and Repulse Bay to expect visits from cruise ships and further develop their touristic services. Historical factors such as the past economic history of an area thus bear an impact on the infrastructure available for Arctic cruise shipping. Northern Norway and the Kola Peninsula have been developed since the 18th century, for instance.

The industry could also gain from investments already made in other activities. For example, Pashkevich and Stjernström (2014) underlined that military airstrips could be used to bring in civilian visitors to an area, a military health care service in a remote location could provide other visitors with basic emergency services, and a transportation network built for natural resources exploitation could be used to develop a tourist destination. In the Canadian Arctic, there are no public ports with berths except Churchill and while air connections do exist to most communities, air fares are very expensive and represent another limiting factor. Moreover, most infrastructures in the Canadian Arctic were put in place in the 1950s to build the DEW line based on the aircraft of the time. As a result, many northern settlements still have 2 500 or 3 000 foot gravel air strips ideal for DC-3s but ill-suited for Boeing 737s that Canadian North, First Air, and Air Yukon use. Unlike the neighboring state of Alaska or even Greenland, Iceland, Norway, Svalbard, or Russia, the Canadian Arctic has few paved and long runways, limiting the type and size of aircraft that northern carriers can use. For instance, there are very few airfields in the Canadian Arctic that are used to embark or disembark cruise passengers at the exception of Resolute Bay, Kugluktuk, Kuujjuaq, or Iqaluit. Canadian International airports such as Edmonton, Toronto, and St. John are much more developed, but it is Ottawa International Airport that is the busiest.

It will be discussed later how the Canadian Coasting Trade Act of Canada, by prohibiting foreign vessels from operating from a voyage embarking one Canadian port and ending that same voyage in Canadian waters without leaving the territory, has an impact on the modus operandi of companies and this has an impact on the choice of airports and airliners. Contrary to the trends that we observe in the Arctic in comparison with Canadian airports such as Iqaluit or Kugluktuk but not Ottawa or Edmonton, airports in Bergen (Norway), Kangerlussuaq (Greenland), Reykjavik (Iceland), and Longyearbyen in Svalbard are much busier.

The role of governance, policy, and regulations

Despite a polar-class certification, incidents can happen because of poor charts, weather, or sea ice, even with ice-strengthened vessels, as the sinking in 2007 of the *Polar Explorer* reminded the industry. In comparison, the low concentrations or absence of sea ice in most other areas of the Arctic allows cruise operators to organize voyages on vessels with a carrying capacity of more than 1 000 passengers. Arctic destinations such as Svalbard, Iceland, Norway, or Alaska are regularly visited by vessels owned or operated by CLIA members and without a polar class, such as Carnival Cruises, Princess Cruises, AIDA Cruises, etc. However, new environmental regulations that have been or could soon be implemented such as a heavy fuel oil (HFO) ban and CO_2 emissions regulations could pose more important challenges for cruise operators. For example, the ban on heavy fuel oil that was introduced for Svalbard with full effect from 2015 and compulsory pilotage, also introduced in 2015, have meant that ships using heavy fuel oil and those without a pilot on board are no longer permitted to sail in Svalbard's protected areas.

Whether it is linked to these new environmental regulations and global awakening, several cruise tourism operators operating in the whole Arctic are slowly replacing older vessels with new ones that will more easily comply with current regulations. For instance, Hapag Lloyd, while it is too early to assess their polar classification, will add three new vessels in the coming years: the *Hanseatic Spirit* built by Norwegian shipyard Vard is expected to be launched in the second quarter of 2021; the *Hanseatic Nature* in spring 2019 and the *Hanseatic Inspiration* scheduled for fall 2019. The French company Ponant announced that its new polar exploration vessel, the world's first hybrid electric icebreaker powered by liquefied natural gas (LNG) will be named *Le Commandant Charcot* after the notable French polar explorer Charcot, and should be launched in 2021. Finally, the Canadian company, already operating in the Canadian Arctic, One Ocean Expedition, added a new vessel to its fleet – the *RCGS Resolute* – in November 2018. A document from the Maritime Executive website presents an impressive list of expedition ships intended for polar waters and informs that many new operators are seeking to get into the business while existing players are enlarging their fleet (The Maritime Executive, 2018).

The Canadian permitting requirements process is complex and in some cases incredibly inefficient (Pashkevich et al., 2015), but its robustness is essential and important in ensuring the safety of shipping in Canadian waters despite its loopholes enabling ships like the *Crystal Serenity* to ply Arctic waters. There are similarly also a high number of requirements to sail in the Russian Arctic (Shirokiy, 2015). From the industry perspective, the convoluted permitting system is a major development barrier for the Canadian Arctic (see Dawson et al., 2014, 2017). A US provisional AECO member mentioned that despite their high interest for Arctic expedition cruises in Canada, the permitting process was too complex.

The requirement to work with various territories with inconsistent requirements and departments within the Canadian government make getting permits for the

Canadian Arctic the most complexes and tedious in the world. Going the route of IAATO or AECO would help hugely (Pashkevich et al., 2015). The permitting process appears to be their biggest challenge and enough of a reason for them to not currently go to Canadian Arctic. For instance, a discussion with a company then present but now out of the Canadian Arctic market, underlined that it would return when permitting becomes easier. For example, the process in Greenland seems to be more streamlined in comparison with Canada where the requirement to work with various territories with inconsistent requirements and departments within the Canadian government makes getting permits for the Canadian Arctic the most complex and tedious in the world (Dawson et al., 2017).

These regulatory challenges for expedition cruise operators in the Canadian Arctic highlight the need, from the industry perspective, to streamline the number of permitting, licensing, clearance, inspection, review, certification, impact, registration, and reporting requirements and the costs associated to them. This permitting system could be a serious concern for operators because they could easily oversee one or more requirements, which could result in a company unintentionally being non-compliant – a situation that has happened on several occasions over the past decade. In 2017, an update to the 2005 Transport Canada document, Guidelines for the Operation of Passenger Vessels in Canadian Arctic Waters (TP 13670E) was released and this could assist new operators in better understanding the complex permitting system in Arctic Canada. However, no effort was made to streamline regulations or the regulatory process, rather the document provides an outline of all of the required permits and an updated (but static) list of contact persons. Although updating this information document is a good start, it would be more useful to create a centralized permitting system or a one-window electronic approach in which operators facilitate the permitting process (Dawson et al., 2017; Kostin, 2018).

Another factor that limits cruise tourism development in Arctic Canada is the Coasting Trade Act (1992, c. 31), which imposes a significant tax on foreign-flagged vessels that engage in an itinerary that only occurs within Canadian waters. Since all cruise ships operating in Artic Canada are foreign flagged, the net result of this legislation is that cruise operators always begin or end their voyages outside Canada (typically Greenland) in order to avoid paying this tax (Dawson et al., 2014; Lasserre & Têtu, 2015). There are local economic ramifications considering the ships spend additional time outside of Canada and spend money in communities there (ibid.). The side effect of avoiding paying the tax associated to the Coasting Trade Act is that cruise operators must arrange for their passengers to cleared by customs (Canadian Border Service Agency – CBSA) when they enter the country from Greenland considering there are no permanent border services in the high Canadian Arctic. Cruise operators must pay for CBSA agents to fly to and stay in the community of entry in order to clear passengers into Canada. However, there is a recent example of a Canadian cruise operator requesting exception from the Coasting Trade Act tax for operating a voyage solely within Canadian waters with some success. One Ocean Expeditions Inc. made a request to the Canadian Transportation Agency in February 2018 for a license to use the *Akademik Ioffe* to offer a cruise starting and ending in Canada from Cambridge Bay to Iqaluit. The company asked the Canadian Transportation Agency whether there was a Canadian ship available to provide the service, and identical or similar adequate marine service available from any person operating one or more Canadian ships. Canadian Transport Agency staff gave notice of the application to the Canadian marine industry and no Canadian ships were offered. Therefore, the Agency determined that there were no suitable Canadian ships available and that there is no identical or similar adequate marine service available. As a result, in February 2018 and according to the Canadian Transportation Agency, One Ocean Expeditions Inc. was granted a Coasting Trade License beginning on June 27, 2018 and ending on September 25, 2018. This process was incredibly arduous and most operators, especially new to Canada, would be challenged to navigate existing regulatory systems. Requiring special permits for foreign-flagged vessels to operate across the Arctic is not unique to Canada. In the Russian Arctic, foreign-flagged vessels must also obtain permission and the permitting system is also challenging. Most cruise companies operating in Russia prefer to get a Russian agent to deal with officials and the required paperwork for cruise because of the amount of time and the lack of clarity with respect to the Russian permitting process. For example, only the Russian prime minister signs permission applications for foreign cruise ships or any other vessels coming in Russian internal waters (Pashkevich et al., 2015).

Discussion and conclusion

Merchant networks and industries have developed in northern Scandinavia and Iceland for several centuries now; Svalbard was actively developed from the end of the 19th century while Denmark sought to develop Greenland since the 18th century. In the Soviet Union, central planning enabled the government to develop infrastructure in Siberia. These are key elements partly explaining the competitiveness of the Euro-Russian Arctic cruise tourism destinations. Partly, since it was pointed out Siberian ports did not transform into a large cruise market. Also influential are melting sea ice and the opening of the Arctic passages, infrastructure differences, and policy and regulatory mechanisms that are often designed to enhance protections but which have side effects of limiting development.

In Canada, there are current plans to develop small craft harbors, and a wharf is under construction in Iqaluit due for completion in 2020, but the equipment lags far behind port infrastructure that can be found in Greenland. Arctic communities that invested in port facilities have increased their attractiveness and competitiveness for cruise tourism.

Influenced by various forces of change, among them the effects of climate change and melting of summer sea ice in the Arctic, all these factors contributed to the emergence of a cruise tourism industry in the Arctic, expanding accessibility throughout the last 25 years but not without important contrasts. The risks associated with sea ice, ice ridges, multiyear ice accidents and spills, intense cold and damage to vessels are viewed as manageable risks by cruise operators offering voyages in Svalbard, but in the Canadian Arctic, sea ice remains an important physical hazard (Stewart et al., 2007; Pizzolato et al., 2014). Melting of sea ice in the Arctic at a faster speed than predicted in last decades then played an important role in the emergence of a cruise tourism industry. Sea ice is a major constraint for cruise tourism in the Arctic, and various policies of Arctic states as well as International Regulations such as the International Convention for the Safety of Life at Sea (SOLAS) of 1974 and the recently International Maritime Organization's Polar Code have specific provisions for vessels operating in polar waters that must respect hull standards, better known as polar-classification requirements. However, there are various level of sea-ice concentration in the Arctic and popular cruise destinations such as most destinations of Alaska, even in the north; in Iceland; and along the coast of Norway experience a high level of cruise activity due to low concentration of sea ice or absence of such a constraint. In Svalbard, Franz Josef Land, and in southern Greenland, sea-ice conditions allow bigger vessels to sail without or with weak polar hulls. In the Canadian Arctic Archipelago, sea-ice dynamics and highly variable trends are a concern for safety and security and a major physical barrier for most cruise operators to expand their business activities whether it is the cost of icebreakers or double strengthened hulls, insurances, etc. All these factors contribute to increasing the cost of doing business in the north.

While various Arctic states have their own regulations regarding shipping in their respective waters, the customs clearances and translation fees associated with the permitting process are also often underlined as time consuming. The scientific community has underscored how time consuming the permit process is in the Canadian Arctic and this itself is one of the major limiting factors for cruise tourism development in that region. This consuming permit process in the Canadian Arctic is also pointed out by several cruise operators operating in the Canadian Arctic, who have complained that the existing permit process failed to take into account the fact that itineraries are always changing due to weather and ice which make the Canadian Arctic very expensive for the consumer compared to other Arctic regions. The Canadian Coasting Trade Act of 1992 that prohibits foreign vessels, even if it is a Canadian company, from operating a voyage embarking in one Canadian Port and ending that same voyage in Canadian waters without paying significant duty taxes is also seen as an important barrier by several cruise operators. Admitting the presence of world-class ports and airports in the Canadian Arctic, the coasting trade act regulations would prevent them from fully benefiting from the economic benefits of the cruise industry. However, the granting for a rare occasion to the Canadian company One Ocean Expeditions a Coasting Trade License to operate a voyage starting and ending in Canadian ports in summer/fall of 2018 is promising.

Historical events can explain the development evolution and resultant competitiveness of cruise tourism destinations across the Arctic. The current trends in melting of sea ice in the Arctic is also another important factor driving the attractiveness of a destination and giving a good indication of what the intensity of the traffic would be. This is also true given the facts that a homogenous definition of a tourist among Arctic states is still lacking and different data collection timelines are collected. The presence of the AECO in the Euro-Russian Arctic is a good way to manage impacts of cruise tourism and its expansion to the Canadian Arctic and Greenland would be another way to enhance monitoring of cruise tourism in the Arctic. The specificities of the Canadian Arctic and Greenland at some extent, by the presence of Indigenous communities that historically live and travel in the area require broader consultations when establishing such guidelines. By aiming for a sustainable and respectful regional development of communities and societies, investments will be needed in transportation infrastructure; enhancing environmental, historical, and cultural education of visitors as well as locals can improve safety and security; and improvement of capacity building, reduction of time-consuming permit process, and improving reliable and extensive data collection will be the next challenges. Senior researchers (Johnston et al., 2017; Huijbens & Lamers, 2017) have also pointed out the urgent need to improve marine tourism data collection to bring the Canadian Arctic up to date with other Arctic tourism regions that already collect key tourism statistics to facilitate better decision-making and to support sustainable development in the region. The identification of these needs also underlines the need for more studies focusing on cruise tourism trends across the Arctic using comparable and reliable data. Currently, tourism statistics are collected using very different methods in each Arctic region and in a very ad hoc manner across Arctic Canada in particular.

Note

1 The DEW line (Distant Early Warning) is a series of radar sites built in the 1950s to detect potential incoming Soviet bombers or missiles.

References

AECO. (2019). *Association of Arctic expedition cruise operators*. Retrieved January 5, 2019, from www.aeco.no/

Arctic Council. (2019a). *Arctic monitoring and assessment program*. Retrieved January 5, 2019, from www.amap.no/

Arctic Council. (2019b). *Protection of the Arctic marine environment (PAME) – Arctic ship traffic data*. Retrieved January 5, 2019, from www.pame.is/index.php/projects/arctic-marine-shipping/astd

Bornhorst, T., Ritchie, J., & Sheehan, L. (2010). Determinants of tourism success for DMOs & destinations: An empirical examination of stakeholder's perspectives. *Tourism Management, 31*, 572–589.

Bystrowska, M., & Dawson, J. (2017). Making places: The role of Arctic cruise operators in 'creating' tourism destinations. *Polar Geography, 40*(3), 208–226.

CIN. (2018). *Cruise industry news annual report and industry growth forecast*. Retrieved January 10, 2019, from www.cruiseindustrynews.com/annual-cruise-industry-report.html

Coppes, M. (2017). No more crystal serenity in the Northwest Passage. *High North News*. Retrieved January 7, 2019, from www.highnorthnews.com/en/no-more-crystal-serenity-northwest-passage

Cruise Lines International Association (CLIA) (2018. *2018 cruise industry outlook*. Retrieved December 13, 2018, from https://cruising.org/docs/default-source/research/clia-2018-state-of-the-industry.pdf?sfvrsn=2

Dawson, J., Johnston, M. E., & Stewart, E. J. (2014). Governance of Arctic expedition cruise ships in a time of rapid environmental and economic change. *Ocean & Coastal Management, 89*, 88–99.

Dawson, J., Johnston, M. E., & Stewart, E. J. (2017). The unintended consequences of regulatory complexity: The case of cruise tourism in Arctic Canada. *Marine Policy, 76*, 71–78.

Dawson, J., Kaae, B., & Johnston, M. E. (2017). Tourism. In AMAP (2018). *Adaptation actions for a changing Arctic. Perspectives from the Baffin Bay/Davis Strait Region* (pp.223–242). Oslo: Arctic Monitoring and Assessment Programme (AMAP).

Dawson, J., Pizzolato, L., Howell, S. E. L., Copland, L., & M. Johnston (2018). Temporal and spatial patterns of ship traffic in the Canadian Arctic from 1990 to 2015. *Arctic, 71*(1), 15–26.

Dean, R., Lackenbauer, P. W., & A. Lajeunesse (2014). *Documents on Canadian Arctic sovereignty and security – Canadian Arctic defence policy – A synthesis of key documents, 1970–2013*. Retrieved January 12, 2019, from http://pubs.aina.ucalgary.ca/dcass/82112.pdf

Dupré, S. (2009). Les croisières touristiques dans l'Arctique canadien: Une réalité tangible à l'appropriation territoriale encore limitée. *Téoros – Revue de recherche en tourisme, 28*(1), 39–51.

Fay, A., & Karlsdottir, A. (2011). Social indicators for arctic tourism: Observing trends and assessing data. *Polar Geography, 34*(1–2), 63–86.

Government of Greenland. (2016). *Turismeudvikling i Grønland – Hvad skal der til? National Sektorplan for Turisme 2016–2020*. [Tourism Development in Greenland – What Happens? National Sectoral Plan for Tourism 2016–2020]. 76 p. Retrieved July 19, 2019, from https://naalakkersuisut.gl/~/media/Nanoq/Files/Hearings/2015/Turismestrategi/Documents/Turismestrategi%202016-2020%20FINAL%20DK.pdf

Government of Nunavut. (2013). *Tunngasaiji: A Tourism Strategy for Nunavummiut*. Retrieved January 22, 2019, from https://gov.nu.ca/sites/default/files/tourism-strategy-en-2-aug21-web.pdf

Graeger, N. (1996). Environmental Security? *Journal of Peace Research, 33*(1), 109–116.

Hagen, D., Vistad, O. I., Eide, N. E., Flyen, A. C., & Fangel, K. (2012). Managing visitor sites in Svalbard: From a precautionary approach towards knowledge-based management. *Polar Research, 31*(1), 1–18.

Huijbens, E., & Lamers, M. (2017). Sustainable tourism and natural resource conservation in the Polar Regions: An editorial. *Resources, 6*(45), 1–7.

Johnston, M., Dawson, J., De Souza, E., & Stewart, E. J. (2017). Management challenges for the fastest growing marine shipping sector in Arctic Canada: Pleasure crafts. *Polar Record, 53*(1), 67–78.

Kostin, K. B. (2018). Foresight of the global digital trends. *Strategic Management, 23*(1), 11–19.

Lamers, M., & B. Amelung (2010). Climate change and its implications for cruise tourism in the Polar Regions. In M. Luck, P. T. Maher, & E. J. Stewart (Eds.), *Cruise tourism* in *Polar Regions: Promoting environmental and social sustainability?* (pp.147–163). London: Earthscan.

Lasserre, F., & Têtu, P. L. (2015). The cruise tourism industry in the Canadian Arctic: Analysis of activities and perceptions of cruise ship operators. *Polar Record*, *51*(1), 24–38.

Lasserre, F., & Têtu, P. L. (2018). Extractive industry: The growth engine of Arctic shipping? In P. W. Lackenbauer, & H. Nicol (Eds.), *Whole of government through an Arctic lens* (pp.239–268) Antigonish, NS, Canada: St. Francis Xavier University & Mulroney Institute of Government. Retrieved July 15, 2019, from http://operationalhistories.ca/wp-content/uploads/2018/05/Whole-of-Government-throught-an-Arctic-Lens-eBook.pdf

Lenmelin, R. H., Johnston, M. E., Dawson, J., Stewart, E. J., & Mattina, C. (2012). From hunting and fishing to cultural tourism and ecotourism: examining the transitioning tourism industry in Nunavik. *The Polar Journal*, *2*(1), 39–60.

Marquez, J. R., & Eagles, P. F. J. (2007). Working towards policy creation for cruise ship tourism in parks and protected areas of Nunavut. *Tourism in Marine Environments*, *4*(2–3), 85–96.

Nunavut Tourism. (2011). *Nunavut Visitor Exit Survey 2011*. Nunavut Tourism and Government of Nunavut, Iqaluit.

Nymand, J., & Fondahl, G. (2014). *Arctic human development report: Regional processes and global linkages*. Report prepared for the Nordic Council of Ministers. Copenhaguen: Norden.

Pashkevich, A., Dawson, J. & Stewart, E. (2015). Governance of expedition cruise ship tourism in the Arctic: A comparison of the Canadian and Russian Arctic. *Tourism in Marine Environments*, *10*(3–4), 225–240.

Pashkevich, A., & Stjernström, O. (2014). Making Russian Arctic accessible for tourists: Analysis of the institutional barriers. *Polar Geography*, *37*(2), 137–156.

Pizzolato, L., Howell, S. E. L., Dawson, J., Laliberté, F., & Copland, L. (2016). The influence of declining sea ice on shipping activity in the Canadian Arctic. *Geophysical Research Letters*, *43*, 12146–12154.

Pizzolato, L., Howell, S. E. L., Derksen, C., Dawson, J., & Copland, L. (2014). Changing sea ice conditions and marine transportation activity in Canadian Arctic waters between 1990 and 2012, *Climate Change*, *123*, 161–173.

Shirokiy, S. (2015). *Problems and perspectives of tourism development in the high Arctic: Case of Franz Josef Land*. (Master Thesis in Tourist Studies). The Arctic University of Norway Retrieved from https://munin.uit.no/bitstream/handle/10037/10082/thesis.pdf?sequence=1

Stewart, E. J., & Dawson, J. (2011). A matter of good fortune? The grounding of the clipper adventurer in the NWP, Arctic Canada. *Arctic*, *64*(2), 263–267.

Stewart, E. J., Dawson, J., & Johnston, M. (2015). Risks and opportunities associated with change in the cruise tourism sector: Community perspectives from Arctic Canada. *The Polar Journal*, *5*(2), 403–427.

Stewart, E. J., Dawson, J., Howell, S. E. L., Johnston, M. E., Pearce, T., & Lemelin, H. (2013). Local-level responses to sea ice change and cruise tourism in Arctic Canada's Northwest Passage. *Polar Geography*, *36*(1–2), 142–162.

Stewart, E. J., & Draper, D. (2008). The sinking of the MS explorer: Implications for cruise tourism in Arctic Canada. *Arctic*, *61*(2), 224–231.

Stewart, E. J., Draper, D., & Dawson, J. (2010). Monitoring patterns of cruise tourism across Arctic Canada. In M. Lueck, P. T. Maher, & E. J. Stewart (Eds.), *Cruise tourism in Polar Regions: Promoting environmental and social sustainability?* (pp. 133–145). London: Earthscan.

Stewart, E. J., Howell, S. E. L., Draper, D., Yackel, J., & Tivy, A. (2007). Sea ice in Canada's Arctic: Implications for cruise tourism. *Arctic, 60*(4), 370–380.

Stewart, E. J., Liggett, D., & Dawson, J. (2017). The evolution of polar tourism scholarship: Research themes, networks and agendas. *Polar Geography, 40*(1), 59–84.

Têtu, P. L. (2019). The Northern marine transportation corridors in the Canadian Arctic: An initiative adapted to marine tourism? *The Canadian Geographer, 63*(2), 225–239.

Têtu, P. L., Pelletier, J. F., & Lasserre, F. (2015). The mining industry in Canada north of the 55th parallel: A maritime traffic generator? *Polar Geography, 38*(2), 107–122.

The Maritime Executive. (2018). *The rise and rise and rise of polar cruising.* Retrieved July 15, 2019, from www.maritime-executive.com/features/the-rise-and-rise-and-rise-of-polar-cruising

Tivy, A., Howell, S. E. L., Alt, B., McCourt, S., Chagnon, R., Crocker, G., Carrieres, T., & Yackel, J. J. (2011). Trends and variability in summer sea ice cover in the Canadian Arctic based on the Canadian Ice Service Digital Archive, 1960–2008 and 1968–2008. *Journal of Geophysical Research: Oceans, 116*(3), 1–25.

U.S. Coast Guard. (2017). *Major icebreakers of the world.* Retrieved from www.dco.uscg.mil or https://tinyurl.com/ycyz2ord

XST. (2019). *Xpert Solutions Technologies.* Retrieved from http://xst.ca/

Young, O. R. (2005). Governing the Arctic: From Cold War theater to Mosaic of cooperation. *Global Governance: A Review of Multilateralism and International Organizations, 11*(1), 9–15.

Part II

The impact of the advent of the Polar Code

7 Arctic shipping law: from atomised legislations to integrated regulatory framework

The Polar Code (r)evolution?

Laurent Fedi

Introduction

According to scientists, climate change is affecting the Arctic and Antarctic oceans both with a progressive decline of annual sea-ice coverage and thickness (IPPC, Polar Regions 2014). In the last decade, the Northern Sea Route (NSR) and the Northwest Passage (NWP) have easily been opened and 2018 will confirm the same pattern of low ice extent (NSIDC, 2018). Moreover, the Arctic Ocean should be ice free in summer within this century, allowing expanded human activities and shipping. Seaborne tourism, fishing and oil and gas exploration above all, should follow the same development trend (AMSA, 2009, 2013; Lasserre, 2009). Nonetheless, these new economic opportunities (Ørts, Grønsedt, Lindstrøm, & Hendriksenn, 2016) also involve numerous maritime risks, notably: shipwrecks, pollution, operational discharges or invasive species (Henriksen, 2014). Furthermore the specific features of operational conditions in the Arctic, extreme environment and remoteness in particular, increase the level of conventional shipping risks (Lasserre, Beveridge, Fournier, Têtu, & Huang, 2016; Haavik, 2017; Fedi et al., 2018a).

Accordingly, Arctic shipping raises the question of an appropriate legal framework in view of maritime transportation growth and related demand for high safety and environmental standards. This topical question is not new and several studies have explored in depth Arctic shipping law at the national (Becker, 2010; Rothwell, 2013) or international level (Stokke, 2007; Deggim, 2009) and its ways of reform (Chircop, 2013; Molenaar, 2014). Since 1 January 2017, the 'International Code for Ships Operating in Polar Waters' commonly named the 'Polar Code' (IMO, 2014) has entered into force and the Arctic navigation, managed until this date through national or regional provisions, came into a new age with a harmonised and mandatory regulatory instrument designed to frame a universal regime for polar waters (Fedi & Faury, 2016). Notwithstanding some weaknesses, the new code represents a strategic step toward safer maritime transportation and its implementation seems timely, taking into consideration the higher number of accidents that occurred recently in the Arctic (Allianz, 2017; 2018). The purpose of this chapter is twofold: firstly, it aims at analysing to which extent the adoption of the Polar Code shall positively influence the Arctic navigation and mitigate associated risks. Secondly, it identifies the remaining gaps and suggests recommendations for addressing such risks.

After this introduction providing some background information on the main context of the legal aspects of Arctic shipping, the chapter is structured as follows: the first section provides an overview of Arctic shipping law before the new IMO Polar Code. Adoption and implementation issues of the Polar Code are addressed in the second section. The third section contemplates the basic structure of Arctic shipping law and its interaction with the international legal framework in the aftermath of the code implementation. Finally, conclusions are provided in the final section.

The Arctic shipping law before the Polar Code

Before the adoption of the IMO Polar Code, hereinafter 'PC', Arctic shipping law could be qualified as disparate and atomised. 'Disparate' on the one hand insofar as several initiatives were launched by different regional or international United Nations (UN) bodies such as the Arctic Council and the IMO. 'Atomised' on the other hand since coastal Arctic states enacted unilateral legislations pursuant to the 1982 United Nations Convention of the Law of the Sea (UNCLOS, 1982).

The Arctic Council initiatives

Established by the 1996 Ottawa Declaration, the Arctic Council brings together the 'Arctic Eight' which are Canada, Denmark (for Greenland), Finland, Iceland, Norway, the Russian Federation, Sweden and the United States. Rather a political body than a regulatory one, the Arctic Council pursues complementary objectives and especially sustainable development and environmental protection in the Arctic. Pursuant to its broad mission, the Council has carried out various studies and launched key initiatives related to shipping. The Arctic Marine Shipping Assessment report (AMSA, 2009) was certainly the most significant pillar as regards marine shipping issues, setting out a number of recommendations for the development of safer Arctic shipping including the protection of interests of indigenous people and the preservation of the fragile marine environment. These recommendations turned into concrete actions notably through the Arctic SAR, the 2013 Agreement on Cooperation on Marine Oil Pollution Preparedness and Response in the Arctic (MOPPR), and the 2013 Arctic Ocean Review Final Report (AOR).

Entered into force 1 January 2013, the Agreement on Cooperation on Aeronautical and Marine Search and Rescue in the Arctic (Arctic SAR, 2011) is a binding agreement on maritime, aeronautical, offshore search and rescue covering more than 13 million square miles of the Arctic Ocean and aiming to coordinate assistance among all Arctic states in SAR operations. The Arctic SAR Agreement is the regional translation of IMO SAR and OPRC Conventions (Molenaar, 2014). Each state is in charge of a respective area for the central Arctic Ocean and has to maintain adequate and sufficient SAR capability. A second legally bind-ing agreement was adopted in 2013, the MOPPR, organising mutual assistance among Arctic states in response to oil pollution incidents that exceed the capac-ity of a single state to respond promptly and effectively on its own. Pursuant to the MOPPR, Arctic states must conduct monitoring activities to identify spills, to notify them to other states, to maintain spill response systems and to under-take training and joint exercises. Focused on oil pollution and not including other harmful substances, this new agreement takes advantage of specific guidelines, the 'Recommended Practices in Oil Pollution Prevention' (EPPR, 2013), dealing with operational and administrative aspects.

Moreover, the recent AOR is focused on Arctic marine operations and shipping in light of current achievements and future challenges to be addressed (AMSP, 2015). Even though the Arctic Council has obtained successful policy outcomes, *inter alia* the SAR and MOPPR agreements, certain questions on growing navi-gation should indeed be resolved in the medium run. The first one is the identi-fication and protection of ecologically important Arctic marine areas including 'Particularly Sensitive Sea Areas' (PSSAs) and other fragile ecological zones (IMO, 2002; 2005). The IMO PSSA status involves stricter controls on oil dis-charges, noxious liquid substances, sewage and garbage. Whereas the Antarctic Sea is already a special area under MARPOL Annex I, II, V (IMO, 1990; 1992), the Arctic Ocean is not and should benefit from the same protective regime. The Baltic Sea represents the unique Arctic zone recognised as PSSA out of 13 (IMO, 2004b). With Arctic sea ice melting, more areas are likely to be open to shipping and with greater environmental impacts. The recent report on the Identification of Arctic Marine Areas of Heightened Ecological and Cultural Significance (AMAP/CAFF/SDWG, 2013) identified 97 areas within the Arctic Large Marine Ecosys-tems (LMEs). Among the sets of criteria for identifying these sensitive and eco-logically important areas, the IMO PSSA criteria were used.

Law of the Sea and national regulatory regimes

General international law is applicable in the Arctic region (Rothwell, 2013) and the Law of the Sea in particular which is codified by the LOSC. Entered into force in 1994, this text constitutes the key legal foundation for the regulation of the Arctic Ocean. All Arctic coastal states are parties to the LOSC except the US even if they recognised the LOSC provisions as customary international law (Roach & Smith, 2012). The 2008 Ilulissat Declaration issued by Canada, Denmark (Green-land), Norway, the Russian Federation and the US illustrated their commitment to the LOSC regime as regards 'rights and obligations concerning the delineation of the outer limits of the continental shelf, the protection of the marine environment, including ice-covered areas, freedom of navigation, marine scientific research and other uses of the sea' (Ilulissat, 2008).

The provisions of relevance dealing with Arctic navigation are not numerous while very important. The LOSC sets out general rules applicable to all waters and contains some specific provisions for ice-covered areas. Firstly, concerning the general rules, states have different navigational rights which can be summarised as follows: the right of innocent passage in territorial seas (art. 24 LOSC), the right of transit passage in international straits (art. 38 LOSC), the right of archipelagic sea-lanes passage within routes normally used for international navigation (art. 53 LOSC) and finally the freedom of navigation within Exclusive Economic Zones (EEZs) (art. 58 LOSC). The legal issue lies in the scope of application and the substantive law of coastal states dealing with international shipping (Chircop, 2013). The transit passage through straits used for international navigation illustrates a relevant example especially in Russian and Canadian waters. Positioned in strategic sea routes, Canada and Russia consider waters enclosed by straight baselines as historic internal waters. Canada has declared that the Arctic Archipelago and the NWP were internal waters considering the latter not as a strait used for international navigation. The US and the European Union (Memorandum on Arctic Policy, 2009; European Parliament, 2010) have contested this position by arguing the regime of transit passage applied to passage through those straits (Roach & Smith, 1996; Molenaar, 2014).

Secondly, as regards 'ice-covered areas', pursuant to art. 234 LOSC, coastal states are entitled to adopt and enforce

> non-discriminatory laws and regulations for the prevention, reduction and control of marine pollution from vessels in ice-covered areas within the limits of the EEZ, where particularly severe climate conditions and the presence of ice covering such areas for most of the year create obstructions or exceptional hazards to navigation, and pollution of the marine environment could cause major harm to or irreversible disturbance of the ecological balance. Such laws and regulations shall have due regard to navigation and the protection and preservation of the marine environment based on the best available scientific evidence.

Intended for the primary purpose of vessel source pollution, this provision should not allow states to enact rules on maritime safety although some authors consider that art. 234 entitles a regulation pursuing a primary environmental protection objective and a secondary safety purpose (Molenaar, 2014). The boundary is not 'crystal clear' as illustrated by the 2010 Northern Canada Vessel Traffic Services Zone Regulation (NORDREG, 2010) imposing mandatory reporting for foreign ships equivalent to 300 GRT or more, towing or carrying dangerous or pollutant goods and entering or leaving Canadian waters. In addition, the coastal legal framework cannot be stricter than 'general admitted international rules and standards' (GAIRAS) and thereby in accordance (Molenaar, 2014). To summarise, whereas art. 234 confers unilateral rights to the coastal states, they are invited to cooperate through IMO to define rules for the protection of the environment and maritime safety (Henriksen, 2014).

One ultimately recalls that states exercise jurisdiction over their ports that are under their territorial sovereignty. The International Court of Justice stated this principle in the 1986 *Nicaragua* case: 'by virtue of its sovereignty, . . . the coastal state may regulate access to its ports', meaning that foreign ships have no general right of access to seaports (Lowe, 1977; Molenaar, 2014). Moreover, the LOSC defines the rights of protection of the coastal state in the territorial seas, whether the right to take the necessary steps to prevent any breach of the conditions to which admission of ships to internal waters or such a call is subject (art. 25(2)), and to prevent and monitor ships' pollution (art. 211(3)). Nevertheless, in case of a force majeure event, a state is not entitled to deny access of a foreign ship in distress to port pursuant to the IMO Resolution A.949(23) on places of refuge (IMO, 2003).

International maritime law and key instruments

Due to their global scope of application, the IMO instruments dealing with safety and environmental protection are mostly applicable in the Arctic. Since its creation in 1948, the IMO has indeed adopted numerous key mandatory codes and non-binding tools such as guidelines and recommendations. These texts govern topical issues especially maritime safety such as the International Convention on the Safety of Life at Sea (SOLAS) (IMO, 1974); or the International Convention on Standards of Training, Certification and Watchkeeping for Seafarers (STCW) (IMO, 1978a); pollution prevention with the 1973 International Convention for the Prevention of Pollution from Ships (MARPOL), as modified by the 1978 Protocol (IMO, 1978b); the International Convention on the Control of Harmful Antifouling Systems on Ships, (IMO, 2001); the International Convention for the Control and Management of Ships' Ballast Water and Sediments (IMO, 2004a); liability and compensation concerns such as the International Convention on Civil Liability for Oil Pollution Damage (1969). The international standards laid down in the above IMO instruments are applicable *mutatis mutandis* to Arctic navigation. Nevertheless, few IMO instruments set out specific provisions dealing with Arctic and polar waters as a whole and the *Exxon Valdez* oil sick in 1989 raised the necessity to adopt construction, design, equipment and manning (CDEM) standards for navigation in ice-covered areas (Jensen, 2008). In order to bridge this gap, the IMO has enacted special provisions during the last two decades while this trend started at the end of the 20th century.

The IMO's initiatives for an appropriate response to Arctic navigation

The IMO has enacted different resolutions aiming at providing an adapted and progressive response to Arctic shipping and, more generally, for vessels operating in remote areas. One often ignores that the IMO launched initiatives in the 1980s with the 'Guide for Cold Water Survival' revised twice in 1996 and 2006 (IMO, 2006). This Guide aimed to prevent and minimise hazards of cold exposure (air and water) and define survival techniques in cold waters. It was also the case of the voluntary 'Arctic Shipping Guidelines' in 2002 (IMO, 2002), which provided specific recommendations to SOLAS and MARPOL in terms of maritime safety and pollution prevention standards appropriate to the harsh Arctic climatic conditions (Jensen, 2008). Furthermore, these guidelines dealt with construction, equipment norms and operational procedures designed to ensure safety in case of normal and emergency situations (Henriksen, 2014). It was acknowledged that safe operation in such conditions required specific attention to human factors, especially training (Deggim, 2013). In addition, they recommended that only ships with a polar-class designation, based on the IACS 'Unified Requirements for Polar Class Ships' (IACS, 2011), or a comparable alternative standard of ice strengthening should operate in polar ice-covered waters. They were amended to include Antarctic waters and became the 'Polar Guidelines' in 2009 (IMO, 2009a). In the meantime, IMO enacted the 2008 'Guidelines on Voyage Planning for Passenger Ships in Remote Areas' just one week after the sinking of the passenger vessel *MS Explorer* in Antarctic waters (IMO, 2008). Beyond voyage planning, these recommendations underlined the key role of information concerning weather conditions, extent and type of ice and icebergs in the vicinity of the intended route. They pointed out the operational limitations of vessels confronted with ice-covered areas or icebergs, aggravating factors (darkness, swell, fog) and the measures to be taken before entering such waters (Deggim, 2009). Finally, in 2010, a modification of the STCW Convention on 'Guidance Regarding Training of Masters and Officers for Ships Operating in Polar Waters' was adopted. These Manilla Amendments set out, *inter alia*, requirements on ice characteristics and ice areas, ship performance in ice and low temperature, equipment limitations, voyage planning, safety and environmental requirements and emergency procedures (Chircop, 2013).

Notwithstanding their relevance, the main weakness of these instruments was for most of them their non-legally binding nature. Up against increased international shipping in polar waters, several states such as Norway, Denmark and the United States have taken the initiative to turn the 'Polar Guidelines' into a mandatory code and submitted their proposal to the IMO (IMO, 2009b).

The IMO Polar Code adoption and implementation

In November 2014, the MSC adopted the safety provisions of the *International Code for Ships Operating in Polar Waters* (Resolution MSC 385(94)) and in May 2015, the MEPC validated the environmental requirements (Resolution MEPC 264(68)). The PC is the first global mandatory framework applicable to Arctic and Antarctic waters. Its main requirements are related to safety, environmental protection and seafarer competence. The PC is not a standalone instrument and it is implemented through amendments to three key conventions: SOLAS, MARPOL and STCW respectively as illustrated in Figure 7.1. Divided into two main parts, Part I deals with maritime safety and Part II with pollution prevention, the PC combines mandatory and non-mandatory provisions. 'Part I-A on Safety Measures' (12 Chapters) and 'Part II-A on Pollution Prevention' (5 Chapters) represent the mandatory rules and the recommendations are stated in Part I-B and

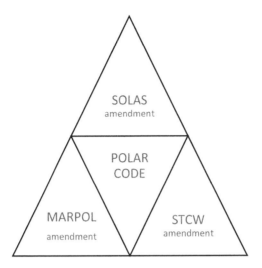

Figure 7.1 The three conventions featuring in the Polar Code

Source: Fedi, L., based on the IMO Polar Code (IMO, 2014)

Part II-B. The PC applies to ships differently, depending on their construction type and how they will be operated in Polar areas.

Scope of application of the Polar Code

Since 1 January 2017, the PC has entered into force for new vessels, built on or after this date, and after 1 January 2018 for existing vessels from the first intermediate or renewal survey. It applies to ships that intend to operate on domestic or international voyages in Polar Regions. These vessels have to be certified under both SOLAS 74 and MARPOL 73/78. State-owned vessels, smaller vessels, leisure and fishing boats are excluded from the first version of the PC. Nevertheless, fishing vessels must comply with the PC environmental protection provisions (DNV-GL, 2017).

Regarding its geographical application, IMO is applicable to the waters north of latitude 60°N for the Arctic and the waters south of latitude 60°S for the Antarctic. Some areas are excluded from its scope of application, notably Russia's Kola Peninsula, the White Sea, the Sea of Okhotsk and Alaska's Prince William Sound where the famous MS *Exxon Valdez* sank in 1989.

Risk proceduralisation and risk mitigation

Two main features characterise the new PC: it is risk and goal based (Henriksen, 2014; Fedi et al., 2018a). On the one hand, it emphasises the key hazards inherent to polar navigation affecting the probability of risk occurrence, more severe consequences or both (PC Introduction point 3). Whilst the list of hazard sources includes sea ice and topside icing, it is not limited to the sole ice concern. Low temperatures, extended periods of darkness or daylight, high latitude, 'vagaries' of weather conditions, remoteness, lack of data (charts), lack of crew experience, lack of SAR equipment, reduced availability of navigational aids and the sensitivity of the environment are the main identified hazards with specific risk exposure. This identification of hazards can be considered as risk mapping. Furthermore, in addressing risks in polar waters which were not 'adequately mitigated' by previous IMO provisions (Henriksen, 2014), the PC strives to implement risk mitigation and risk management. As a result, the PC follows a holistic approach that frames the global environment of ships in harsh conditions (Fedi & Faury, 2016).

As regards the PC's contributions to Arctic risk appraisal, some scholars demonstrated that the new IMO instrument shaped 'proceduralisation' of risk thanks to preventive safety measures and mandatory standards (Fedi et al., 2018a). As shown in Figure 7.2, this proceduralisation means the PC sets out procedures for better risk appraisal, risk control and risk mitigation in Arctic waters through ships' certification, polar water operational manual (PWOM), voyage planning and qualification and training of officers. This new framework contributes significantly to reinforce the vessel's suitability for Arctic navigation and strengthens its 'polarseaworthiness' (Cullen, 2015). According to Fedi, Faury and Gritensko,

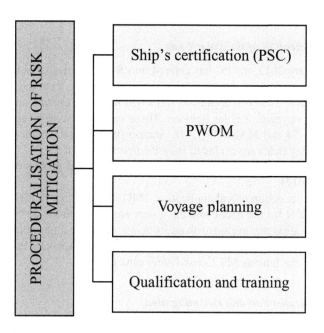

Figure 7.2 The Polar Code and proceduralisation of risk mitigation

Source: Fedi, L. based on Fedi, Faury and Gritsenko (2018a) and Polar Code (IMO, 2014)

the PC can be considered as a 'tool box' for underwriters and new Arctic entrants in particular insofar as it provides a set of operational risk management tools (2018).

The Polar Code safety measures

The safety provisions represent the first part of the PC and are primarily focused on key aspects of Polar navigation. The PC notably imposes structural requirements for ships operating in ice-covered areas, considering low temperatures and remoteness. Accordingly, the ship's navigational and communication equipment have to be designed with these polar constraints. The manning and training part sets out minimum obligations for crew officers (Chap. 12 PC).

To summarise, the PC sets out the concept of 'operational limitations' of a vessel operating in polar waters where sea ice and low temperature are hazardous (MARSH, 2014). The vessel's capabilities and operational limitations are certified by two fundamental new prerequisites. The first one is the Polar Ship Certificate (PSC) showing evidence that the ship has been satisfactorily surveyed (structure, equipment, fittings, radio station arrangements and materials) and has received her ice class (A, B, C) according to her ability to sail in ice-covered areas. *Category A* encompasses ships designed for operation in polar waters in at least medium first-year ice (ice thickness between 70 and 120 cm) corresponding to IACS polar ice classes PC1 to PC5. *Category B* designates ships designed for operation in polar waters in at least thin first-year ice (ice thickness between 30 and 50 cm) and corresponding to IACS classes PC6 and PC7. *Category C* covers vessels designed to operate in open waters or in ice conditions less severe than those included in the Categories A and B. Moreover the certification requires an assessment to establish procedures in accordance with operational limitations of the ship taking into account anticipated scenarios of operating, environmental conditions and hazards the ship may face. The methodologies used for evaluating operational capabilities and limitations in ice are based on the 'Polar Operational Limit Assessment Risk Indexing System' (POLARIS) developed by the International Association of Class Societies (IACS) and some Arctic nations such as Canada, Denmark, Finland, Russia and Sweden (IMO, 2016; Kujala et al., 2016; Fedi et al., 2018a; Fedi et al., 2018b). Other methodologies than POLARIS can be used as decision-making support systems such as the 'Arctic Ice Regime Shipping System' (AIRSS) defined by Canada or the 'Ice Passport' by Russia. The second requirement is the 'Polar Water Operational Manual' (PWOM) that sets out specific procedures for mitigating risks by ensuring that the vessel operates within or beyond formal limitations or capabilities (Chap. 2 PC). The Manual includes procedures for normal operations and in case of incidents.

The PWOM is completed by a 'Voyage planning' (Chap. 11 PC) requiring that the ship and the crew are provided with sufficient information to ensure safe operations both for the ship and persons on board and also environmental protection. For instance, when a route is chosen, a maximum amount of information on hazards, hydrography, navigation aids, extent and type of sea ice, vicinity of icebergs, areas with densities of marine mammals, places of refuge or remoteness from SAR capabilities is collected (Chap. 11 PC).

Regarding the other safety rules, their purpose also satisfies objectives of accident prevention. In essence, navigational equipment has to be adapted, the ship's structure has to maintain its integrity 'based on global and local response due to environmental loads and conditions' (Chap. 3 PC). Here the impact of low air temperature on crew and equipment performance, survival time and material properties is significant. Pursuant to the PC, a ship intended to operate in low air temperature will undertake voyages to areas where the lowest 'Mean Daily Low Temperature' (MDLT) is below $-10°$ C. A 'Polar Service Temperature' (PST) shall be defined and being at least $10°$ C colder than the lowest MDLT for the intended area. Then, ship's systems and equipment must be fully functional at the defined PST. In the same way survival equipment must be totally operational at the PST during the maximum expected time of rescue. To do so, the PC imposes the definition of the 'maximum expected time of rescue' which determines the nature and amount of survival devices the ship must carry on board. Moreover, additional communication and navigation equipment shall be installed in order to proceed safely to high latitudes (Chap. 10 PC).

Ultimately, the training obligations are stated at the end of the first Part of the PC. They are focused on deck officer (master, chief officer and officer in charge of navigational watch) and tankers and passenger ships are prioritised. Amending the STCW Convention, two levels of training have been implemented as of 1 July 2018. The 'Basic Training' concerns open waters with an ice concentration less than 1/10 and 'Advanced Training' is focused on other ice-covered waters with an ice concentration more than 1/10.

The Polar Code environmental protection and pollution prevention

Compared to the PC safety provisions, environmental requirements are fewer in number and show an actual lack of ambition (Fedi & Faury, 2016). Nevertheless, the safety provisions aim to reduce the likelihood of accidents having impacts on the fragile Arctic environment and its ecosystems. Stated in Part II of the PC, the environmental provisions are mainly based on the mandatory (I, II) and non-mandatory MARPOL (Annexes III, IV, V) with the aim of preventing impacts of harmful substances from shipping on the environment (IMO, 1978b). While fishing vessels are exempt from the PC safety and training requirements, they have to comply with environmental provisions stated in the PC Part II since they are MARPOL-certified ships.

As regards oil pollution (MARPOL Annex I) which is considered as one of the major threats to the Arctic Ocean, all discharge of oil is prohibited. Specific construction norms apply to new Category A and B ships that must have additional protection to fuel tanks, oil residue tanks and oily bilge water holding tanks. In the same way, pursuant to Annex II, any discharge into the Arctic waters of noxious liquid substances or mixtures containing such substances shall be prohibited. For the prevention of pollution by noxious liquid substances in packaged form (MARPOL Annex III), the PC is silent while it paradoxically mentions the related chapter (Fedi & Faury, 2016). Concerning sewage (MARPOL Annex IV), discharge is restricted near ice, that is to say more than three nautical miles are required for treated sewage and 12 for untreated sewage. New category A and B ships and passenger vessels are not allowed to discharge untreated sewage except if they have an approved sewage treatment plant. Surprisingly, garbage discharge is allowed subjected to 12 NM from land and when ice concentration is higher than 1/10. Moreover, food wastes shall not be discharged onto the ice and discharge of animal carcasses is also prohibited.

The Arctic shipping law in the aftermath of the Polar Code

As previously explained, the Arctic shipping law has been significantly affected by the adoption of the PC and as a result its future regime is henceforth strongly dependent on the PC evolutions. Due to the tacit acceptance procedure of SOLAS and MARPOL provisions, one can contemplate corrective measures of the current PC shortcomings. At the same time, even though the primary responsibility for enforcement of the PC lies with the IMO flag states, the different Memorandums of Understanding (MoU) in charge of Port State Controls (PSCs) must monitor the implementation of PC requirements. Other stakeholders shall complete this monitoring and be involved in the effectiveness of the new IMO instrument in order to guarantee the required 'polarseaworthiness'. Finally structuring onshore safety and pollution prevention still represent key stakes in the Arctic Ocean at the dawn of the 21st century.

The Polar Code's shortcomings and short-term corrective measures

Some scholars have underlined the PC shortcomings both on safety and environmental obligations (Chircop, Reggio, Snider, & Ray, 2014; Fedi & Faury, 2016). Regarding safety measures, notwithstanding an obvious focus of the PC, one regrets that training requirements are limited to deck officers. Other crew members should at least benefit from the basic training especially in light of different studies on Arctic accidents. At the end of the 20th century a study reported a 19 times higher incident rate in the Arctic compared to open waters (Loughnane, Judson, & Reid, 1995). In addition, the lack of crew experience was identified as primary source of the main root causes of accident (Tikka, Riska, & Liu, 2008). A detailed survey based on 19 years' analysis of Arctic marine accidents from 1993 to 2011 stressed the significance of crew training and competence requirements (Kum & Sahin, 2015). This study also pointed out the fishing vessels and the passenger ships that represented a significant part of the number of injuries and incidents. Consequently, how might one justify why existing fishing vessels operating in the Arctic must comply with Part II environmental requirements and they do not need to comply with Part I safety or training requirements (DNV-GL, 2017)? In addition, some authors have highlighted the neglected issue of voyages in light ice conditions for lower ice-class ships (Fedi et al., 2018a) or polar load lines whilst ice navigation potentially affects the freeboard of a vessel (Chircop et al., 2014). Therefore, others addressed the leeway of goal-based approach granted by some PC safety provisions that could provide the 'necessary flexibility' to ensure appropriate seaworthiness solutions (Henriksen, 2014) or could lead to different interpretations by national authorities (Jensen, 2016).

The low environmental requirements illustrate the 'lack of clear mandate' of the MEPC (Henriksen, 2014) and tough negotiations between active lobbying groups (Sakhuja, 2014). The first PC weakness lies in the absence of banning transport and use of heavy fuel oil (HFO) in the Arctic. Risk managers acknowledge that accidental oil pollution, even of low quantity, can greatly worsen due to the remoteness and the lack of SAR infrastructures (MARSH, 2014). Moreover, surprising as this may seem, the PC does not refer to the mandatory MARPOL Annex VI on air pollution prevention (Fedi & Faury, 2016). There is no doubt that this Annex applies to the Arctic. Nevertheless, while several Emission Control Areas (ECAs) are in effect all around the world such as the North Sea, the Baltic Sea and North America in particular with the use of low sulphur fuel at 0.5% (Fedi, 2013, 2017), the navigation standard in the Arctic remains the global cap at 3.5% of sulphur content till 1 January 2020 where the threshold will drastically reduce to 0.5%. The Arctic Ocean is not protected by the status of ECA that requires lower sulphur threshold (SOx) in marine fuel (Fedi & Cariou, 2015) and mitigates other greenhouse gases (GHG) such as nitrogen oxide (NOx) and particulate matter (PM). In addition, the PC does not address carbon dioxide (CO_2) and black carbon (BC) emissions. Commercial vessels are still burning a poor quality of fuel (Lack & Corbett, 2012; Bows-Larkin, 2015.). Shipping is deemed to contribute between 1–2% of the total BC (Lack et al., 2008) and shipping BC potentially represents up to 50% of BC in some Arctic regions (Dalsøren et al., 2012). The impacts of ships' emissions on Arctic warming are significant and consequently it requires a comprehensive response at the international level and especially from and by IMO (Litehauz, 2012).

Added to this, the PC does not regulate discharges of grey water and loss of containers with packaged dangerous goods. One also observes that the questions of ballast water management and antifouling are simply stated in the PC Additional Guidance Part II-B recommending the application of some guidelines laid down by the BWM and AFS Conventions. Taking into consideration the actual threat of alien aquatic species, it is very surprising that the PC simply invited concerned parties to apply the aforesaid instruments, notably the 'Guidelines for the Control and Management of Ships' Biofouling to Minimise the Transfer of Invasive Aquatic Species' (IMO, 2011 - Resolution MEPC.207(62)) and the 'Guidelines for Ballast Water Exchange in the Antarctic Treaty Area' (IMO, 2007 - Resolution MEPC.163(56)).

To conclude, all these uncovered concerns shall be addressed by future PC developments or thanks to the implementation of mandatory texts such as the BWM Convention that entered into force in September 2017 (Lloyd's

Register, 2017). While deeper environmental awareness is now obvious and urgent, the tacit SOLAS and MARPOL acceptance procedure should facilitate improvements in the medium run.

The Port State Control measures

PC effectiveness in the Arctic will depend on the enforcement of its current provisions (AMSA, 2017; Fedi et al., 2018a) and a strong support from the international community appears necessary, otherwise the PC risks to remain a soft-law instrument (Johannsdottir & Cook, 2014). If IMO parties retain the primary responsibility for harmonising their national legislations in accordance with the PC requirements, PSCs shall be determinant to monitor the actual enforcement through uniform guidelines (Fedi et al., 2018a). Eight regional PSCs are in force all around the word and provide a global coverage (Cariou & Wolff, 2015). The Paris MoU and the Tokyo MoU are particularly important insofar as vessels engaged in intra- or trans-Arctic shipping call at ports covered by these agreements (Molenaar, 2014). Although no specific Arctic PSC has been hitherto created, the fact that seven states out of eight Arctic Council members (Canada, Denmark, Finland, Iceland, Norway, the Russian Federation and Sweden) are parties to the Paris MoU, their respective administration should readily monitor the PC implementation. Through their observer status, the US Coast Guard cooperates with the Paris and Tokyo MoUs (Molenaar, 2014). However, standardised guidelines shall be enacted between the different MoUs in order to guarantee a harmonised enforcement. In 2017, 71 casualties occurred in the Arctic Circle compared to 55 incidents in 2016 (Allianz, 2017; 2018). In view of shipping growth in the years to come, the PC shall be of paramount importance in the region.

The stakeholders' actions through proactive policies: implementing an effective 'polarseaworthiness' and sharing best practices

Climate change is affecting shipping routes in the Arctic with a lengthening of free-ice periods (Stroeve, Markus, Boisvert, Miller, & Barrett, 2014). Nevertheless, ice and related risks shall always be present, especially in wintertime. The PC is a first positive response to an indubitable growing of maritime operations that need a binding framework but its adoption requires an effective implementation by flag states. Other public and private stakeholders have a key role to play in its enforcement. In 2017, the Arctic states launched the 'Arctic Shipping Best Practice Information Forum ('the Forum') aiming to raise awareness of PC provisions and to exchange best practices for Arctic marine operations (AMSA, 2017). Thanks to a public web portal hosted by the Arctic Council, the best available information can be collected on a cross-jurisdictional basis in different key topics, notably: hydrography, meteorology, ice data, crew training, SAR logistics, industry guidelines or operational understanding of ship equipment, systems and structure. This information is useful to assist shipowners to prepare PWOM in particular, to facilitate successful transits and more globally to faster disseminate best practices for PC compliance and 'polarseaworthiness'. Numerous diverse private institutions representing insurers, shipowners, oil companies and 'organizations dedicated to improving safe and environmentally sound marine operations in the Arctic' such as IMO, WMO, IACS, IAPH, IAIN, IMSO and ISU participate in the Forum.

Besides, the Forum initiative is strengthened by some complementary actions and policies. The Association of Arctic Expedition Cruise Operators (AECO) case remains particularly relevant. Since 2009 AECO has clustered the leading cruise companies operating in the Arctic in setting up an actual CSR policy. AECO aims to ensure environmentally friendly, responsible and safe cruise tourism (Falk, 2018). To this end, the Association has enacted several mandatory guidelines for their members who are obliged to comply with them. These guidelines cover topical marine and land issues as regards vulnerable wildlife, beaches clean-up, or biosecurity especially. This sustainable policy highlights that self-compliance to high standards and best practices is an appropriate way to complete the PC that is not deeply environmentally oriented.

Structuring onshore safety and pollution prevention

Structuring onshore safety and pollution prevention for Arctic waters requires greater developments. Two observations can be made on legal and operational grounds. From the legal side, the adoption of the PC affects both IMO flag states and primarily Arctic coastal states. As regards the overarching binding nature of the PC, IMO parties have to implement it. Furthermore, the PC affects the rights of Arctic states to regulate navigation within their zones of sovereignty (Henriksen, 2014). Obviously, they cannot maintain or enact national regulations contradicting the safety requirements of the PC. Besides, the PC environmental provisions raise the question of the consistency and the future of art. 234. As abovementioned, this article grants Arctic states to implement unilateral legislations aiming at protecting and monitoring the environment against ships' pollution sources. Two argumentations are possible as regards the legal consistency of art. 234 with international law. Firstly, Arctic members must enforce and respect the new PC. Consequently, they have to harmonise their legislation in accordance. Canada and Russia have already modified their national legal framework. For instance, Russia has required the polar ship certificate to obtain permits for NSR navigation as of March 2017. Secondly, if these states want to maintain specific environmental requirements not contained in the current PC, they will be entitled to do it as long as they will respect the restrictive criteria laid down in the LOSC and notably the presence of ice 'for most of the year'. Molenaar (2014) observed that due to melting ice, fewer states shall justify their unilateral framework pursuant to art. 234 in coming decades. Finally, the relevance of this specific LOSC provision for domestic polar shipping regulation should be legally constrained by the PC progressive environmental requirements and operationally weakened by climate change.

Regarding the operational side, Arctic states shall invest in SAR infrastructure, maritime disaster response capability and shall reinforce their collaboration. A melting Arctic could lead to an increase in drift of icebergs and affect trade routes. The adoption of the Bering Strait Vessel Traffic Separation Scheme (IMO, 2018) aiming to reduce the risk of marine casualties and increase the efficiency of vessel traffic in the famous international strait represents a paramount initiative between the US and Russia (Alaska State Legislature, 2012). Three precautionary areas and six two-way routes will be created insofar as more ships will use NSR across Siberia and around North America. These are the first ship routeing measures to be agreed at IMO for the Arctic region since the PC entered into force. Finally, these policy actions strengthen in terms of relevance the efficiency of the PC provisions.

Conclusion

This chapter was to assess the evolutions of the Arctic shipping legal framework in light of the existing legislations prior to the PC adoption and after its entry into force. The PC can be considered as the first international standardised and integrated instrument applicable to Polar waters harmonising the previous disparate unilateral legislations. Goal based rather than prescriptive, the PC provides adapted universal standards applicable to all merchant ships. Accordingly the PC represents a legal paradigm shift. Taking into consideration its recent implementation, a certain time will be necessary to accurately evaluate its impacts on maritime safety, environmental protection and indigenous people in the Arctic. What can be asserted is that the first PC version cannot be considered as a disruptive instrument. It remains an evolution of the current international legal framework rather than a 'revolution'. The PC is indeed far from being perfect, it is not an 'exhaustive instrument' (Fedi et al., 2018a) and its weaknesses should be corrected in the short run especially regarding environmental issues. Paradoxically, notwithstanding its situation of vulnerability, the Arctic Ocean still receives a low level of protection either under MARPOL or under specific regimes such as PSSA. The new PC provisions shall rapidly evolve towards stricter environmental standards, nonetheless considering the recent PC amendments, safety concerns still seem the first priority of IMO members.

Moreover the traffic along the Arctic coastal states tends to increase every year. According to the Russian Federal Agency for Maritime and River Transport, cargo volumes on the NSR increased by nearly 40% in 2017. Some Asian countries such as China, Japan and South Korea shall indubitably reinforce their presence in Arctic waters and provide support to their national shipowners. The China's ambitious Arctic Policy aiming to create an 'Arctic Silk Road' clearly illustrates the opportunities represented by the Arctic Ocean and new maritime routes (White Paper, 2018).

Ultimately, even if ice melts in the Arctic, the hazards weighing on ships are still present. It raises the question of potential greater marine claim incidence as illustrated by recent reports. Five hundred and seven shipping incidents including 16 total losses have occurred in just one decade (Allianz, 2018). A worst case-scenario similar to the *Titanic* catastrophe must not be excluded. The author assumes that the specific Arctic shipping law shall progress with the aim of meeting the key challenges at both safety and environmental levels. The fundamental navigational rights and freedoms to access Arctic routes shall be preserved at the same time. Challenges are numerous and the IMO shall be able to refine the PC more rapidly and to definitively implement a proactive policy. If one takes into consideration the lessons from the past, anticipation and prevention are better than cure.

References

Alaska State Legislature. (2012). *Findings and recommendations of the Alaska Northern Waters Task Force 15*. Retrieved July 15, 2019, from http://dot.alaska.gov/stwdmno/ports/assets/pdf/northern_waters_final.pdf

Allianz. (2017). *Safety and shipping review. An annual review of trends and developments in shipping losses and safety*. Retrieved May 3, 2018, from www.agcs.allianz.com/assets/PDFs/Reports/AGCS_Safety_Shipping_Review_2017.pdf

Allianz. (2018). *Safety and shipping review. An annual review of trends and developments in shipping losses and safety*. Retrieved September 12, 2018, from www.agcs.allianz.com/assets/PDFs/Reports/AGCS_Safety_Shipping_Review_2018.pdf

AMAP/CAFF/SDWG. (2013). *Identification of Arctic marine areas of heightened ecological and cultural significance: Arctic Marine Shipping Assessment (AMSA) IIc. Arctic Monitoring and Assessment Programme (AMAP)*, Oslo. 114 pp. ISBN-978-82-7971-081-3.

AMSA. (2009). *Arctic marine shipping assessment 2009 report: Arctic Council (PAME)*, April 2009, second printing. Retrieved May 5, 2018, from www.arctic-council.org/index.php/en/documentarchive/category/20-main-documents-from-nuuk

AMSA. (2013). *Status on Implementation of the 2009 AMSA Report Recommendations, May 2013*. Retrieved July 15, 2019, from https://oaarchive.arctic-council.org/bitstream/handle/11374/57/AMSA_Progress_Report_May_2013.pdf?sequence=1&isAllowed=y

AMSA. (2017). *Arctic Shipping Best Practice Information Forum (the FORUM). Terms of Reference*. (Revisions and final as per PAME II-2017). Retrieved September 1, 2018, from https://pame.is/index.php/fundur1/the-arctic-marine-shipping-best-practices-information-forum

AMSP. (2015). *Arctic Council Arctic marine strategic plan 2015–2025*. Retrieved August 20, 2018, from https://oaarchive.arctic-council.org/handle/11374/413

Arctic SAR (Search and Rescue Agreement) (2011). *Agreement on cooperation on aeronautical and maritime search and rescue in the Arctic, signed by the Arctic ministers on 12 May 2011 in Nuuk*. Greenland.

Becker, M. A. (2010). Russia and the Arctic: Opportunities for engagement within the existing legal framework. *American University International Law Review*, *25*(225), 225–247.

Bows-Larkin, A. (2015). All adrift: Aviation, shipping and climate policy change. *Climate Policy*, *15*(6), 681–702.

Cariou, P., & Wolff, F. C. (2015). Identifying substandard vessels through Port State Control inspections: A new methodology for concentrated inspection campaigns. *Marine Policy*, *60*, 27–39.

Chircop, A. (2013). Regulatory challenges for international Arctic navigation and shipping in an evolving governance environment. In *CMI Yearbook* (pp. 408–427). CMI Headquarters, Antwerp, Belgium.

Chircop, A., Reggio, N., Snider, D., & B. Ray (2014). Polar load lines for maritime safety: A Neglected issue in the international regulation of navigation and shipping in Arctic waters? In *CMI Yearbook*, (pp. 345–356). CMI Headquarters.

Cullen, P. J. (2015). Polarseaworthiness – a new standard of seaworthiness in the polar context? In *CMI Yearbook* (p. 413). CMI Headquarters, Antwerp, Belgium.

Dalsøren, S. B., Samset, B. H., Myhre, G., Corbett, J. J., Minjares, R., Lack, D., & Fuglestvedt, J. S. (2012). Environmental impacts of shipping in 2030 with a particular focus on the Arctic region. *Atmospheric Chemistry Physics Discuss, 12*(10), 26647–26684. doi:10.5194/acpd-12–26647–2012

Deggim, E. (2009). *International requirements for ship operating in polar waters: Meeting of experts on the management of ship-borne tourism in the Antarctic Treaty Area Wellington.* New Zealand, 9 to 11 December 2009.

Deggim, E. (2013). Ensuring safe, secure and reliable shipping in the Arctic Ocean. In P. A. Berkman & A. N. Vylegzhanin (Eds.), *Environmental security in the Arctic Ocean,* Springer: Dordrecht, 2013, 241–254.

DNV-GL. (2017). *Polar Code. Understand the code's requirements to take the right steps for smooth compliance.* Brochure DNV GL SE April 2017, Hamburg, Germany.

EPPR. (2013). *Recommended practices in oil pollution prevention.* Det norske Veritas (DnV), Narayana Press, Denmark. ISBN: 978-82-7971-078-3

European Parliament. (2010). *Opening of new Arctic shipping routes. Directorate general for external policies,* Policy Department.

Falk, E. (2018). *Chartering a sustainable path for a growing industry: Arctic shipping conference 2018* (pp. 17–20). April, Helsinki, Finland.

Fedi, L. (2013). *Air pollution from ships: Towards harmonization or atomization of rules? A plea in favour of a feasible and universal regime for shipping industry, IAME 2013 Conference,* Marseille, France. Retrieved from July 3–5, 2013.

Fedi, L. (2017). The Monitoring, Reporting and Verification (MRV) of ships' CO2 emissions: a European substantial policy measure towards accurate and transparent CO2 quantification. *Ocean Yearbook, 31,* 381–417.

Fedi, L., & Cariou, P. (2015). *Shipping sulphur reduction policy in Europe: An analysis of the 2015 implementation, IAME 2015 Conference,* Kuala Lumpur, Malaysia, August 23–26, 2015.

Fedi, L., Faury, O., & Gritensko, D. (2018a). The impact of the Polar Code on risk mitigation in Arctic waters: A 'toolbox' for underwriters? *Maritime Policy and Management, 45*(4), 478–494. doi:10.1080/03088839.2018.1443227

Fedi, L., Etienne, L., Faury, O., Rigot-Müller, P., Stephenson, S., & Cheaitou, A. (2018b). Arctic navigation; stakes, benefits, limits of the polaris system. *The Journal of Ocean Technology, 13*(4), 54–67.

Fedi, L., & Faury, O. (2016). Les Principaux Enjeux et Impacts du Code Polaire OMI. [The Main Stakes and Impacts of IMO Polar Code]. *Le Droit Maritime Français, 779,* 323–337.

Haavik, T. K. (2017). Remoteness and sensework in harsh environment. *Safety Science, 95,* 150–158. doi:10.1016/j.ssci.2016.03.020

Henriksen, T. (2014). The Polar Code: Ships in cold water – Arctic issues examined. In *CMI Yearbook,* published by CMI Headquarters, 332–344.

IACS (2011). International Association of Classification Societies, requirements concerning polar class, IACS Req. 2011, online: http://www.iacs.org.uk/publications/unified-requirements/ur-i/

Ilulissat Declaration. (2008, May 28). *48 I.L.M. 382*. Retrieved July 5, 2018, from www.oceanlaw.org/downloads/arctic/Illulissat_Declaration.pdf

IMO. (1974). International Convention for the Safety of Life at Sea (SOLAS), Article VIII (a), London 1 November 1974, in force 25 May 1980, UN *Treaty Series, 1184*, 278.

IMO. (1978a). International convention on standards of training, certification and watchkeeping for seafarers, London 7 July 1978, UN *Treaty Series, 1361*, I-23001. Its annex has been amended, Adoption of Amendments to the Annex to the International Convention on Standards of Training, Certification and Watchkeeping for Seafarers (STCW), 1978 STCW/CONF.2/DC/1, 24 June 2010.

IMO. (1978b). International Convention for the Prevention of Pollution from Ships, as modified by the Protocol of 1978 relating thereto (*MARPOL 73/78*), Article 16 (2), London 2 November 1973 and 17 February 1978, in force 2 October 1983, UN *Treaty Series, 1340*, 62.

IMO. (1990). Resolution MEPC.42(30) adopted on 16 November 1990 adoption of amendments to the annex of the protocol of 1978 relating to the international convention for the prevention of pollution from ships, *Designation of Antarctic area as a special area under Annexes I and V of MARPOL 73/78.*

IMO. (1992). Resolution MEPC.57(33) adopted on 30 October 1992 amendments to the Annex of the Protocol of 1978 relating to the international convention for the prevention of pollution from ships, 1973 *Designation of the Antarctic area as a special area and lists of liquid substances in Annex II.*

IMO. (2001). International Convention on the Control of Harmful Anti-fouling Systems on Ships, London 5 October 2001; Entry into force: 17 September 2008, AFS/CONF/26, 18 October 2001.

IMO. (2002). Guidelines for ships operating in Arctic ice-covered waters, *MEPC/Circ. 399* 23 December 2002.

IMO. (2003). Guidelines on places of refuge for ships in need of assistance, IMO Assembly Resolution A.949(23) of 5 December 2003.

IMO. (2004a). *International convention for the control and management of ships' ballast water and sediments*. Retrieved from 16 February, 2004, BWM/CONF/36

IMO. (2004b). Resolution MEPC.136(53) adopted on 22 July 2005 designation of the Baltic Sea area as a particularly sensitive sea area.

IMO. (2005). IMO Assembly Resolution A. 982(24) of 1 Dec 2005, 'Revised guidelines for the identification and designation of particularly sensitive sea areas' (IMO doc. A 24/Res.982), 6 February 2006.

IMO. (2006). Guide to cold water survival, IMO Doc. MSC.1/Circ.1185, 2006.

IMO. (2007). Guidelines for ballast water exchange in the Antarctic treaty area. *Resolution MEPC, 153*(56) adopted on 13 July 2007.

IMO. (2008). Guidelines on voyage planning for passenger ships operating in remote areas. IMO Doc. A 25/Res.999, 3 January 2008.

IMO. (2009a). Guidelines for ships operating in polar waters, Resolution A.1024(26) adopted on 2 December 2009, IMO Doc. A 26/Res.1024, 18 January 2010.

IMO. (2009b). Report of the Maritime Safety Committee on its eighty-sixth session, paragraph 23.32, MSC 86/26 12 June 2009. MEPC concurred with the proposal, Report of the Marine Environment Protection Committee on its fifty-ninth session, paragraph 20.9, MEPC 59/24.

IMO. (2011). Guidelines for the control and management of ships' biofouling to minimize the transfer of invasive aquatic species. Resolution MEPC.207(62) adopted on 15 July 2011.

IMO. (2014). Resolution MSC 385(94) of 21 November 2014 and Resolution MEPC 264(68) of 15 May 2015, International Code for Ships Operating in Polar Waters (Polar Code). Retrieved from https://edocs.imo.org/Final Documents/English/MEPC 68-21-ADD.1 (E).doc

IMO. (2016). *Guidance on methodologies for assessing operational capabilities and limitations in ice.* MSC. 1/Circ 1519, June 6.

IMO. (2018). *Maritime Safety Committee (MSC), Report of the maritime safety committee on its ninety-ninth session,* June 5, 2018.

IPPC. (2014). Climate Change 2014: Impacts, Adaptation and Vulnerability; Contribution of Working Group II to the Fifth Assessment Report of the Intergovernmental Panel on Climate Change, Chapter 28 Polar Regions, *46.* Retrieved May 15, 2018, from www.ipcc.ch/pdf/assessment-report/ar5/wg2/WGIIAR5-Chap28_FINAL.pdf

Jensen, Ø. (2008). Arctic shipping guidelines: Towards a legal regime for navigation safety and environmental protection? *Polar Record, 44*(2), 107–114.

Jensen, O. (2016). The international code for ships operating in polar waters: Finalization, adoption and Law of the Sea implications. *Arctic Review on Law and Politics, 7*(1), 60–82.

Johannsdottir, L., & Cook, D. (2014). *An insurance perspective on Arctic opportunities and risks, hydrocarbon exploration and shipping. Institute of international affairs,* Centre for Arctic Policy Studies.

Kujala, P., Kämäräinen, J., & Suominen, M. (2016). Challenges for application of risk based design approaches for Arctic and Antarctic operations. In *6th International Maritime Conference on Design for Safety,* Hamburg, Germany.

Kum, S., & Sahin, B. (2015). A root cause analysis for arctic marine accidents from 1993 to 2011. *Safety Science, 74,* 206–220.

Lack, D. A., & Corbett, J. J. (2012). Black carbon from ships: A review of the effects of ship speed, fuel quality and exhaust gas scrubbing, *Atmospheric Chemistry Physics, 12,* 3985–4000. doi:10.5194/acp-12-3985-2012

Lack, D. A., Lerner, B., Granier, C., Baynard, T., Lovejoy, E. R., Massoli, P., Ravishankara, A. R., & Williams, E. (2008). Light absorbing carbon emissions from commercial shipping. *Geophysical Research Letters, 35*(L13815).

Lasserre, F. (2009). High north shipping: Myths and realities. *NATO Defense College Forum Paper, 7,* 179–199.

Lasserre, F., Beveridge, L., Fournier, M., Têtu, P. L., & Huang, L. (2016). Polar seaways? maritime transport in the Arctic: An analysis of shipowners' intentions II. *Journal of Transport Geography, 57,* 105–114.

LITEHAUZ. (2012). Investigation of appropriate control measures (abatement technologies) to reduce black carbon emissions from international shipping. Denmark, 20 November, 118 pp., Retrieved July 15, 2019, from www.imo.org/en/OurWork/Environment/PollutionPrevention/AirPollution/Documents/Air%20pollution/Report%20IMO%20Black%20Carbon%20Final%20Report%2020%20November%202012.pdf.

Lloyd's Register. (2017*). Statutory alert: IMO Ballast Water Management (BWM) convention – new implementation dates agreed for installation of ballast water treatment systems.* Retrieved July 7 2017, from http://info.lr.org/l/12702/2017-07-07/45byzv

Loughnane, D., Judson, B., & Reid, J. (1995). Arctic tanker risk analysis project. *Maritime Policy & Management, 22*(1), 3–12.

Lowe, A. V. (1977). The right of entry into maritime ports in international law. *San Diego Law Review, 14*, 597–622.

MARSH. (2014). *Arctic shipping: Navigating the risks and opportunities*. Marsh Risk Management Research. Retrieved January 5, 2017, from www.marsh.com/uk/insights/research/arctic-shipping-navigating-the-risks-and-opportunities.pdf.

Memorandum on Arctic Region Policy. (2009). *45 Weekly Comp. Press. Doc, 47* (Jan.9). Retrieved November 5, 2018, from www.gpo.gov/fdsys/pkg/WCPD-2009-01-19-Pg47-2.pdf

Molenaar, E. J. (2014). Status and reform of international Arctic shipping law. In E. Tedsen et al. (Eds.), *Arctic Marine Governance* (pp.127–157). Berlin Heidelberg: Springer-Verlag.

NORDREG. (2010). *Northern Canada Vessel Traffic Services Zone Regulation, SOR/2010–127, Canada Shipping Act, 2001*. Retrieved July 15, 2019, from https://laws-lois.justice.gc.ca/PDF/SOR-2010-127.pdf

NSIDC. (2018). *National snow and ice data center, Arctic winter warms up to a low summer ice season*. Retrieved May 15, 2018, from http://nsidc.org/arcticseaicenews/

Ørts Hensen, C., Grønsedt, P., Lindstrøm, G. C., & Hendriksenn, C. (2016). *Arctic shipping, commercial opportunities and challenges*. CBS Maritime.

Roach, J. A., & Smith, R. W. (1996). United States responses to executive maritime claims (2nd ed.). The Hague: Martinus Nijhoff Publishers.

Roach, J. A., & Smith, R. W. (2012). *Excessive maritime claims 639* (3rd ed.). The Hague: Brill-Nijhoff Publishers.

Rothwell, D. R. (2013). International law and Arctic shipping. *Michigan State International Law Review, 22*(1), 67–97.

Sakhuja, V. (2014). The Polar Code and Arctic navigation. *Strategic Analysis, 38*(6), 803–811.

Stokke, O. S. (2007). A legal regime for the Arctic? Interplay with the Law of the Sea convention. *Marine Policy, 31*(4), 402–408.

Stroeve, J. C., Markus, T., Boisvert, L., Miller, J., & Barrett, A. (2014). Changes in Arctic melt season and implications for sea ice loss. *Geophysical Research Letters, 41*(4), 1216–1225.

Tikka, K., Riska, K., & Liu, S. (2008). Tanker design considerations for safety and environmental protection of Arctic waters: Learning from past experience. *WMU Journal of Maritime Affairs, 7*(1), 189–204. doi:10.1007/BF03195131.

UNCLOS. (1982). United Nations Convention on the Law of the Sea, Montego Bay, 10 December 1982, in force 16 November 1994, United Nations *Treaty Series, 1833*, 3.

White Paper. (2018). China Arctic Policy. The State Council Information Office of the People's Republic of China, 26 January 2018, First Edition. Retrieved September 1, 2018 from http://english.gov.cn/archive/white_paper/2018/01/26/content_281476026660336.htm

8 Shipping in the Canadian and Russian Arctic

Domestic legal responses to the Polar Code

Kristin Bartenstein and Suzanne Lalonde

Introduction

The entry into force on 1 January 2017 of the *International Code for Ships Operating in Polar Waters* (Polar Code)[1] is described by the International Maritime Organization as "a historic milestone" in its work to "protect ships and people aboard them, both seafarers and passengers, in the harsh environment of the waters surrounding the two poles".[2] The Polar Code is also an important development in support of the IMO's overall mandate to create a regulatory framework for the shipping industry that is fair and effective, universally adopted and universally implemented. While the goal of the Polar Code is to provide universal requirements for safe ship operations in polar waters, both Canada and Russia had already implemented robust regimes for shipping in their respective Arctic waters at the time of adoption of the Polar Code.[3] Its entry into force therefore raises the question of whether the new international and the pre-existing national regimes can be reconciled. It might also resurrect the debate over Canada and Russia's powers in their respective Arctic waters.

Canada and Russia's respective positions regarding the Northwest Passage (NWP)[4] and Northern Sea Route (NSR)[5] are well established. Successive Canadian governments have declared that all of the waters within Canada's Arctic Archipelago are Canadian historic internal waters over which Canada exercises full sovereignty.[6] This assertion of sovereignty necessarily includes the right to control access and govern navigation in the various routes that make up the NWP. For its part, the Soviet government claimed early in the 1960s that a number of the strategic straits that make up the NSR belonged historically to the Soviet Union, now the Russian Federation.[7] More recently, both the 2008 Russian Policy for the Arctic[8] and the 2013 Strategy for the Development of the Arctic[9] have emphasized Russia's sovereignty over the NSR and the need to protect the country's national interests.

Following the transit of the American icebreaker *Polar Sea* in 1985, Canada acted to consolidate its legal position by drawing lines around the outer perimeter of its Arctic Archipelago to "define the outer limit of Canada's *historic* internal waters".[10] Earlier that same year, by a Declaration of its Council of Ministers,[11] the Soviet Union drew straight baselines connecting its Arctic island groups of Novaya Zemlya, Severnaya Zemlya and the New Siberian Islands to the mainland.[12]

As Vincent explains, a coastal state's powers and prerogatives diminish as the distance from shore increases.[13] For this reason, a state exercises the greatest degree of control over its internal waters, defined in United Nations Convention on the Law of the Sea (LOSC) as "waters on the landward side of the baseline of the territorial sea".[14] While the LOSC does not provide a detailed set of international rules governing internal waters, state sovereignty is the key concept, as confirmed by article 2(1) of the Convention[15] and by the International Court of Justice's 1986 *Nicaragua* decision.[16]

Recognized as an integral part of a state's territory, international law thus provides that internal waters are subjected to the full force of the coastal state's legislative, administrative, judicial and executive powers. Foreign ships benefit from what has been termed a presumptive right of entry into the internal waters of a coastal state but as Gidel insists, "the presumption is in favour of a right of access to ports; but [it is a] presumption and not [an] obligation".[17]

Washington, for its part, has consistently maintained that the NWP and critical straits along the NSR are 'international straits'[18] through which the ships and aircraft of all nations enjoy a right of transit passage.[19] Other states have also in the past protested against Canadian and Russian Arctic governance measures[20] and more recently, Germany and China's Arctic policies have promoted freedom of navigation in the Arctic Ocean and 'Arctic shipping routes' with both expressions deemed to include the NWP and NSR.[21]

Under Canada's *Oceans Act*, the Canadian territorial sea,[22] contiguous zone[23] and Exclusive Economic Zone (EEZ)[24] in the Arctic are defined using the baselines established in 1985, which define "the outer limits of any area . . . over which Canada has a *historic* or other *title* of sovereignty".[25] Russia's 1998 *Federal Act on the Internal Maritime Waters, Territorial Sea and Contiguous Zone of the Russian Federation* (*Federal Act on Coastal Waters*) also specifically refers to "[a] system of straight baselines . . . joining . . . a strait . . . between an island and the mainland which have *historically belonged* to the Russian Federation"[26] as one of the starting points from which the breadth of Russia's territorial sea and contiguous zone are measured.[27] Relying on the same system, the 1998 *Federal Act on the EEZ of the Russian Federation* situates the outer limit of Russia's EEZ at 200 nautical miles from this baseline.[28]

The objective of this chapter is first to provide a brief overview of the Canadian and Russian domestic regimes existing at the time of the entry into force of the Polar Code and then to shed some light on any subsequent amendments. In the second part, some legal challenges confronting the Canadian and Russian measures will be identified and possible justifications will be discussed.

Canadian and Russian domestic regimes governing Arctic navigation 'pre Polar Code'

Canada was an active participant in the Polar Code negotiations held under the auspices of the IMO and for good reason: it already had an established domestic regime governing Arctic shipping. Canada had therefore a vested interest in ensuring that any new international rules and standards offered at least the same level of protection or that the Canadian domestic regime could be maintained or, ideally, that both outcomes could be reconciled.[29]

Since the 1970s, Canada has built a regime meant to ensure that Arctic navigation is as safe as possible, for the environment and the communities in the Arctic, but also the vessels, their crews and cargo. The first building block was the 1970 *Arctic Waters Pollution Prevention Act* (AWPPA), adopted in the aftermath of the *SS Manhattan*'s transit of the NWP and which established a zero-discharge rule for Canadian "Arctic waters".[30] These were initially defined as a zone of 100 nautical miles (nm) north of 60 degrees north, off the Canadian mainland and Arctic Archipelago.[31] Today, Canada's "Arctic waters" extend up to 200 nm north of 60 degrees north.[32]

Adopted to operationalize the AWPPA, the *Arctic Shipping Pollution Prevention Regulations* (ASPPR)[33] provided a set of detailed rules on a range of issues including ship construction, the use of ice navigators and limited exceptions for sewage and oil deposits. In addition to these measures geared towards pollution prevention, concerns related to the safety of the vessels travelling in its Arctic waters led Canada to institute a ship reporting system and vessel traffic services called NORDREG, on a voluntary basis beginning in 1977[34] and as a mandatory regulation as of 2010.[35]

In July 1991, the NSR was declared open for transits by foreign vessels. This announcement coincided with the enactment of the *Regulations for Navigation on the Seaways of the NSR*.[36] This detailed regime, intended to ensure the safety of navigation and the protection of the Arctic marine environment, was only the first in a series of regulatory instruments. In 1996, three separate measures governing navigation by foreign vessels through the NSR were adopted: *Guide to Navigating through the NSR*, *Regulations for Icebreaker and Pilot Guiding of Vessels through the NSR* and *Requirements of the Design, Equipment, and Supplies of Vessels Navigating the NSR*.[37]

The 2012 *Federal Law of Shipping on the Water Area of the NSR* (*Federal Shipping Law*)[38] amended in certain important respects the 1998 *Federal Act on Coastal Waters*[39] as well as the 1999 *Merchant Shipping Code of the Russian Federation* (*Shipping Code*).[40] The *Shipping Code* describes the NSR as "a historically developed national transportation communication of the Russian Federation" and adopts a very wide definition of the NSR, from Novaya Zemlya in the west to the Bering Strait in the east, encompassing the internal and territorial waters, the contiguous zone and the Exclusive Economic Zone of the Russian Arctic.[41] Navigation by vessels in the NSR is to be organized on an approval and remuneration basis,[42] subject to compliance with specific rules for such navigation.[43] Administrative responsibilities are in flux as ROSATOM, a government-owned corporation, is taking over from the Northern Sea Route Administration.[44]

Building on these and other instruments,[45] the *Rules of Navigation in the Water Area of the NSR* (*Rules of Navigation*) were promulgated on 17 January 2013.[46] After an introductory "General" section, the Rules are divided into nine parts, including Part II "Procedure of the navigation of ships in the water area of the

NSR" (procedure for obtaining permission to navigate) and Part VIII "Requirements to ships pertaining to the safety of navigation and protection of the marine
environment from the pollution from ships". Part VIII defines specific requirements in relation to, for instance, emergency equipment, storage tanks for the
collection of waste, minimum levels of fuel, fresh water and provisions. Most
importantly, the "[d]ischarge of oil residues into the water area of the NRS is
prohibited".[47] Given this long-established and detailed domestic regime, it is no
surprise that Russia was also deeply involved in the IMO process that led to the
adoption of the Polar Code.[48]

Integration of the Polar Code into the Canadian domestic regime

The entry into force of the Polar Code led to a significant reform of Canada's
regulatory regime on Arctic shipping with the replacement as of January 2018 of
the ASPPR by the *Arctic Shipping Safety and Pollution Prevention Regulations*
(ASSPPR).[49] These new regulations seek to achieve three distinct objectives, the
first of which is to incorporate the Polar Code requirements into Canadian law so
as to make them mandatory for Canadian-flagged vessels. However, in several
significant respects, the ASSPPR provisions go beyond mere incorporation. Some
of the new provisions are specifically designed to make Polar Code requirements
mandatory for foreign-flagged vessels as well, while others impose unilaterally
defined requirements on both Canadian and foreign-flagged vessels.

ASSPPR requirements incorporating the Polar Code

The Canadian approach to the domestic reception of treaty norms such as the
Polar Code is essentially dualist: no treaty is self-executing and "all require legislative implementation if they are to enjoy direct legal effect in Canadian law".[50]
The Polar Code is based on the flag-state principle, which means that Canada
bears the responsibility of ensuring that vessels registered in Canada comply with
the Polar Code's provisions whenever they navigate in "polar waters" as defined
in the Polar Code (see Figures 8.1 and 8.2).[51]

The incorporation of the mandatory provisions of Polar Code into Canadian
law (Part I-A on safety measures and Part II-A on pollution prevention measures)
follows the same two-pronged approach with part 1 of the ASSPPR devoted to
safety requirements and part 2 to pollution prevention requirements.

The safety-related measures of the Polar Code became internationally mandatory as a new additional chapter to the SOLAS Convention,[52] Chapter XIV. This
new chapter is incorporated into Canadian law by reference, according to section 6(1) of the ASSPPR.[53] Thus, the safety requirements of Chapter XIV are now
applicable to all Canadian vessels that fall within the scope of application of the
ASSPPR, which mirrors the definition in the SOLAS Convention.

By contrast, the pollution prevention provisions of the Polar Code, included
in the MARPOL Convention,[54] were selectively incorporated into the ASSPPR.

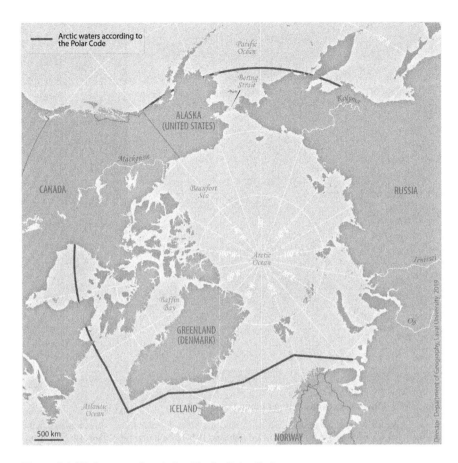

Figure 8.1 "Polar waters" as defined in the Polar Code

Since the Canadian regime already included requirements related to the four pollutants regulated by the Polar Code (waste,[55] oil,[56] sewage[57] and garbage[58]), only those Polar Code requirements that increased the Canadian level of protection were incorporated. Critically, any Polar Code provisions that would have weakened Canada's zero-discharge principle and its restricted exceptions were omitted.

ASSPPR requirements for foreign-flagged vessels

The ASSPPR make a significant number of the Polar Code provisions applicable to foreign-flagged vessels as well, provided they navigate in waters under Canadian jurisdiction. Indeed, a foreign vessel, unless it is a state vessel,[59] is required to comply with roughly the same obligations as a Canadian vessel[60] whenever it is navigating in one of the 16 "shipping safety control zones" (SSCZ) that cover the entire Canadian "Arctic waters" (see Figure 8.3).[61]

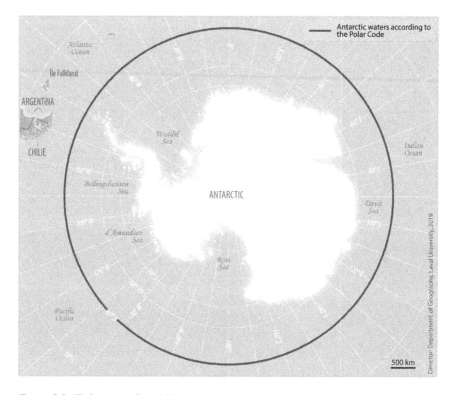

Figure 8.2 "Polar waters" as defined in the Polar Code

Source: Adapted from *International Code for Ships Operating in Polar Waters*, Amendments to the International Convention for the Safety of Life at Sea, 1974, Resolution MSC.386(94), 21 November 2014, in *Report of the Maritime Safety Committee on Its Ninety-Fourth Session*, Annex 6, IMO Doc MSC 94/21/Add.1, Introduction, article 5, p. 32–33

More specifically, the ASSPPR refer to "Canadian vessels [navigating] in polar waters" and "foreign vessels [navigating] in a shipping safety control zone".[62] In the first case, Canada acts as a flag state and its requirements follow Canadian vessels whenever they are in the Polar Code area,[63] i.e. in Canadian Arctic waters, in Arctic waters outside Canada's jurisdiction or in Antarctic waters. In the second case, Canada acts as a coastal state and its requirements apply to foreign vessels only insofar as these vessels are under Canada's jurisdiction, i.e. in its "Arctic waters". As the Polar Code creates obligations for flag states only, the jurisdictional basis for these coastal state requirements cannot be the Polar Code, at least not directly.

As explained above, a coastal state has complete sovereignty in its internal waters.[64] By contrast, the right of innocent passage in territorial waters,[65] the right of transit passage in international straits[66] and a slightly modulated freedom of

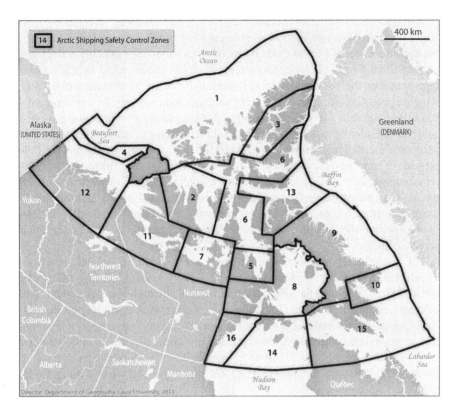

Figure 8.3 "Arctic Waters" with the "shipping safety control zones"

Source: *Shipping Safety Control Zones Order*, C.R.C., c. 356, SOR/2010–131, s. 8 (schedule 2)

navigation in the EEZ[67] place considerable limitations on its ability to determine the conditions under which navigation can take place. Overlaying these general regimes is the specific jurisdiction conferred upon coastal states bordering "ice-covered waters".[68] This so-called 'Arctic exception' provides the coastal state with exceptional prescriptive and executive powers yet their scope of application remains uncertain.[69] This legal complexity is further compounded by challenges to Canada's claim that the waters of the Arctic Archipelago are Canadian historic internal waters.[70]

As Canada considers that it enjoys full sovereignty over the waters of the archi-pelago, nothing in its view impedes its legal ability to determine the conditions under which navigation, including by foreign-flagged vessels, can take place within it. Outside the archipelago, Canadian "Arctic waters" encompass the terri-torial sea and the EEZ and as such, Canada's regulations need to take into account the right of innocent passage and freedom of navigation. While the coastal state has some jurisdiction in its territorial sea to adopt laws and regulations for the protection of the marine environment against threats posed by navigation,[71] it is unclear whether this jurisdiction also includes safety-related measures. However, the fact that under the Polar Code the safety provisions are explicitly recognized as contributing to environmental protection[72] lends considerable strength to the argument that the coastal state's jurisdiction should be interpreted extensively. Another potential hiccup is the fact that although requirements for environmental protection can relate to the construction, design, manning or equipment of vessels (CDME measures), they are only permitted if they give effect to "generally accepted international rules or standards" (GAIRS).[73] The Canadian ASSPPR provisions may however qualify as GAIRS insofar as they mirror Polar Code requirements. In the EEZ, according to the modulated regime of freedom of navigation, the coastal state may take measures, but only if they are "conforming to and giving effect to generally accepted international rules and standards".[74] Again, as the relevant ASSPPR provisions mirror Polar Code requirements, the condition seems to be met.

The ASSPPR requirements might be more difficult to defend, however, should the competing view prevail that the NWP (located within the Arctic Archipelago) is an international straight through which all ships enjoy the right of transit passage. The only GAIRS measures that a state bordering an international strait may impose relate to substance discharge,[75] seemingly excluding any safety-related and CDME measures. This raises the question of whether such measures might be justified under Article 234. This question is also raised by the ASSPPR requirements that are not directly based on the Polar Code, discussed below.[76]

ASSPPR provisions imposing additional requirements

Additional Canadian safety-related provisions apply to vessels navigating in a SSCZ.[77] Their scope of application, extending even to non-SOLAS vessels, is broader than the Polar Code-based regulations and in keeping with other components of Canada's Arctic shipping regime, including NORDREG.[78] The substantive requirements, for their part, build on Canada's pre-existing zone/date system (ZDS), which, for each SSCZ, limits vessel operations to a certain navigational period, according to the vessels' capabilities and limitations in ice.[79] Operation outside the ZDS is possible if deemed safe according to a mandatory risk assessment.[80] In this case, vessels need to report to Canadian authorities before entering the SSCZ.[81] Medium-sized non-SOLAS vessels of at least 300 but less than 500 gross tonnage navigating in a SSCZ outside the ZDS under the AIRSS are required to have an ice navigator on board.[82]

Several of the ASSPPR pollution prevention requirements also go beyond the Polar Code, mainly by maintaining, through the non-incorporation of Polar Code allowances, the level of protection established by the "zero-discharge" regime of the AWPPA. This is the case for waste[83] as well as oil and oily mixtures from machinery spaces for certain types of ships,[84] to which the AWPPA discharge prohibition remains applicable.[85] Carriage of several noxious liquid substances by certain categories of vessels is prohibited,[86] unless the tanks conform to detailed technical specifications.[87] Furthermore, a discharge restriction for sewage is imposed upon vessels of more than 15 but less than 400 gross tonnage and not certified to carry more than 15 persons.[88] While cargo residue may be discharged under certain conditions[89] by Canadian vessels operating in polar waters outside Canada's Arctic waters, all vessels navigating within Canadian Arctic waters are strictly prohibited from doing so.[90]

The application of these unilaterally defined safety and pollution prevention requirements to Canadian vessels is incontrovertibly justified under Canada's flag-state jurisdiction.[91] Questions arise, however, when it comes to foreign vessels. As the requirements are not directly based on the Polar Code, and although they align the Canadian regime with the Polar Code's spirit, they might not qualify as GAIRS. Within its internal waters in its Arctic Archipelago, Canada considers it has the jurisdiction to impose whatever type of measure it considers necessary. Outside the archipelago, in the territorial sea and the ZEE, restrictions under the default regimes of innocent passage and freedom of navigation bear on Canada's ability to determine the level of protection and the type of measures required. The Canadian pollution prevention requirements are mostly discharge prohibitions or restrictions. The safety provisions, for their part, are operational measures. Under the innocent passage regime, CDME requirements that are not GAIRS cannot be applied to foreign vessels.[92] The same is true under the freedom of navigation regime, for *any* requirement that is not a GAIRS.[93] Thus the question of whether Article 234 of the LOSC can justify these non-GAIRS requirements is of critical importance:

> Coastal States have the right to adopt and enforce non-discriminatory laws and regulations for the prevention, reduction and control of marine pollution from vessels in ice-covered areas within the limits of the exclusive economic zone, where particularly severe climatic conditions and the presence of ice covering such areas for most of the year create obstructions or exceptional hazards to navigation, and pollution of the marine environment could cause major harm to or irreversible disturbance of the ecological balance. Such laws and regulations shall have due regard to navigation and the protection and preservation of the marine environment based on the best available scientific evidence.

The ambiguous wording casts doubt on whether the provision applies to the territorial sea. Should it be considered not to, the coastal state would paradoxically have broader competencies in its EEZ under Article 234 than in its territorial sea.[94] A more rational interpretation – favoured by Canada[95] – views Article 234 as extending to the territorial sea.[96] A related question is whether it also extends to international straits – and the NWP, if it is so categorized – superseding the generally prevailing transit passage regime. American and Canadian scholars are divided on this issue, a consequence of the inability to resolve the politically sensitive question of the status of the NWP at the time Article 234 was negotiated.[97] It should however be noted, as McRae emphasizes, that article 234 is not included in the sections of part XII of the Convention that are subject to the international straits regime.[98]

The "prevention, reduction and control of marine pollution from vessels" referred to in Article 234 clearly justifies discharge prohibitions. However, given the focus on "pollution" and the obligation of the coastal state to pay "due regard to navigation", it is uncertain whether environment-related safety measures as well as operational and CDME measures would also be covered. Vehement denunciation of Canada's unilateral decision to make NORDREG mandatory in 2010 as *ultra vires* of article 234 attests to this uncertainty.[99] Arguments in favour of a broad interpretation of Article 234 include promoting consistency across regimes, as the link between safety measures and environmental protection exists in other international instruments,[100] and furthering the primary objective of the provision, the protection of the particularly sensitive Arctic environment from the hazards of navigation.[101] A broad interpretation would also be in keeping with the fact that Article 234 was negotiated specifically with the aim of providing a jurisdictional basis for Canada's AWPPA, which included CDME standards along with discharge restrictions.[102] Canada may thus argue with some confidence that it has the necessary jurisdiction to impose unilateral requirements on foreign vessels.

Integration of the Polar Code into the Russian domestic regime

The Russian response to the entry into force of the Polar Code has thus far been more modest than the Canadian one, perhaps a reflection of Russia's differing approach to the integration of international law. Yet Russian domestic measures governing Arctic shipping raise similar questions to those confronting the Canadian regime.

Russian constitutional law

Referring to the broad definition of the NSR adopted in 2012,[103] Gavrilov declares that although "Russia has not explicitly extended its full sovereignty to the entire area of the NSR, it has de facto placed the navigation of foreign vessels therein under its absolute control",[104] irrespective of whether it occurs in internal waters, the territorial sea or the EEZ. This broad assertion of authority prompts the expert to query whether Russian actions are consistent with "norms of international law" and "treaties to which Russia is a party, all of which are to prevail over Russian national laws".

Russia's 1993 Constitution[105] marked the culmination of an important development in Russian constitutional and political practice aimed at giving a more prominent place to international legal standards.[106] The relationship between international law and the Russian legal system is redefined at article 15(4):

> The generally recognized principles and norms of international law and the international treaties of the Russian Federation shall constitute part of its legal system. If an international treaty of the Russian Federation establishes other rules than those stipulated by the law, the rules of the international treaty shall apply.

This fundamental shift is apparent in the Russian laws and regulations successively promulgated to govern navigation in the NSR. Article 14 in the 1998 *Federal Act on Coastal Waters* provided that "[n]avigation . . . shall be carried out in accordance with this Federal Act, other federal laws and the international treaties to which the Russian Federation is a party". The 2012 *Federal Shipping Law*,[107] however, reverses the hierarchy in the applicable norms: "Navigation in . . . the Northern Sea Route . . . is carried out according to generally recognized principles and norms of international law, international treaties of the Russian Federation, the present Federal Law, other federal laws".

Thus, the general regimes of the LOSC governing the territorial sea, contiguous zone and EEZ and the IMO-negotiated Polar Code all have direct legal effect in Russia and constitute "part of its legal system".[108] Furthermore, in case of incompatibility between the Polar Code requirements and the Russian *Rules of Navigation*, Russia's Constitution seems to prioritize the international rules.

Legislative developments since the entry into force of the Polar Code

At time of writing, only two Russian legislative initiatives could be discovered in response to the entry into force of the Polar Code. The most relevant is a very short list of amendments to the 2013 *Rules of Navigation*.[109] The first amendment replaces the words "category of ice strengthening" with "ice class", an expression used throughout the Polar Code. The third amendment adds a new subparagraph 7 to paragraph 4 and the requirement that a "Polar Ship Certificate, as provided for by the International Code for Ships Operating in Polar Waters" be attached to any application for permission to navigate in the water area of the NSR.

This modest regulatory activity is perhaps due to Russia's monist approach to international law: as the Polar Code requirements already form part of the rules governing navigation in the NSR, no further legislative modifications were deemed necessary. Certainly such an interpretation would help reconcile the fairly limited safety requirements under Part VIII of the Russian *Rules of Navigation* (as amended) with the much more detailed and comprehensive requirements and guidance provided in the IMO's Polar Code.[110]

However, like Canada's ASSPPR, the Russian domestic regime imposes requirements that go beyond those adopted in the Polar Code. There is, for instance, no equivalent in the Polar Code to the "Rules of the icebreaker assistance of ships" set out in Part III of the Russian *Rules of Navigation* or the "Rules of the pilot ice assistance of ships" detailed in Part IV. Thus the same fundamental legal questions are at play in the Russian situation: what legal basis authorizes Russia to impose domestic requirements mirroring those of the Polar Code upon foreign vessels navigating in its different maritime zones? Even more critically, how can Russia justify imposing nationally defined, unilateral requirements upon foreign ships transiting through Russian Arctic waters?

As discussed above in regard to Canada's new ASSPPR, and insofar as the Russian requirements mirror those imposed by the Polar Code, Russia as a coastal state can also rely on established prescriptive and executive powers. In its internal waters, Russia has full and exclusive sovereign authority to govern navigation, including by foreign-flagged vessels. In its territorial sea, notwithstanding the right of innocent passage, it can adopt measures aimed at "preserving the environment" and "preventing, reducing and controlling pollution".[111] Like Canada, Russia will undoubtedly be a strong proponent of the interpretation according to which safety requirements must be regarded as necessary for the effective protection of the marine environment.[112] As for the rule according to which CDME measures may only be imposed on foreign vessels if they are GAIRS,[113] to the extent that Russia's requirements reflect the internationally negotiated Polar Code standards, it will not be a bar to effective domestic action.

Article 26 of the LOSC would also seem to offer a legal justification for the unilateral imposition of icebreaker escort and ice pilotage by Russian authorities.[114] While "[n]o charge may be levied upon foreign ships by reason only of their passage through the territorial sea", charges levied "as payment . . . for specific services rendered to the ship" are permitted, provided they are without discrimination.[115] Article 26 arguably supposes that the services rendered are required by the prevailing conditions, making mandatory icebreaker escort in ice-free waters or for vessels with icebreaking capacity highly problematic. For this reason, the assessment of the need for icebreaker assistance is an essential component of the Russian regime.[116]

In recognition of the modulated freedom of navigation conferred upon all ships in the EEZ, coastal states can adopt laws and regulations "for the prevention, reduction and control of pollution from vessels", provided they give "effect to generally accepted international rules and standards established through the competent international organization".[117] Thus it is of critical importance that Russia's requirements governing navigation in its EEZ reflect and operationalize Polar Code standards.

As for the NSR, Russia's capacity to regulate foreign navigation hinges on its legal status. If in its entirety it is an area of Russian internal waters, then Russia's sovereignty enables it to adopt and impose nationally defined requirements. If it is a patchwork of internal waters, territorial sea and EEZ, then the rules defined above would apply. However, if as Washington has consistently argued, the NSR includes a number of strategic straits subject to the "right of transit passage", Russia's regulatory powers would be severely curtailed. States bordering straits can designate sea lanes and prescribe traffic separation schemes to ensure the safety of navigation and are also entitled to adopt laws and regulations for the "prevention, reduction and control of pollution" but only by giving effect to "applicable international regulations".[118]

It appears from the foregoing that the legal bases justifying distinct Russian requirements that go beyond the Polar Code and other international standards, at least outside Russia's internal waters, are relatively difficult to identify. Like Canada, Russia could certainly invoke the special regulatory and enforcement powers conferred upon it by article 234 for ice-covered areas. However, as article 234 confers these supplementary powers only "for the prevention, reduction and control of marine pollution from vessels" and insists that "due regard to navigation" must be given, Russia would face the same uncertainties as Canada.

According to Gavrilov, different arguments supporting Russia's action can be found in academic literature.[119] Vylegzhanin, for instance, justifies the exercise of Russian authority over vessels from "a historical point of view":[120] "the discovery and exploration of many Arctic spaces [conferred upon the] discoverer . . . in accordance with then-current international law principles, a sufficient title in order to extend the authoritative powers of the Russian state to the discovered spaces".[121] According to Vylegzhanin, not only has Russia effectively exercised its authority in the Arctic for many centuries, but its domestic legislation has clearly claimed and defined these rights and prerogatives, without objection from foreign states or international legal doctrine.[122]

Another line of argument stems from the idea that Arctic states enjoy special legal rights and obligations with respect to shipping and other issues in the region. Gavrilov underlines that the NSR is "an indivisible transportation system whose legal regime does not differ depending on the areas of its passing".[123] This view is clearly reflected in the 2012 *Federal Shipping Law*, which describes the NSR as "a historically developed national transport communication of the Russian Federation".[124] The same law offers a very broad definition of the NSR water area[125] given that, as Gavrilov explains, the NSR does not have a "constant or fixed track line" but changes according to weather and ice conditions.[126]

Poval and Vylegzhanin both insist that foreign vessels cannot safely navigate through Arctic waters without relying on the coastal state's infrastructure, icebreaking assistance, ice observations, communication technologies, search and rescue and other services.[127] For this reason, Poval stresses that "the regulation of use of the route's lines should on reasonable grounds be a prerogative of the Russian Federation as a state whose coast lies near that route".[128] The "logistic inseparability and indivisibility of the NSR" and the "peculiarities of the region through which it passes" justify, according to Gavrilov, "the leading role of the Arctic coastal states in specifying the legal regime of the Arctic marine areas".[129]

This interpretation, claims Gavrilov, is directly supported by article 234 of the LOSC. He argues that this 'Arctic exception' together with both the Russian and Canadian laws and regulations should be treated and respected as a *lex specialis* in relation to the regulation of navigation in Arctic coastal areas as they provide for higher environmental and safety standards than those established internationally and thus offer a more robust and effective protection of the Arctic marine environment. He closes his analysis by emphasizing that "no objections from other countries have arisen concerning the Russian control" and that while exercising their authority, neither Russia nor Canada "is interested in undermining the potential for international commerce through their Arctic waters".[130]

Conclusion

As Chircop et al. rightly observed before the entry into force of the Polar Code, Russia and Canada

> are able to shrug off international concerns [that the exercise of their jurisdiction exceeds their powers under the LOSC] because of their unique historic water claims, the challenging safety and environment protection demands of regional navigation and the ambiguity in Article 234.[131]

This pragmatic assessment is still valid after the entry into force of the Polar Code, even as the relationship between the latter and article 234 adds a further layer of complexity. The fact that the Polar Code imposes internationally established, uniform standards on polar navigation has indeed raised the question of whether the Arctic coastal states retain their *lex specialis* jurisdiction. Russia and Canada met with resistance when they sought to include in the Polar Code a clause specifying that domestic jurisdiction under article 234 would remain intact.[132] While ultimately both the new SOLAS Chapter XIV and the (amended) MARPOL include clauses giving precedence to the LOSC,[133] the case could still be made that article 234 does not cover all of the Canadian and Russian requirements. Although the legal debate may not be resolved, it is likely that international navigation will in practice conform to these additional national requirements, not least because enhanced safety and effective pollution prevention is also in the interest of the ship operators.

Notes

1 *International Code for Ships Operating in Polar Waters*, Amendments to the International Convention for the Safety of Life at Sea, 1974, Resolution MSC.*386*(94), 21 November 2014, in Report of the Maritime Safety Committee on Its Ninety-Fourth Session, Annex 6, IMO Doc MSC 94/21/Add.1, and Amendments to the Annex of the Protocol of 1978 relating to the International Convention for the Prevention of Pollution from Ships, 1973, Resolution MEPC.265(68), 15 May 2015, in Report of the Marine Environment Protection Committee on Its Sixty-Eighth Session, Annex 11, IMO Doc MEPC 68/21/Add.1.
2 See www.imo.org/en/mediacentre/hottopics/polar/pages/default.aspx.
3 For a thorough comparison, see Chircop, A. et al. (2014). Course convergence? Comparative perspectives of the governance of navigation and shipping in Canadian and Russian Arctic waters. *Ocean Yearbook, 28*, 291.
4 The NWP spans the waters within the Canadian Arctic Archipelago between Baffin Bay and the Beaufort Sea. As Rothwell explains, the NWP is in reality a series of connected straits passages. Rothwell, D. R. (1993). The Canadian-U.S. Northwest

Passage dispute: A reassessment. *Cornell International Law Journal, 26*, 331 at 352. According to Pharand, the NWP consists of five basic routes, of which only two, referred to as the northern routes, are known to be suitable for deep-draft ships: Pharand, D. (1988). *Canada's Arctic Waters in International Law* (pp. 189–201). Cambridge: Cambridge University Press, (see also map at 190–191).

5 According to a recent study, a minimum definition of the NEP [Northeast Passage] is that it is made up of all the marginal seas of the Eurasian Arctic, i.e., the Chukchi, the East Siberian, the Laptev, the Kara and the Barents Sea. As such, the NSR makes up approximately 90 percent of the NEP. Østreng, W. et al., (2013) *Shipping in Arctic waters: A comparison of the Northeast, Northwest and Trans Polar Passages.* London: Springer-Praxis, at 18. The NSR was designated as a separate part of the NEP and as an administered, legal entity under full Soviet jurisdiction and control by the Council of People's Commissars of the USSR on 17 December 1932. According to the official definition, the NSR stretches from Novaya Zemlya in the west to the Bering Strait in the east and its different sailing lanes cover 2,200 to 2,900 nautical miles of ice-infested waters. Ibid., at 13.

6 Department of Foreign Affairs, Trade and Development, Government of Canada, "Canada's Arctic Foreign Policy", last modified June 3, 2013. Retrieved from www.international.gc.ca/arctic-arctique/arctic_policy-canada-politique_arctique.aspx?lang=eng.

7 Office of Ocean Affairs. (1992). *Limits in the seas No. 112: United States responses to excessive national maritime claims*. Washington, DC: US State Department, at 71. See also Rothwell, D. R. (1996). *The Polar Regions and the development of international law*. Cambridge: Cambridge University Press, at 209. The Soviet government certainly appears to invoke the concept of history in regard to its northern seaway, see *Aide mémoire* from the Soviet Ministry of Foreign Affairs to American Embassy Moscow, 21 July 1964, reproduced in Brubaker, R. D. (1996). The legal status of straits in Russian Arctic waters – internationality. *INSROP Working Paper No. 57*. Retrieved from www.arctis-search.com/tiki-download_wiki_attachment.php?attId=104.

8 Russian Federation (2008). *Basics of the state policy of the Russian Federation in the Arctic for the period till 2020 and for a further perspective*. Retrieved from www.arctis-search.com/Russian+Federation+Policy+for+the+Arctic+to+2020.

9 Russian Federation. (2013). *Russian strategy of the development of the Arctic zone and the provision of national security until 2020*. Retrieved from www.iecca.ru/en/legislation/strategies/item/99-the-development-strategy-of-the-arctic-zone-of-the-russian-federation.

10 Clark, J. (1985). *Statement in the House of Commons by secretary of state for external affairs*, 10 September 1985, reproduced in (1986) *Canadian Yearbook of International Law* 24 at 326. Emphasis added.

11 Office of Ocean Law and Policy, Bureau of Oceans and International Environmental and Scientific Affairs, US Department of State. (1988). *Limits in the seas, No. 109*. Retrieved from www.state.gov/documents/organization/58383.pdf.

12 Scovazzi, T. (1988). New Developments Concerning Soviet Straight Baselines. *International Journal of Estuarine and Coastal Law, 3*, 37 and Golitsyn, V. (1989). The Arctic – On the Way to Regional Cooperation. *Marine Policy Report, 1*, 91.

13 Vincent, P. (2008). *Droit de la mer*. Bruxelles: Éditions Larcier, at 12.

14 *United Nations Convention on the Law of the Sea*, 10 December 1982, 1833 *UNTS* 396, article 8(2).

15 Ibid.

16 *Military and Paramilitary Activities in and against Nicaragua (Nicaragua v. United States of America)*, I.C.J. Reports 1986, 14 at 111, paragraph 212.

17 Gidel, G. (1932). *Le droit international public de la mer*, vol. II. Châteauroux: Établissements Mellottée. At 45, quoted in Lucchini, L. and Voelckel, M. (1990). *Droit de la mer* (vol 2.2). Paris: Pédone, at 287.

18 While Part III of the LOSC reflects the consensus ultimately reached during UNC-LOS III on the scope and nature of the legal regime applicable to international straits, no precise definition of what constitutes an 'international strait' could be agreed upon. Consequently, the International Court of Justice's ruling in the 1949 *North Corfu Channel* case remains an important, albeit ambiguous point of reference: "[T]he decisive criterion is rather its geographical situation as connecting two parts of the high seas and the fact of its being used for international navigation". *Corfu Channel Case*, I.C.J. Reports 1949, 4 at 28.
19 This was emphasized in the White House (2009). *National Security Presidential Directive and Homeland Security Presidential Directive*, Section III "Policy", Subsection B "National Security and Homeland Security Interests in the Arctic" at paragraph 5. Retrieved from www.fas.org/irp/offdocs/nspd/nspd-66.htm. This position was subsequently reiterated in the White House (2013). *National Strategy for the Arctic Region*, Section 3 "Strengthen International Cooperation", third bullet point. Retrieved from https://obamawhitehouse.archives.gov/sites/default/files/docs/nat_arctic_strategy.pdf.
20 See for example the acknowledgement made in 1978 by Erik Wang, director of legal operations, Department of External Affairs, Canada, cited in McDorman, T.L. (1983). The new definition of 'Canada Lands' and the determination of the outer limit of the continental shelf. *Journal of Maritime Law and Commerce, 14*, 195 at 215. Willy Østreng reports that Russia's regulatory powers are challenged by the European Union in Østreng, W. (2010). The Northeast and Northern Sea Route. *Arctic Knowledge Hub*. Retrieved from www.arctis-search.com/The+Northeast+Passage+and+Northern+Sea+Route+2.
21 See Federal Foreign Office, "Guidelines of the Germany Arctic Policy", September 2013, fifth bullet point. Retrieved from www.bmel.de/SharedDocs/Downloads/EN/International/Leitlinien-Arktispolitik.pdf?__blob=publicationFile. See also State Council Information Office of the People's Republic of China, "China's Arctic Policy", 26 January 2018, Part IV, Section 3, Sub-Section (1). Retrieved from http://english.gov.cn/archive/white_paper/2018/01/26/content_281476026660336.htm.
22 *Oceans Act*, S.C. 1996, c. 31, article 4.
23 Ibid., article 10.
24 Ibid., article 13(1).
25 Ibid., article 5(3) "Baselines where historic title". Emphasis added.
26 *Federal Act on the Internal Maritime Waters, Territorial Sea and Contiguous Zone of the Russian Federation*, Federal Law No. 155-FZ, 31 July 1998, article 4, fifth bullet point. Retrieved from www.un.org/Depts/los/LEGISLATIONANDTREATIES/PDFFILES/RUS_1998_Act_TS.pdf.
27 See ibid., articles 2(1) and 22.
28 *Federal Act on the EEZ of the Russian Federation*, November 1998, article 1(3). Retrieved from www.un.org/Depts/los/LEGISLATIONANDTREATIES/PDFFILES/RUS_1998_Act_EZ.pdf.
29 *Regulatory Impact Analysis (Objectives)*, Canada Gazette, 2017, part I, Vol. 151, No. 26, 2867, at 2869.
30 *Arctic Waters Pollution Prevention Act*, R.S.C., 1985, c. A-12, as amended, section 4(1).
31 *Arctic Waters Pollution Prevention Act*, St Can 1969–1970, c 47, article 3.
32 AWPPA (note 30), section 2.
33 *Arctic Shipping Pollution Prevention Regulations*, C.R.C., c. 353 (repealed).
34 Department of Transport, Vessel Traffic Reporting Arctic Canada Traffic Zone (NORDREG). Retrieved from https://web.archive.org/web/20070206015755/www.ccg-gcc.gc.ca:80/cen-arc/mcts-sctm/mcts-services/vtrarctic_e.htm (archived content, as of 6 February 2007).

35 *Northern Canada Vessel Traffic Services Zone Regulations*, SOR/2010–127.
36 See Franckx, E. (2015). The 'new' Arctic passages and the 'old' Law of the Sea. In H. Ringbom, (Ed.), *Jurisdiction over Ships: Post-UNCLOS developments in the Law of the Sea* (pp. 194–216). Leiden: Brill Nijhoff, at 200.
37 Ibid., at 200–201.
38 *Federal Law of Shipping on the Water Area of the NSR*, Federal Law No. 132-FZ, 28 July 2012 (unofficial translation). Retrieved from www.arctic-lio.com.
39 See note 26.
40 1999 *Merchant shipping code of the Russian Federation*, 30 April 1999. Retrieved from http://folk.uio.no/erikro/WWW/HNS/rmc.pdf.
41 Ibid., article 5.1(1).
42 Gavrilov, V. V. (2015). Legal status of the Northern Sea Route and legislation of the Russian Federation: A note. *Ocean Development and International Law*, *46*(3), 256 at 257.
43 *Shipping Code* (note 40), article 5.1(4).
44 'Vladimir Putin signed a law on ROSATOM's powers in Northern Sea Route development' ROSATOM, 28 December 2018). Retrieved from www.rosatom.ru/en/press-centre/news/vladimir-putin-singed-a-law-on-rosatom-s-powers-in-northern-sea-route-development/?sphrase_id=615108.
45 Ibid., article 5(2) and (4).
46 *Rules of navigation in the water area of the Northern Sea Route*. Retrieved from www.nsra.ru/files/fileslist/120-en-rules_perevod_cniimf-13_05_2015.pdf. A few minor amendments were introduced on 9 January 2017. Retrieved from www.nsra.ru/files/fileslist/122-en-transl_asmp.pdf.
47 Ibid., paragraph 65.
48 On the role of Russia and, incidentally, Canada during the negotiations of the *Polar Code*, see Bognar, D. (2016). Russian proposals on the Polar Code: Contributing to common rules or furthering state interests?. *Arctic Review on Law and Politics*, *7*(2), 111 at 113f.
49 *Arctic Shipping Safety and Pollution Prevention Regulations*, C.R.C., c. 354.
50 Van Ert, G. (2010). Dubious dualism: The reception of international law in Canada. *Valparaiso University Law Review*, *44*(3), 927 at 928, footnote omitted.
51 See *Polar Code* (note 1), chapter 5.
52 *International Convention for the Safety of Life at Sea* (SOLAS) 1 November 1974, 1184 *UNTS* 278, as amended.
53 ASSPPR (note 49), section 6(1).
54 *International Convention for the Prevention of Pollution from Ships* [MARPOL], 17 February 1978, 1340 *UNTS* 61, as amended.
55 ASSPPR (note 49), section 14.
56 Ibid., sections 15 and 16.
57 Ibid., sections 17–22.
58 Ibid., sections 23–26.
59 Ibid., section 3.
60 Ibid., sections 6(1) and 7(1) (for the safety-related measures) and section 13 (for the pollution prevention measures).
61 See *Shipping Safety Control Zones Order*, C.R.C., c. 356.
62 ASSPPR (note 49), sections 6 (1) and 13.
63 LOSC (note 14), article 94.
64 Ibid., article 2 (indirectly), see notes 14 through 17 and accompanying text.
65 Ibid., articles 17 ff. and 211(4).
66 Ibid., articles 37 ff.
67 Ibid., articles 56 (1)(b)(iii) and (2), 58 (2) and 211(5) and (6).
68 Ibid., article 234.

69 Bartenstein, K. (2011). The 'Arctic exception' in the Law of the Sea convention: A contribution to safer navigation in the Northwest Passage?. *Ocean Development and International Law, 42*(1–2), 22.

70 See supra notes 6, 10 and 25 and accompanying text.

71 LOSC (note 14), article 21(1)(f) and 211(4).

72 *Polar Code* (note 1), Preamble, recital 5.

73 LOSC (note 14), article 21(2).

74 Ibid., article 211(5).

75 Ibid., article 42(1)(b).

76 See notes 94 etc. and accompanying text.

77 ASSPPR (note 49), section 7. Indeed, even Canadian vessels are only concerned if they navigate in one of Canada's SSCZ.

78 NORDREG (note 35), section 2.

79 ASSPPR (note 49), section 8(1) and schedule 1.

80 Ibid., section 8(2). The assessment may be based on the *Polar Code*'s POLARIS method or, for a transitional period, Canada's Arctic Ice Regime Shipping System (AIRSS) (see Transport Canada, Arctic Ice Regime Shipping System (AIRSS) Standard. Retrieved 19 July 2018 from www.tc.gc.ca/eng/marinesafety/tp-tp12259-menu-605.htm.

81 ASSPPR (note 49), section 9(1).

82 Ibid., section 10. The STCW certificate is in any case mandatory for SOLAS vessels and for non-SOLAS vessels of 500 gross tonnage or more operating within the SSCZ (*Polar Code* [note 1], chapter 12; see also *International Convention on Standards of Training, Certification and Watchkeeping for Seafarers*, 7 July 1978, 1361 *UNTS* 2, as amended [STCW Convention], article VI).

83 *Polar Code* (note 1), chapter 5 (II-A).

84 Ibid., chapter 1.1.2 (II-A).

85 AWPPA (note 30), section 4(1).

86 Vessels defined under section 12 of the ASSPPR (note 49) as "designed for operation in polar waters in at least medium first-year ice, that may include old ice inclusions" and vessels not included in this category that are "designed for operation in polar waters in at least thin first-year ice, which may include old ice inclusions".

87 ASSPPR (note 49), section 18. Under the *Polar Code* (note 1), chapter 21.3 (II-A) an approval possibility exists even if the distance requirement is not met.

88 ASSPPR (note 49), section 21.

89 Ibid., section 26.

90 AWPPA (note 30), section 4(1).

91 LOSC (note 14), article 94.

92 Ibid., article 21(2).

93 Ibid., article 211(5).

94 Bartenstein (note 69) at 28 ff.

95 See Chircop, A. (2016). Jurisdiction over ice-covered areas and the Polar Code: An emerging symbiotic relationship? *Journal of International Maritime Law, 22*, 275, at 280.

96 To this effect, see also Pharand, D. (2007). The Arctic waters and the Northwest Passage: A final revisit. *Ocean Development and International Law, 38*(1–2), 3 at 47. See also Fauchald, O. K. (2011). Regulatory frameworks for maritime transport in the Arctic: Will a Polar Code contribute to resolve conflicting interests? In J. Grue, & R. H. Gabrielsen (Eds.), *Marine transport in the high north* (pp. 73–91). Oslo: Novus forlag, at 77. Against: Chircop, A. (2009). The growth of international shipping in the Arctic: Is a regulatory review timely. *International Journal of Marine & Coastal Law, 24*, 355 at 371.

97 For details, see Franckx, E., & Boone, L. (2017). Article 234: Ice-covered areas. In A. Proelss, (Ed.), *United Nations Convention on the Law of the Sea – A commentary* (pp. 1566–1585). Munich: Beck, at 1570, paragraph 4.

98 McRae, D. (1987). The negotiation of article 234. In F. Griffiths, (Ed.), *Politics of the Northwest Passage* (pp. 98–114). Kingston & Montreal: McGill-Queen's University Press, at 110.
99 United States and INTERTANKO, *Northern Canada Vessel Traffic Services Zone Regulations*, 22 September 2010, IMO Doc. MSC/88/11/2, paragraph 2; Singapore, "Statement by the delegation of Singapore", in IMO, *Report to the Maritime Safety Committee on its Eighty-Eight Session*, 19 January 2011, IMO Doc. MSC 88/26/ Add.1, Annex 28; for Germany, see IMO, *Report of the Maritime Safety Committee on its Eighty-Eighth Session*, IMO Doc. MSC 88/26, 15 December 2010, paragraph 11.35.
100 *Polar Code* (note 1), Preamble, recital 5. The link has long been recognized in the SOLAS Convention (note 52), chapter V, regulation 10.1.
101 Bartenstein, note 69 at 24 ff. and 41 ff. For a broad teleological interpretation, see Fauchald (note 96) at 77 (indirectly) and 80 and Chircop (note 95) at 280.
102 See Lalonde, S. (2004). Increased traffic through Canadian arctic waters: Canada's state of readiness. *Revue Juridique Thémis*, *38*(1), 49 at 61 and 64. See also Howson, N.C. (1988). Breaking the ice: The Canadian-American dispute over the Arctic's Northwest Passage. *Columbia Journal of Transnational Law*, *26*(2), 337 at 354.
103 See definition at note 41 above.
104 Gavrilov (note 42) at 257.
105 *Constitution of the Russian Federation*, 12 December 1993, in force since 25 December 1993. Retrieved from www.constitution.ru/en/10003000-01.htm.
106 See Danilenko, G. M. (1994). The new Russian constitution and international law. *American Journal of International Law*, *88*(3), 451 at 458.
107 See note 38.
108 Gavrilov (note 42) at 257.
109 *Amendments to the rules of navigation in the water area of the NSR*, Annex to the Order of the Ministry of Transport, 9 January 2017. Retrieved from www.nsra.ru/ files/fileslist/122-en-transl_asmp.pdf.
110 Only three brief paragraphs in Article 60 of the *Rules of navigation* (note 46) are devoted to safety issues: the need to have on board "sea nautical charts and manuals" for the ship's entire route, "supplementary emergency equipment" which is deemed to include "one search light with power of at least two kW" (with spare lamps), "warm clothes for each person on board" with three spare sets and "hydrosuits" for every admissible person. This contrasts with the 12 detailed chapters of Part I-A of the *Polar Code* (note 1), on mandatory "Safety Measures".
111 LOSC (note 14), articles 21(1)(f) and 211(4).
112 See discussion above at notes 72 and 100 and respective accompanying text.
113 LOSC (note 14), article 21(2).
114 See *Rules of navigation* (note 46), Parts III and IV.
115 LOSC (note 14), article 26(1) and (2) respectively.
116 See *Rules of navigation* (note 46), Parts III and IV, in particular paragraph 23.
117 LOSC (note 14), article 211(5).
118 LOSC (note 14), article 42(1)(b).
119 Gavrilov (note 42) at 257.
120 Ibid.
121 Vylegzhanin, A. N. (2007). Features of the legal regime of subsoil use in the arctic. In A. N. Vylegzhanin, (Ed.), *International legal fundamental principles of the subsoil use: Manual*. Moscow: Norma, at 121 as quoted by Gavrilov (note 42) at 258.
122 Ibid.
123 Gavrilov (note 42) at 260.
124 *Federal Shipping Law* (note 38), article 2.
125 See the definition at note 38.

126 Gavrilov (note 42) at 257.
127 Poval, L. M. (2011). International legal issues: Concerning the division of the Arctic economic spaces. *Arctic and North, 3*, 3 at 9 and Vylegzhanin, A.N. (2012). Introduction. In A. V. Zagorsky, & A. V. Nikitin (Eds.), *International cooperation in the sphere of environmental protection: Preservation and sustainable management of biological resources in the Arctic Ocean.* Moscow: Russian Political Science Association, at 6. Both are referred to by Gavrilov (note 42) at 260.
128 Poval (note 127) as quoted by Gavrilov (note 42) at 260.
129 Gavrilov (note 42) at 260 (quoting Vylegzhanin [note 127]).
130 Ibid., at 261.
131 Chircop et al. (note 3) at 326.
132 Canada, *Development of a mandatory code for ship operating in polar waters: Proposed framework for the code of ships operating in polar waters,* DE 53/18/2, 20 November 2009, IMO Doc. DE 53/18/2 (2009), 7, paragraph 2.11 and Russian Federation, *Procedure of Accounting for National Regulations,* 1 February 2011, IMO Doc. DE 55/12/23 (2011), paragraph 5. See Rayfuse, R. (2014). Coastal state jurisdiction and the Polar Code: A test case for Arctic oceans governance. In T. Stephens, & D. L. VanderZwaag (Eds.), *Polar oceans governance in an era of environmental change* (pp. 235–252). Cheltenham: Edward Elgar, at 245.
133 SOLAS (note 52) Chapter XIV, regulation 2, paragraph 5 and MAROPL (note 54), article 9(2).

Part III

Arctic shipping and port development

9 An analysis of the Arctic ports

Olivier Faury, Brigitte Daudet,
Pierre-Louis Têtu and Jérôme Verny

Introduction

There are numerous facets of the Arctic Ocean, a diversity reflected by the difference of population density, climate conditions, economic development, geography constraints.

This regional diversity leads to a variety of ports. Focusing on ports typologies
according to their activity, we may find that some ports are predominantly dedicated to the exportation of raw materials, the supply of population and/or to the
transshipment of goods.

The low number of ports is stressed by numerous academics as the weak point
of the Arctic development. The implementation of a port network along the Arctic
shore is paramount at four levels: economic, social, safety and strategic.

At an economic layer, Arctic ports ease the value creation of this ocean. The
Arctic is considered as a significant reserve of oil, gas and minerals. From the economic vision, ports are used to export cargo and develop mines and hydrocarbons
fields (USGS, 2008).

Ports, as value providers, provide the opportunity for a population to settle in a
place, being supplied in cargo in the case of remoteness, and the population settlement can participate in maintaining the port's infrastructures. In the Arctic, due to
harsh conditions and the remoteness of some communities, ports are the only way
to be supplied and to maintain a link with the rest of the country.

If ports offer an opportunity for social and economic development, they also
provide a safe place for repair if needed. The low density of ports along the shore
does not provide enough refuge areas, a parameter stressed as one of the major
brakes for the development of Arctic navigation.

From a more geopolitical point of view, ports are tools for maintaining sovereignty by offering coastal states faster reaction in case of intrusion. However, it is
highly correlated with the fleet of vessels' ability to face harsh sailing conditions.

If ports have numerous goals, they are impacted by geographic parameters
such as climate, draft, location and hinterland parameters with an impact on their
accessibility.

In the Arctic, climate conditions are paramount and may have an impact on
the attractiveness of ports and thus, on their economic capacity to maintain

their infrastructures. The draft of ports – the length of berth and the loading or unloading tools – are key parameters in the port's development. Most Arctic ports have a draft lower than 12 m, limiting the type of vessels able to call. Moreover, not all Arctic ports have the same berth length or even a berth, and consequently, not all Arctic ports have handling cranes for both containers and raw materials.

Looking at the interaction between goals and external factors, we may find a high diversity of ports in the Arctic. Regarding the Russian section between the Kola and the Yamal Peninsula, ports are more or less dedicated to the exportation of raw materials, the eastern part being less used, potentially due to a higher remoteness and harsher sailing conditions. The Canadian section seems to be mainly composed of ports dedicated to the supply of goods to local populations with a low level of infrastructures. Yet, even if Churchill is not technically speaking an Arctic port, its development appears as highly strategic for Canadian authorities (Sevunts, 2017; Malone, 2018; Ng, Andrews, Babb, Lin, & Becker, 2018). Regarding the American ports in Alaska, based on World Ports (2019), most of them are based in the sub-Arctic area including Anchorage, the most important port. Considering in this analysis ports on the Arctic shore of states, only the port of Red Dog and Kotzebue are Arctic ports.

The aim of this chapter is to define and provide an analysis of the different typology of existing ports within the Arctic, to look at the way they interact in order to fill their various goals.

Hence, after a literature review that defines the components of a port, we will focus on the type of Arctic ports. The fourth section concentrates on the port systems for each Arctic country before a prospective analysis of ports' potential evolution, followed by the conclusion.

Literature review

As explained by Vigarié (1979), a port is an anthropogenic place with infrastructures created by humans. Geographers considered that the localisation of ports is influenced by positive conditions provided by physical parameters (Miossec, 1998). For 3000 years, the main human settlements have been along the shore in areas offering a place protected from unpredictable wind, storms and marine currents. Ports are, first, places of refuge. According to Boorstin (1988), ports were created in the Eastern Mediterranean because some population had expressed the desire to leave their own territory in order to discover and conquer other ones (Boorstin, 1988). Fernand Braudel reminds us that the first thalassocracy had a will to develop a commercial outpost able to manage the call of commercial vessels (Braudel, 1993). The anthropisation of the shore became more organised with berths, dams and other infrastructures to make the port the hyphen between sea and land (Corlay, 1998). Buchet (2004) stressed that for Egyptians ports became political tools in order to increase the power of the state, while Greeks and Romans implemented the first network of cities-ports in the Mediterranean and Black Seas. Vigarié (1983) shed a light on the existing relation between hinterland, port and foreland and named it ports triptych. Because a port is a bridge between two different organization (maritime and inland), it is characterized by an ecosystem of services.

Port economy

At the origination of ports, the frontier between war and trade was thin and so were the services provided whether for war or commercial vessels and crew. Interests for war and commercial vessels were often mixed, creating cities with the management of vessels and cargo as their main purposes (Daudet & Alix, 2012).

The management of the relation between ports and cities has been analysed during the last 30 years and mainly by the International Association of Cities and Ports (AIVP, 2018).

Loading, unloading, storage, exchange and transformation of goods make ports transit areas where cargo settles during the time of their physical evacuation as demonstrated by the literature produced by the English geographer and economist Bird (1971).

Whatever may be its main activity – cruise, war, trade or fishing, or pleasure yachting – a port is an area made of infrastructures and superstructures and infrastructures and superstructures which define the nature of the main activity and the services associated with it. The port can be a deepwater sea port or a river port (Fischer, 1963; Roa Perera et al., 2013). It can, at the same time, focus on finished goods, raw materials or cruising.

Ports are strategic tools, symbols of a state's sovereignty (Vigarié, 1995). Most ports around the world are managed by public authority with state services maintaining the service provided (Grosdidier de Matons, 1999). During the last decades a non-negligible part of this authority has been transferred to private firms specialising in creating Public Private Partnerships (PPPs) (Grosdidier de Matons, 2012). As stressed by Grosdidier de Matons (2012), these PPPs created new ecosystems where the economic, financial and legal concerns of public and private stakeholders are strongly linked to one another.

From a sociologist point of view, ports are a place where numerous different types of population co-exist (AIVP, 2008). Ports are also a place with numerous jobs dedicated to the management of ports such as dredging, towing, boatage, marine or maritime agents at sea. On land, tasks such as transit agents, stevedores, underwriters, custom agents constitute a network of professionals dedicated to the port's development, interacting with the unions (Hislaire, 1993).

In our day, the specialization of port terminals leads to the implementation of dedicated infrastructures which posit ports as loading, unloading interfaces for specific vessels such as in the port of Sabetta in Russia. This is mainly the case for ports focusing on raw materials such as crude oil or LNG (Alix & Guy, 2007). These ports do not require the same level of service density as cross-functional ports. Some new value chains consider the port terminal as the link between the hinterland and the foreland (Alix, 2018).

Transshipment ports dedicated to the exportation of raw materials benefit from a strategic geographical position. As an example, we could quote the case of LNG ports that ground the development on the exploitation of gas fields or the case of

Australian ports managing coal dedicated to the Chinese market (Alix & Lacoste, 2013). This strategy of Australian ports posits them as an antechamber of the Chinese steelworks.

Ports are paramount economic and strategic tools in the globalization of international trade. As an example, Dutch ports represent 6 points of the Netherland GNP. Shanghai and Ningbo represent together one billion tons. In West Africa, Cotonou and Lomé represent 85% of the Benin and Togo custom revenues (Daudet, 2015). Looking at the competition between ports, productivity, reliability, competitiveness are qualitative and quantitative indexes providing a way to rank ports.

Focusing on the Arctic, the navigation within this ocean is mainly composed of flows between two Arctic ports or between an Arctic and a non-Arctic port (Pelletier & Guy, 2012; Humpert, 2014; Tianming, Zabelina, Erokhin, & Ivolga, 2017; Kiiski, Solakivi, Töyli, & Ojala, 2016; Gritsenko & Kiiski, 2016), transiting being a very small share of the amount of goods loaded (Doyon et al., 2016).

Flows are mainly made of raw material (Humpert, 2014; Kaiser, Pahl, & Horbel, 2018) and supply materials for communities (Pelletier & Guy, 2012; Gritsenko & Efimova; 2017) or infrastructures construction. Yet, whatever may be the type of flows, ports are at the core of the Arctic development, as highlighted by Ragner (2000), Kitagawa, Izumiyama, Kamesaki, Yamaguchi & Ono (2001), Didenko and Cherenkov (2018) and Farré et al. (2015). As seen previously, ports fulfil various needs (Kaiser et al., 2018), they provide a refuge for vessels if a claim occurs, ease the exportation of cargo and the supply of population, and are a means to maintain their sovereignty upon a disputed area.

Due to the harsh climate conditions, the Arctic attractiveness is highly dependent on the safety issue (Faury, 2015; Fedi, Faury, & Gritsenko, 2018). Hence, the low number and density of ports able to be a refuge for vessels freeze the motivation of shipowners and underwriters to enter into this market (Sarrabezoles, Lasserre, & Hagouagn'rin, 2016; Gritsenko & Efimova, 2017).

The exportation of raw materials from these remote fields are paramount for the development of the Arctic coastal states (Têtu, Pelletier, & Lasserre, 2015; IES Report, 2010). Besides, due to the remoteness of raw materials, the optimal way to bring parcels for the update or building of a port is often by sea, which can, by consequence, enhance the amount of cargo loaded (Doyon et al., 2016). Hence, from an economic point of view, the development of ports is mainly grounded on raw materials exploitation (Zelentov, 2012; Bennett, 2014; Pelletier & Guy, 2012; Pahl & Kaiser, 2017).

The Arctic population is not homogenous from one region to another, even in the same country (Csonka & Schweitzer, 2014; Kaiser et al., 2018). Population centres can be in remote area where few roads, railways or barges may supply them in necessary goods (Pelletier & Guy, 2012). Hence, besides the expensive airlift services, sealift appears to be the most reliable means of transportation (Doyon et al., 2016), stressing the importance of ports for those local communities (Smirnova, Lipina, Kudryashova, Krejdenko, & Bogdanova, 2016; Têtu et al., 2015).

As stressed by Pahl and Kaiser (2017), the Arctic is a place with a wide variety of ports (Serry, 2011) and few of them can be considered as deepwater ports (Pahl & Kaiser, 2017). For example, some Canadian ports are mainly used by local communities for their own supplies, hence port infrastructures are sometimes limited in mooring and loading operations take place on the beach. Gritsenko and Efimova (2017) stress the possibility for a project such as Sabetta to be unprofitable. One of the reasons is to be found within the high level of investment needed (Gritsenko & Efimova, 2017) but the volatility of the raw materials on which the return of investment is based can be another factor. The additional cost for an Arctic port is mainly due to their remoteness and to the harsh sailing conditions as a direct consequence of the unpredictability of the ice blanket (Gunnarsson, 2013).

Hence, remoteness, harsh climate, additional maintenance cost, low draft, limited hinterland and density of population, sovereignty issues and the variation of raw materials value shapes the Artic ports development (Pahl & Kaiser, 2017).

Aware of the diversity of the various analyses regarding ports within the Arctic, it appears that as far as we know, no one has looked at their diversity, trying to define if they can be considered as ports, and the way they interact in order to reach their goal.

As seen, the definition of a port in the literature is complex and the Arctic is an area with a wide variety of ports, impacted by numerous exogenous and endogenous factors. It also seems that there is not a single universal definition or typology of ports through the literature. As far as we know, no analysis has tried to define if they all can be considered as ports and the way they interact with each other.

Arctic constraints

Arctic ports face climate, economic, human and geographic challenges. Each one is strongly interrelated and if they have the same final effect, a potential loss of attractiveness, their pathway to reach this situation is different.

Climatic constraints have a direct impact on the attractiveness of the port and its ability to generate revenue on a yearly basis (Gritsenko & Efimova, 2017). The presence of ice all along the year or at least a part of it may hinder the call of certain vessels (Ng et al., 2018). Besides, the use of icebreakers enhances the cost of handling goods which increases the price cost of raw materials. The ice pressure, extreme cold, low visibility due to the fog and long period of darkness impose the use of additional tools to secure the navigation (IMO, 2014).

Economic constraints are shown by a limited hinterland and a dependency toward one type of raw materials, with a fluctuating value. A limited hinterland could restrain the ability of a port to generate profit, attract new flows and gain independency toward an oil field or a mine. Moreover, the remoteness, related to the geography of the Arctic, has a negative impact on the building and maintenance cost of port infrastructures (Ng et al., 2018). The combination of the high cost and variable revenue could raise the question of the profitability of certain ports and hence the implementation of such infrastructures.

With the remoteness that impacts negatively the development of ports, a low draft may hamper its attractiveness (Figuereido De Oliveira & Cariou, 2011). The low draft imposes the use of smaller vessels and prohibit the use of vessels that would allow scale economies.

Port management necessitates experience, competency and a steady population. Yet, the climatic, economic and geography factors do not ease a population settlement. Numerous Arctic ports are far from the others' economic centre and increasing their population is one of their biggest challenges.

The different types of ports within the Arctic

These constraints plus the variety of the Arctic Ocean gave birth to a wide variety of ports. As seen above there are different ways to classify ports. In this subsection we decided to look at their task.

The first group would be composed of regional hubs as described by Monios et al. (2019). Their goal is to transship the cargo via a shuttle to a bigger vessel that will reach the final consumer. These ports, in the Arctic or just at its frontier, are the link between smaller ports within the Arctic and foreigner ports. It appears that as far as we know, Murmansk is, for now, the only existing case. This port is ice free on a yearly basis, allowing non-ice class calls yearly, and it is able to load and manage vessels bigger than a Panamax. Moreover, Murmansk is connected with the rest of the Russian network. Looking at Pelletier and Guy (2012) or Têtu et al. (2015), respectively Montréal or Québec would be its equivalent in Canada if they were within the Arctic area.

The second group would be made of ports focused on the export of raw materials. They are, for some of them, managed by both state and private stakeholders. As an example, the port of Sabetta in the Yamal Peninsula has been built from scratch in order to export the production coming from the LNG plant. This port, covered by ice most of the year, is dredged in order to welcome the ARC7 YamalMax LNG carrier. Looking at the Canadian port we could quote the case of Deception Bay that ships their raw materials to China or to the port of Quebec City; or Milne Inlet which directly supplies Belgium and Japan.

The third group would deal with local communities and supply them in goods required for their survival. Due to geographical remoteness, the melt of the permafrost and its impact on the cost of roads or railways, the sea trades are the optimal way to supply communities, although a significant share of the supply is airborne. Usually vessels managing this transportation are smaller vessels or barges and fill the role of shuttle between ports.

The different port systems reflect the states' Arctic strategy

In the Arctic Ocean, producing crude oil, LNG or extracting minerals implies additional costs and so does the transportation. Thus, in order to maintain a price cost as low as possible and to provide a service as reliable as possible, the flows of cargo are organised though an array made of hub and spoke.

If each coastal country integrates a hub and spoke, the final objective is not the same regarding the country analysed.

The Russian port system, which appears to be dedicated to the exportation of raw materials and to reinforce the Russian sovereignty (Sokolov, 2013), needs to attract new population to favour its development. Hence, investments occurred during previous years such as in the ports of Sabetta or Novy in the Yamal Peninsula. As a result, 2018 saw 10 million tons of goods shipped along the Russian shore (mainly coming from Russian ports).

The main sea trade activity along the Russian shore is included between the Kola Peninsula and the Yenissei River whereas the eastern part is rather poor in term of infrastructures compared to the western shore. The main reason for this discrepancy can be found in the climate and population differences: the western part benefits from less difficult climate conditions and a lower ice extent and thickness.

The production of oil and gas is a paramount for the Russian economy, thus, the valorisation of Arctic fields is the core of the Russian strategy (IES Report, 2010). However, the production cost of a Brent barrel in this region is between 90 USD (Klimenko, 2014) and 100 USD (Harsem & Knutheen, 2011) and the transportation between Prirazlomnoye and Murmansk, as an example, is around 40 USD (Klimenko, 2014). Hence, the implementation of a port system able to diminish the negative impact of transport cost is strategic for private and public stakeholders.

Thereby, the previous years saw the implementation of a Russia port system with ports dedicated to the exportation of raw materials (Sabetta, Novy, Varandey, Indiga and Dudinka), managing exportation and transshipment (Murmansk, Arkhangelsk) on the western part of the Arctic. If the western part of the Russian shore is well developed, it is not the case of the eastern part as stated by Frolov (2015). The ports of Khatanga, Tiksi, Pevek, Dudinka and Dixon Island need to be updated (Frolov, 2015). This difference can be explained by the higher number of inhabitants in the area comprised within the Yamal and the Kola Peninsulas (Kaiser et al., 2018).

The Canadian system seems to be more focused on the supply of northern communities compared to the Russian. Looking at Pahl and Kaiser (2017), 18 ports out of 286 in Canada are in the Arctic. Yet most of them are dedicated to the supply of cargo and are considered by Pahl and Kaiser (2017) as being small or very small. Pelletier (2014) stressed that most of the supply is doomed to the northern communities. The sealift is managed from St Lawrence ports. He also shed a light on the fact the ice conditions impose the use of specific vessels.

Economic development of the Canadian Arctic is grounded on mining exploitation, and maritime infrastructure such as ports or bulk terminals are essentially based on private investments. This is the case with Glencore Xstrata's Raglan mine, serviced by a bulk terminal in the North of Quebec at Deception Bay; Raglan is 40 kilometres northwest of another mining project owned by the Canadian Royal Company called Nunavik Nickel, which also operates a terminal in Deception Bay. Investigations on this nickel project highlight the fact that a Chinese provincial state-owned company called Jilin Jien Nickel is an investor on this mining project. On Baffin Island, south of the community of Pond Inlet, a Canadian company called Baffin Land, jointly owned by Arcelor-Mittal and Nunavut Iron Ore Company, exploits the Mary River Iron Ore Mine. Throughout the years, limited investments by Canadian officials and respective governments in infrastructure in the Canadian North explain why Ottawa lags behind other Arctic states that substantially invest in their shipping networks and ports.

Norway posits its ports as potential hubs and develops its hinterland in order to attract flows coming from Scandinavia and Europe (Staalesen, 2018a). Among them, Kirkenes is promoting the idea of transforming into the future Arctic Norwegian hub. The mutation of Kirkenes from a port dedicated to the exportation of minerals to a port able to manage containers, timber, minerals is conditioned upon the construction of the Baltic railway. Kirkenes is a perfect example of the danger of a port strategy totally based on raw materials. The year 2015 saw the definitive closure of the Sydvaranger mine by Tschudi (Lasserre, 2018) and that opened a new challenge for this port. Thus, in order to maintain the infrastructure, Kirkenes provided a transshipment service for Russian tankers coming from Varandey (Staalesen, 2016) but this situation did not last and the flows went back to Murmansk. In order to maintain an activity independent from exogenous economic factors and from raw materials, Kirkenes focused on the development of the Baltic railway (Staalesen, 2018a). This railway is supposed to link the extreme north with Berlin, providing a new service for containers through the north (Staalesen, 2018b). To do so, the project is to build a railway linking both cities with a tunnel under the Gulf of Finland.

The American strategy seems to be close to the Norwegian, with the will to place Alaskan ports as future hubs in prediction of the use of the NSR and/or the NWP as transit lanes (Portlet, 2019). However, the port infrastructures development is quite low compared to the other Arctic states.

Iceland appears as a potential challenger and is betting on the opening of the Transpolar Sea Route in order to position its ports as potential hubs for goods coming from Asia and dedicated to Europe or America (Ómarsson, 2010).

Regarding Greenland, the ice conditions and the distance between each community shape the ports to be mainly focused on supply. Moreover, some ports may not be accessible during a part of the year (Borch et al., 2016), making the use of airplanes mandatory. However, the port of Nuuk benefited from a 50% capacity increase (Mac Gwin, 2017). As explained by Mac Gwin (2017), this project is part of a bigger one, including airport facilities and the integration of the Royal Arctic Line (RAL) activities. According to Pahl and Kaiser (2018), most of the port in this area are small or very small ports, with low draft, except for Nuuk and Kangaamiut with 12,5 m and 17 m depth respectively.

The potential evolution of the Arctic ports

As explained by Monios, Wilmsmeier, & Ng (2019) and stressed by Rodrigue and Notteboom (2010), the position of a port within a network is not steady and the Arctic ports do not shirk this rule.

As explained previously, we can consider that two types of ports co-exist in the Arctic: ports dedicated to the supply of communities and ports focused on the export of raw materials. Looking at the way Canadian communities are supplied and how Russian ports in the western part are already organised, it appears that some ports posit themselves as second-tier hubs (Monios, Wilmsmeier, & Ng, 2019). This organization is determined by external parameters such as ice conditions that impose the use of specific vessels. These vessels are costlier to build and operate, and with a lower loading capacity than vessels used in the tempered waters (Mulherin et al., 1996). Moreover, these vessels lose manoeuvrability while sailing in tempered waters. Hence, the creation of regional hubs appears as a solution to optimize the transportation of goods.

Numerous announcements have been made by private and public stakeholders. Each country places at least one port as a potential Arctic hub. Some participants, such as Iceland, bet on the use of the Transpolar Route (TPR) by the Chinese to ship containers to Europe and Asia. This lane would avoid the cost of Russian icebreakers by sailing though the international Arctic waters.

On the Russian part, Novatek announced the creation of a regional hub for the transshipment of LNG produced by the LNG plant in the Yamal Peninsula (Staalesen, 2018c) in the sub-arctic port of Bechevinka in the Kamchatka Peninsula. In the western part, the LNG sealift has been shipped directly to the port of Zeebrugge and Montoir. Yet, the possibility of a transshipment has been tried with success in a Norwegian fjord, managed by Tschudi (owner of Kirkenes port) (Staalesen, 2018a). Based on the Kola Peninsula, Murmansk is clearly the main regional hub of this area, as explained in chapter (Chapter 10), for the export of crude oil coming from Novy port, Varandey terminal and the offshore platform of Prirazlomnoye. In order to maintain its dominant position, Murmansk developed a Free Trade Zone (FTZ) and has been developing a supply of cruise ships with a 72-hour free visa for visitors. Yet, the cruise service may remain a low economic layer for the ports in regards of raw materials. However, the FTZ is considered as a strategic tool for the ports development. Competing with Murmansk, Arkhangelsk is a secondary regional hub, hence the implementation of a FTZ may provide a strong economic development to this port and the dredge of the port would make of Arkhangelsk a deepwater port, a sine qua non for its future development (Louppova, 2018)

On the other side of the border, in Norway, Kirkenes, which knew economic development thanks to the mine of Sydvaranger, is looking at various options. As explained above, one of them relies on the potential investment in the Baltic railway which would increase its hinterland and loading capacity. Yet, this project is partly conditioned by the use of the NSR as a transit lane and by the huge investment it represents. The use of Kirkenes as a transshipment hub is more feasible in a short-/mid-term option. Kirkenes has already been used by Lukoil for the transshipment of crude oil coming from Varandey before being handled in Murmansk and the success of the ship-to-ship LNG transshipment in a Norwegian fjord can be an opportunity for Kirkenes. Considering that the cruise vessels are not the main activity of Kirkenes, the implementation of a FTZ would support the economic activities related to hydrocarbons industry and to the potential Baltic railway (Chapter 11).

The biggest island of the Arctic area, Greenland has the same gamble as Iceland. However, at the opposite of the volcanic island, they face very limited port infrastructures. Borch et al. (2016) considered this issue as a consequence of the low density of population. As Iceland, Greenland is betting on the ice melting for transforming itself into a potential Arctic hub and continuing mineral exploration (Borch et al., 2016). The general downward trend of the ice already provided the possibility to access Ulissat all year long in recent years. Yet, the presence of ice represents an important risk for navigation as in any other part of the Arctic, and the size of Nuuk Port, smaller than its competitors, may represent a strong challenge for the port. However, part of the development of Nuuk can be to lean on the cruise industry.

On the North American continent, the scattered communities and the development of extraction sites led to the setting up of 18 ports. We could quote the case of Iqaluit that planned to become a deepwater port. According to Aarluk Consulting, Gartner Lee Consulting and Anderson (2005), dredging this port would provide a competitive service to fishing and cruise vessels. Moreover, its situation at the limit of the Northwest Passage would place this port as the hyphen between the Arctic and the tempered waters.

In the USA, the ports along the Arctic are closer to the nomination of oil terminals. They are managed by private stakeholders and dedicated to the exportation of raw materials coming from their oil fields. The only port in Alaska that can be a hub is Anchorage, which can be considered more as a sub-Arctic port. Yet, as explained in chapter (Chapter 11), Dutch Harbor, Kodiak Island, Anchorage and Valdez already have a Free Trade Zone, but because Anchorage can be perceived as being at the gate of the Arctic.

Conclusion

Arctic ports are considered as highly strategic for Arctic states at different levels. They fulfil economic, social and strategic requirements. Besides, the way they are organised reflects the general strategy of the state. The Russian port system is clearly made for the exportation of raw materials. The Norwegian port of Kirkenes is looking for a second breath and trying to develop its hinterland and provide a transshipment services to Russian companies. Iceland and Greenland are, till now, using their ports for fishing, supply of communities and cruise activities but are waiting for an ice-free Arctic to posit themselves as international hubs for containerised cargo. Canadian ports are the only one with Russia to own a complex port system made of exportation ports and second-tier hubs. The aim is twofold: suppling communities and easing the exportation of crude oil and minerals. Finally, the USA seems to be out of the competition, except if we look at the sub-Arctic ports.

From a prospective vision, the next step seems to be the creation of Arctic hubs to optimise the management of cargo. Here again, all coastal states are racing, yet Russia seems to be the leader compared to the other countries, thanks to the exploitation of the raw materials in the western shore of the Russian Arctic. Besides, if all the other countries have projects in process, they are until now projects and are mainly conditioned by the ice conditions, the will of maritime companies to use this shipping lane and the way to fund them.

This analysis is not doomed to provide a general vision on the way the different Arctic ports of one system interact. Yet, future analysis could dig deeper on the geographic position of such system and their capacity to generate output at a lower cost.

References

Aarluk Consulting, Gartner Lee Consulting & Anderson, C. (2005). *Strategic plan for the Iqaluit deepwater port project.* Retrieved from www.tunngavik.com/documents/publications/2005-08-00%20Iqaluit%20Deepwater%20Port%20Strategic%20Plan.pdf

Alix, Y., (sous la direction) (2018). *Prospective maritime et stratégies portuaires.* Caen: Editions EMS. Mai 2018. 288p.

Alix, Y., & Guy, E. (2007). Pour une reconsidération des critères d'attractivité territoriale: le cas des projets d'implantation de terminaux portuaires méthaniers au Québec. *Organisations et Territoires, 16*(2 & 3), 115–122. Université du Québec à Chicoutimi.

Alix, Y., & Lacoste, R. (sous la direction) (2013). *Logistique et transport des vracs.* Caen: Editions EMS. Juin 2013. 526p.

Association Internationale Ville et Port. (2018). Next Generation. 16ème Conférence mondiale de l'AIVP. Québec. Canada. 11 au 14 juin 2018.

Association Internationale Ville et Port (2008). *Portcities 13:28 GMT.* 285p.

Bennett, M. (2014). North by northeast: Toward an Asian-Arctic region. *Eurasian Geography and Economics, 55*(1), 71–93, doi:10.1080/15387216.2014.936480

Bird, J. (1971). *Seaports and seaport terminals.* London: Hutchinson Press.

Boorstin, D. (1988). *Les découvreurs.* Editions Robert Laffont. Paris; 2 vol. 1024p.

Borch, O. J., Andreassen, N., Marchenko, N., Ingimundarson, V., Gunnarsdóttir, H., Iudin, I., Petrov, S., Jakobsen, U., Dali, B. (2016). *Maritime activity in the high north: current and estimated level up to 2025: MARPART Project Report 1.* Lieu ? éditeur ?

Braudel, F., (1963, 2013), *Grammaire des civilisations.* Flammarion. Collection Champs histoires. 752p.

Buchet, C. (2004). *Une autre histoire des océans et de l'homme.* Robert Laffont. Paris. 220p.

Corlay, J. P. (1998). Facteurs et cycles d'occupation des littoraux. In A. Miossec, (Ed.), *Géographie humaine des littoraux maritimes* (pp. 97–170) (Sous la dir.). Paris: CNED-SEDES.

Csonka, Y., & Schweitzer, P. (2014). *Societies and cultures: Change and persistence. Arctic human development report.* Retrieved from https://rafhladan.is/bitstream/handle/10802/9093/AHDR_chp_3.pdf?sequence=4

Daudet, B. (2015). *Métropoles portuaires africaines. Note prospective et stratégique.* Association Internationale Ville & Port. 30p.

Daudet, B., & Alix, Y. (2012). Gouvernance des territoires ville-port: empreintes locales, concurrences régionales et enjeux globaux. *Revue Organisations & Territoires, 21*(3), 41–54.

De Oliveira, G. F., & Cariou, P. (2011). A DEA study of the efficiency of 122 iron ore and coal ports and of 15/17 countries in 2005. *Maritime Policy & Management, 38*(7), 727–743.

Didenko, N. I., & Cherenkov, V. I. (2018). Economic and geopolitical aspects of developing the Northern Sea Route Arctic: History and Modernity IOP Publishing IOP Conf. Series: *Earth and Environmental Science, 180*(2018), 012012. doi:10.1088/1755–1315/180/1/012012

Doyon, J. F., Lasserre, F., Pic, P., Têtu, P. L., Fournier, M., Huang, L., & Beveridge, L. (2016). Perceptions et stratégies de l'industrie maritime de vrac relativement à l'ouverture des passages arctiques. *Géotransports, 8*, 5–22.

Farré, A. B., Stephenson, S., Chen, L., Czub, M., Da, Y., Demchev, D., Efimov, Y., Graczyk, P., Grythe, H., Keil, K., Kivvekä, N., Myksvoll, M., O'Leary, D., Olsen, J., Pachithran, A. P., Petersen, E., Raspotnik, A., Ryzhoc, I., Solski, J., Suo, L., Troein, C., Valeeva, V., Van Faury, O. (2015, August). Risk management in the Arctic from an underwriter's perspective. In *Proceedings of the IAME 2015 Conference, Kuala Lumpur, Malaysia, August* (pp. 23–27).

Fedi, L., Faury, O., & Gritsenko, D. (2018). The impact of the Polar Code on risk mitigation in Arctic waters: a "toolbox" for underwriters? *Maritime Policy & Management, 45*(4), 478–494.

Fischer, A. (1963). Les ports maritimes. Essai de classification. *L'Information Géographique, 27*(3), 105–114.

Frolov, I. E. (2015). Development of the Russian Arctic zone: Challenges facing the renovation of transport and military infrastructure. *Studies on Russian Economic Development, 26*(6), 561–566.

Grosdidier de Matons, J. (1999). *Droit, economie et finances portuaires.* Paris: Presses de l'Ecole Nationale des Ponts et Chaussées.

Grosdidier de Matons, J. (2012). *Les concessions portuaires.* Fondation SEFACIL. Caen: Ed. EMS.

Gritsenko, D., & Efimova, E. (2017). Policy environment analysis for Arctic seaport development: the case of Sabetta (Russia). *Polar Geography, 40*(3), 186–207.

Gritsenko, D., & Kiiski, T. (2016). A review of Russian ice-breaking tariff policy on the Northern Sea Route 1991–2014. *Polar Record, 52*(2), 144–158.

Gunnarsson, B. (2013). The future of Arctic marine operations and shipping logistics. www.chnl.no/publish_files/Ch_2_Gunnarssons_Paper.pdf.

Harsem, N. Ø., & KnutHeen, A. E. (2011). Factors influencing future oil and gas prospects in the Arctic. *Energy Policy, 39*(2011), 8037–8045. doi:10.1016/j.enpol.2011.09.058.

Hislaire, L. (1993). *Dockers, corporatisme et changement.* Transport Actualités GEP Communication.

Humpert, M. (2014). Arctic shipping: An analysis of the 2013 Northern Sea Route season. *The Arctic Institute*, 1–14.

IES Report State Institute of Energy Strategy. (2010). *Energy strategy of Russia for the period up to 2030. Institute of energy strategy.* Retrieved from www.energystrategy.ru/projects/docs/ES-2030_(Eng).pdf

IMO. (2014). Resolution MSC 385 (94) of 21 November 2014 and Resolution MEPC 264 (68) of 15 May 2015, International Code for Ships Operating in Polar Waters (Polar Code). Retrieved from https://edocs.imo.org/Final Documents/English/MEPC 68–21-ADD.1 (E).doc

Kaiser, B. A., Pahl, J., & Horbel, C. (2018). Arctic ports: Local community development issues. In N. Vestergaard, B. Kaiser, L. Fernandez, & J. Nymand Larsen (Eds.), *Arctic marine resource governance and development. Springer polar sciences.* Springer: Cham.

Kiiski, T., Solakivi, T., Töyli, J., & Ojala, L. (2016). Long term dynamics of shipping and icebreaker capacity along the Northern Sea Route. *Maritime Economics & Logistics.* doi:10.1057/s41278-016-0049-1

Kitagawa, H., Izumiyama, K., Kamesaki, K., Yamaguchi, H., & Ono, N. (2001). *The Northern Sea Route, the shortest sea route linking East Asia and Europe.* Tokyo: Ship and Ocean Foundation.

Klimenko, E. (2014). Russia's evolving Arctic strategy. Drivers, challenges and new opportunities. *SIPRI Policy Paper.* Stockholm International Peace Research Institute.

Lasserre, F. (2018). Kirkenes, bout du monde norvégien ou place commerciale transfrontalière? Illustration de l'effet frontière. *Regards géopolitiques – Bulletin du Conseil québécois d'Études géopolitiques, 4*(2), 19–28.

Louppova, J. (2018, June 18) Russia to build a new deep-sea port in the north. *Port Today.* Retrieved from https://port.today/russia-build-new-deep-port-north/

Mac Gwin, K. (2017, September 27). Newly opened Greenland port facility "a milestone" for the country as it works to improve its sea and air ties to the other countries. *High North News.* Retrieved from www.highnorthnews.com/en/new-nuuk-port-facility-open-business

Mulherin, N. D., Eppler, D. T., Proshutinsky, T. O., Farmer, L. D., & Smith, O. P. (1996). *Development and results of a Northern Sea Route transit model* (No. CRREL-96-5). Hanover, NH: Cold Regions Research and Engineering Lab.

Ng, A. K., Andrews, J., Babb, D., Lin, Y., & Becker, A. (2018). Implications of climate change for shipping: Opening the Arctic seas. *Wiley Interdisciplinary Reviews: Climate Change, 9*(2), e507.

Ómarsson, S. A. (2010). *An Arctic dream: The opening of the Northern Sea Route: Impact and possibilities for Iceland* (Doctoral dissertation). Bifröst University, Island.

Pahl, J., & Kaiser, B. A. (2018). Arctic port development. In *Arctic marine resource governance and development* (pp. 139–184). Springer, Cham.

Pelletier, J. F. (2014). *Marine transportation North of the 55th parallel report* (T8080–120253). Ottawa: Public Works and Government Services, Canada.

Portlet. (2019). *Alaskan deepwater sea ports to support trans – Arctic shipping.* Retrieved from https://portlets.arcticportal.org/u-s-alaska/227-alaskan-deepwater-sea-ports-to-support-trans-arctic-shipping

Malone, K. G. (2018). 'We are free:' Churchill celebrates return of train service with prime minister. *Canada's national observer* (November 2nd). Retrieved January 4 from https://www.nationalobserver.com/2018/11/02/news/we-are-free-churchill-celebrates-return-train-service-prime-minister

Miossec, A. (1998). *Les littoraux, entre nature et aménagement.* Paris. Sedes.

Monios, J., Wilmsmeier, G., & Ng, A. K. Y. (2019). Port system evolution – the emergence of second-tier hubs, *Maritime Policy & Management, 46*(1), 61–73.

Pahl, J., & Kaiser, B. (2017). Arctic Port development. In N. Verstergaard, B. A. Kaiser, L, Fernandez & J, Nymand Larsen (Eds.), *Arctic marine resource governance and development. Springer, springer Polar Sciences* (pp. 139–184). doi:10.1007/978-3-319-67365-3_8

Pelletier, J. F., & Guy, E. (2012). *Évaluation des activités de transport maritime en Arctique canadien. les Cahiers scientifiques du transport. No 61/2012* – Pages 3–33. JEL: R41, R48

Ragner, C. L. (2000). *Northern Sea Route cargo flows and infrastructure – present state and future potential* (FNI report, 13, 2000).

Roa Perera, I., Peña, Y., Amante García, B., & Goretti, M. (2013). Ports: definition and study of types, sizes and business models. *Journal of Industrial Engineering and Management (JIEM), 6*(4), 1055–1064.

Rodrigue, J. P., & Notteboom, T. (2010). Foreland-based regionalization: Integrating intermediate hubs with port hinterlands. *Research in Transportation Economics, 27*(1), 19–29.

Sarrabezoles, A., Lasserre, F., & Hagouagn'rin, Z. (2016). Arctic shipping insurance: towards a harmonisation of practices and costs?. *Polar Record, 52*(4), 393–398.

Serry, A. (2011). Dynamiques du transport maritime en Baltique orientale. *Territoire en mouvement Revue de géographie et aménagement. Territory in movement Journal of geography and planning*, (10), 36–48.

Sevunts, L. (2017). China's Arctic road and Belt gambit. *The Barents Observer*. Retrieved October 3, from https://thebarentsobserver.com/en/arctic/2017/10/chinas-arctic-road-and-belt-gambit

Smirnova, O. O., Lipina, S. A., Kudryashova, E. V., Krejdenko, T. F., & Bogdanova, Y. N. (2016). Creation of development zones in the Arctic: methodology and practice. *Arctic*, (25), 129.

Sokolov, V. (2013). *The Russian Arctic strategy 2020*. Retrieved from www.star.nesdis.noaa.gov/star/documents/meetings/Ice2013/dayOne/Sokolov_Russian.pdf

Staalesen, A. (2016). Very good cooperation with Lukoil. *The Barents Observer*. Retrieved January 21, from https://thebarentsobserver.com/en/2016/01/very-good-cooperation-lukoil

Staalesen, A. (2018a). Barents town envisions Arctic hub with link to China. *The Barents Observer*. Retrieved February 6, from https://thebarentsobserver.com/en/arctic/2018/02/barents-town-envisions-arctic-hub-link-china

Staalesen, A. (2018b). Finland says new Arctic railway should lead to Kirkenes. *The Barents Observer*. Retrieved March 9, from https://thebarentsobserver.com/en/arctic/2018/03/finland-says-new-arctic-railway-should-lead-kirkenes

Staalesen, A. (2018c). New Arctic transshipment hub is built in former submarine base. *The Barents Observer*. Retrieved May 18, from https://thebarentsobserver.com/en/industry-and-energy/2018/05/new-arctic-transshipment-hub-built-former-submarine-base

Têtu, P. L., Pelletier, J. F., & Lasserre, F. (2015). The mining industry in Canada north of the 55th parallel: a maritime traffic generator?. *Polar Geography, 38*(2), 107–122.

Tianming, G., Zabelina, K., Erokhin, V., & Ivolga, A. (2017 September 11). *One belt one road and Northern Sea Route: Perspectives and risks for China to participate*. Conference "Collaboration between China and Russia: One Belt One Road Initiative". Moscow.

USGS. (2008). *Circum-arctic resource appraisal: Estimates of undiscovered oil and gas north of the Arctic Circle*. Retrieved from https://pubs.usgs.gov/fs/2008/3049/fs2008-3049.pdf

Vigarié, A. (1995). *La mer et la géostratégie des Nations*. Paris: Economica. 432p.

Vigarié, A. (1983). *Le navire, le port et la ville*. Transports et mutations actuelles. Paris: Sedes.

Vigarié, A. (1979). *Ports de commerce et vie littorale*. Paris: Editions Hachette. 495p.

World Ports. (2019). Alaska, United States: Satellite Map of Ports. Retrieved January 5 from, www.worldportsource.com/ports/USA_AK.php

Zelentov, V. V. (2012). Development of Arctic transportation in Russia. *Asia-Pacific Journal of Marine science & Education, 2*(2), 9–16.

10 Analysis of the Russian Arctic port system using AIS data

Olivier Faury, Yann Alix, Arnaud Serry,
Ronan Kerbiriou and, Jean-François Pelletier

Introduction

Ports are essential to the development of Arctic shipping. Their numbers and density are strategic factors for the development of the Northern Sea Route (NSR). From the underwriters' point of view, they render navigation along the Russian shore safer. They are, also, part of the geopolitical strategy of Russia aimed at reinforcing its sovereignty on this area. Finally, and it is the point we will focus on during this chapter, the Russian Arctic ports are the gateways for the production of the mines and oil and gas fields.

The Russian economy is highly dependent on raw material exports, more precisely, on oil and gas. Europe accounts for 80% of Russian hydrocarbons exports. Yet, Russia faces three issues: the first is the fact the pipeline has to cross Belorus and/or Ukraine to reach their final customer. The second is the remoteness of the oil and gas fields and the last is the age and the cost of the Transneft network.

For many years after the USSR collapsed in 1991, most of the port infrastructures were abandoned and the flow of cargo decreased, but in recent years the investments dedicated to ports have renewed. The Rosmoport Report (2013) places the development of the Arctic at the core of the Russian strategy.

The western part of the Arctic basin is the most exploited area and is the wealthiest part of the Russian shore. This area regroups the largest ports such as Murmansk, Arkhangelsk, Sabetta and Novy and has benefited from most investments, with various objectives. Ports such as Murmansk and Arkhangelsk appear as regional transshipment hubs for hydrocarbon exportation. Others, such as Sabetta or Novy, are presently dedicated to exporting the oil and gas production from their respective hinterlands.

If these ports appear to be disconnected, this chapter demonstrates that they are highly connected to each other. Much more, the Russian Arctic ports act as in a broader system, dedicated to sustaining the Russian economy. Murmansk is the gateway for this port system and is intrinsically linked to both Russian and foreign ports.

The chapter begins with a short literature review and goes on to examine present and future flows. Our objectives are to demonstrate the existence of a Russian port system, to analyze the way it functions and to provide a prospective vision of this port system's development.

Literature review

The Russian part of the Arctic has been subject to numerous analyses focusing on its shipping attractiveness (Faury & Cariou, 2016), profitability and renewal of the fleet of icebreakers (Gritsenko & Kiiski, 2016; Bukharin, 2006) and on port development (Ragner, 2000; Kitagawa, 2001). The renewed interest for this region is explained by the ice melt (Comiso, 2012), the oil and gas reserves located within this region (Grigoriev, 2015; IES report, 2010; Thorez, 2008) and the numerous investments planned and realized by public and private stakeholders (Fadeev et al., 2011) in order to reach the target of cargo loaded defined by the Russian government (Rosmoport Report, 2013).

The harsh conditions impose the implementation of special infrastructures at a higher cost. Thus, to make these investments profitable, a minimum flow of cargo is required, as stated by the Arctic Council report (2009).

Different types of flows are planned to augment present traffic volumes, including transit and intra flows. While the actual volumes anticipated for each type of trade are different (Lasserre & Têtu, 2017), further port development is required so as such volumes can be attained.

Ragner (2000) claims the low number and density of ports is the main reason for the under exploitation of the NSR as a transit lane. However, ice thickness and extent are a constraint on the development of the NSR. Most cargo transported along the NSR originates from oil and gas fields located in remote areas. Additional constraints include the draft of ports (Figuereido & Cariou, 2011). The harsh climate and the permafrost inevitably enhance the capital costs of infrastructures (Salameh, 2009).

The presence of ice along the Russian shore requires the use of icebreakers or polar-class vessels (IMO, 2014). This technical requirement, related with the geographical constraints, imposes a limit to vessel size, thus, the loading capacity of such vessels is lower than those commonly used in warm waters (Mulherin et al., 1996). This parameter may have an impact on the transportation cost of a crude oil barrel, whose breakeven price is already higher compared to other parts of the world.

Aware of the strategic importance of port development for the Russian economy, numerous articles have been drafted with a different scope from one scholar to another. Governance (Gritsenko & Efimova, 2017), output capacity, the safety aspect of the port (Search and Rescue ports), their social impact and their connection with their hinterland are among the main topics analysed (Bambulyak et al., 2015a,b).

Few academic studies of different Russian ports consider them as part of a global system dedicated to the exportation of raw materials. Most studies look at each port and focus on the investments made at each location. None consider the existing ports as a means of providing a more efficient service to export the raw materials and their connectivity within a world network.

We use the concept of system developed by Cetin and Cerit (2010) and Von Bertalanffy (1972), defining system as a group of elements interacting with each other and with their environment. Moreover, a system can change in time, becoming a dynamic system. In the field of transportation, Rodrigue (2017) defined transport **systems** as the support and drivers of mobility. They are composed of infrastructures, modes and terminals, enabling individuals, institutions, corporations, regions and nations to interact and function.

According to Cetin and Cerit (2010) and Von Bertalanffy (1972), two sorts of system exist: the open and the closed system. The former has permeable frontiers with a supra system; whereas a closed system has permeable frontiers. Cetin and Cerit (2010) also consider that a system is defined by five elements: the performance of the system, its environment, its resources, the components and the management of the system.

The development of the Russian Arctic ports is considered as the cornerstone of the Russian Arctic strategy (Energy Strategy of Russia for the period up to 2030) (hereafter IES, 2010). If we apply these definitions to the Russian Arctic ports as the components of the system, their performance is assessed via their capacities to export the oil and gas from their remote and harsh environment, posing challenges to their governance. Besides, if we consider the investments made in previous years, this system can be considered as a dynamic one, constantly evolving with the implementation of new projects aimed at increasing its potential output.

An analysis based on Automatic Identification System (AIS) data

AIS data

The Automatic Identification System (AIS) is a system designed to monitor ship movements that was made obligatory by the International Maritime Organization (IMO) in 2004. AIS presents various advantages for maritime transportation actors: improvements in safety as well as progress in the management of fleets and navigation. The data acquired from AIS systems also constitute a new means of information for the maritime community, or the wider public (L'évêque, 2016).

The broadcasting of AIS data in real time makes a tangible contribution to the scientific community (Serry, 2017). This data was first used for works based principally on the subject of security or on coastal spaces. Subsequently it has spread to many other fields including international maritime law, physics, signal processing, geopolitics and others. One of the most fruitful areas of research is in the analysis of shipping networks. "Thanks to the availability of AIS data, it is possible to identify, quantify and map navigation lanes of vessels" (Le Guyader et al., 2011). Examples include the study of vessel behavior due to meteorological circumstances for improved emissions estimation (Perez, 2009) and analysis of the voyage times for a population of ship movements (Mitchell & Scully, 2014).

The method used here involves a spatial analysis within a geographical information system (GIS) combined with a database server, that makes it possible to reconstruct each vessel's trajectory in such a way as to identify the navigation lanes then to match the daily traffic in its temporal and quantitative dimensions. It is then possible to analyze whole maritime networks. Our platform (CIRMAR) receives, decodes, cleans, stores and analyzes AIS messages. Data is collected on the port of destination, the navigation status, the draft of the ship and ETA (estimated time of arrival). In this way it is possible to identify the maritime networks. Vessel movements were analyzed for 2017.

Results of AIS data study in Russian Arctic ports

Figure 10.1 clearly shows that the traffic is concentrated on a handful of ports: Sabetta, Varandey, Arkhangelsk and Murmansk. The main node of the network is Murmansk which has the highest number of ports calls in 2017 (1 656) and is the only one connected to all the other ports of the region. Therefore, Murmansk appears as a regional hub port.

Regional flows are strongly dominated by the "Murmansk-Varandey" connection with "Murmansk-Arkhangelsk" occupying a secondary linkage. The other links of the network are clearly smaller.

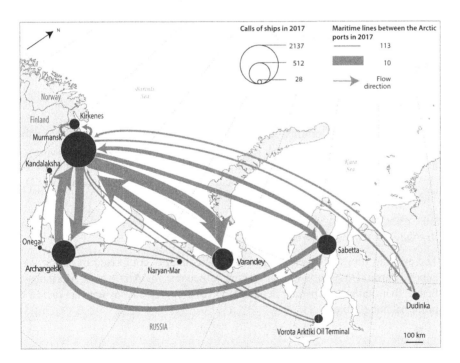

Figure 10.1 Maritime network in the western Russian Arctic (2017)

Source: Authors (2018) based on HIS

We have excluded the Prirazlomnoye extraction profile from our analysis since the research is focused on ports. Moreover, the flows coming from Prirazlomnoye are transshipped in Murmansk.

Murmansk and Varandey

The two-way flows of cargo between these two ports are made up of crude oil coming from the Lukoil and Rosneft production sites (via its new subsidiary Basneft). In 2017, 8,2 Mt of crude oil were shipped in Varandey and transshipped in Murmansk.[1] There is a potential for this trade to grow further since the output capacity of Varandey is 12 Mt per year (Bambulyak & Frantzen, 2009).

Sabetta and Murmansk

Because of the Yamal LNG plant, the trade between Sabetta and Murmansk is earmarked for becoming the bigger flow. The year 2017 saw the beginning of the LNG plant production and the flows of goods between both ports were made up of 7,99 Mt of LNG, and the LNG Project 2 will augment the flows. The main structure of the project is built within the Kola Bay and shipped directly to Ob Bay. Even before the completion of the second plant, Sabetta shall be able to export 16,5 Mt of LNG per year. There is therefore a potential for output to increase as high as 30,7 Mt by 2020 and 50 Mt by 2030.[2] However, some of this future production from the LNG plant will be shipped to Zeebrugge when the ARC7 ships used by NOVATEK and its partners are not able to sail directly to Asia (mainly during winter).

The Vorota Artiki oil terminal

The Vorota Artiki oil terminal ships crude oil coming from Gazpromneft, a subsidiary of Gazprom. The 5,5 Mt shipped come from the Novoportovskoye oil field via a 105 km pipeline. The transshipment takes place in the Kola Bay on the "UMBA", a 300 000 dwt Floating Production Storage and Offloading (FPSO). The total output may grow to 8 Mt per year.

Arkhangelsk and Murmansk

The existing flows between these two ports is mainly comprised of tanker and general cargo. Both ports are competing to become the Arctic hub. Murmansk, thanks to its natural deepwater depth and its ice-free status today appears to be the principal hub (Table 10.1).

Dudinka and Murmansk

The cargo leaving Dudinka for Murmansk is the production of Norilsk Nickel company. Staalesen (2017) emphasizes the importance of Murmansk for the

Table 10.1 Number of vessels per type from Murmansk to Arkhangelsk in 2017

Vessel type	Number of type of vessel
Tanker	58
General Cargo	35
Bulk Carrier	2
Tug	2
Heavy-load Carrier	1
Icebreaker	1
Limestone Carrier	1
Work and Supply Ship	1
Total General	101

Source: Authors (2018)

Table 10.2 Number of vessels per type from Arkhangelsk to Murmansk in 2017

Vessel type	Number of type of vessel
Tanker	63
General Cargo	30
Tug	2
Bulk Carrier	1
Heavy-load Carrier	1
Icebreaker	1
Work and Supply Ship	1
Total General	99

Source: Authors (2018)

exportation of nickel while the investment planned is expected to enhance the number of shipments between both ports.

Figure 10.1 sheds light on the way the transportation of raw materials (LNG, crude oil and nickel) is managed between the Yenissei River and the Kola Peninsula. It indicates the central position of the port of Murmansk. The numerous investments have exploited the deep water and the absence of ice to make Murmansk the main transport hub. Coupled with the determination of the Russian government to develop this area, this has created a regional port system dedicated to the exportation of raw materials and contributing to the development of the Russian economy.

The dissymmetry stressed in Figure 10.1 can be explained by the nature of Murmansk and its Arctic hub position towards other Russian Arctic ports. Varandey, with its 63 and 58 tanker calls, is clearly at the top of the ports.

The dominance of European ports is coherent in that 80% of Russian raw materials are dedicated to the European market.[3] If the presence of Australia can appear as strange, looking at the EIA report, Oceania and Asia are the second largest customer for Russia. Moreover, the presence of Australian ports on both sides of the Figure 10.3 demonstrate that it is not exceptional.

MURMANSK: THE EXISTING HUB

Murmansk is the connecting point between the Arctic ports and the rest of the world port network. The flows coming in and out of Murmansk reveal the numerous links with non-Arctic ports. The ships involved are mainly tankers (Figure 10.2).

Figure 10.2 reveals a typology of port connections with Murmansk:

- Numerous domestic relations with other Russian ports both inside the Arctic and also in the Baltic Sea (St. Petersburg, Ust Luga) or Black Sea (Novorossiysk). The reason for these national connections is the lack of pipelines connecting the oil fields to these ports.
- Important relations with European ports clearly are concentrated on the Northern Range and dominated by Rotterdam. This concentration of flows with the Northern Range can be explained by the demand for Russian oil.
- More distant relationships with Australian, South-American and Asian ports.

To complete this analysis, we focus on ports having at least one tanker call linking Murmansk with other ports in 2017 (Figure 10.2). A strong relationship between Murmansk and European ports appears in both directions, indeed the Murmansk maritime foreland seems to be centered on western Europe. The second port region in relation with Murmansk covers Baltic ports the others areas being Southern Europe, and Black Sea. Due to oil and gas fields exploitation, Sabetta, Varandey and Arkhangelsk also appear in Figure 10.2.

Figure 10.3 provides a more detailed analysis of the main ports in relation with Murmansk. Because of the tanker shuttle, Varandey is the port with the most

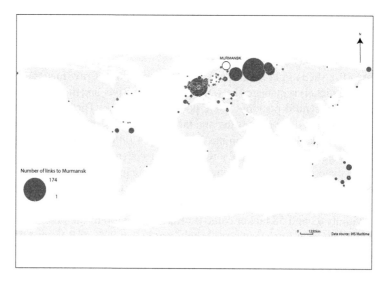

Figure 10.2 Tanker connections from or to Murmansk

ORIGIN

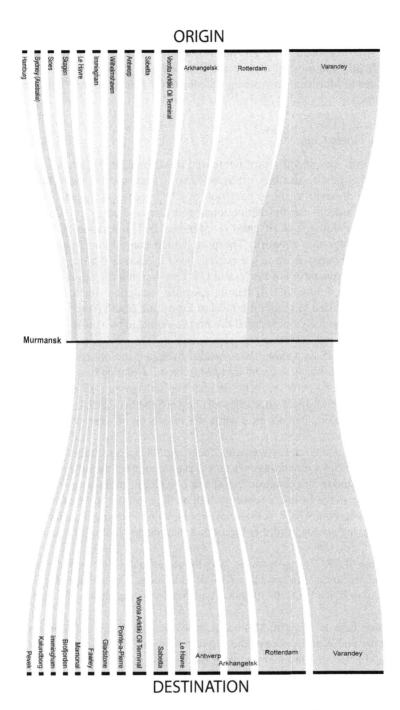

Hamburg
Sydney (Australia)
Sines
Skagen
Le Havre
Immingham
Wilhelmshaven
Antwerp
Sabetta
Vorota Arktiki Oil Terminal
Arkhangelsk
Rotterdam
Varandey

Murmansk

Pevek
Kalundborg
Immingham
Brofjorden
Mamonal
Fawley
Gladstone
Pointe-a-Pierre
Vorota Arktiki Oil Terminal
Sabetta
Le Havre
Antwerp
Arkhangelsk
Rotterdam
Varandey

DESTINATION

Figure 10.3 Murmansk: Origins and destinations of tanker ships in 2017

Source: Authors (2019)

regular liaisons with Murmansk. Rotterdam comes in second place and this can be easily be explained by the fact that Rotterdam manages mainly incoming flows of crude oil,[4] and most of them come from Russian ports. The third port highly connected to Murmansk is Arkhangelsk due to the existing shuttle between those two ports.

Sabetta: the next hub

Sabetta is a very specific port compared to Murmansk (Figure 10.4). One of the reasons lies on the fact it has been built from scratch over the last few years and doomed to the exportation of LNG coming from the LNG plant. Sabetta is a deep-sea multi-functional port constructed in the Ob estuary of the Yamal Peninsula (Gritsenko & Efimova, 2017) because of its new role in the gas logistics network. The port, which can remain open year round despite the extensive ice in the region, is a key element in the Russian strategy for the exportation of the Yamal LNG project and the development of the Northern Sea Route. It will handle specially designed Arctic LNG carriers shipping liquefied gas from the field to European, South American and Asian markets. When fully operational the port is expected to handle 30 Mt of LNG per year.

Regarding AIS data exploitation results, Sabetta is mainly connected by some direct links to Arkhangelsk and not to Murmansk, a relation that is due to a regular shuttle service between them.[5] Its external linkages are different to those of Murmansk (Figure 10.3) since ships arriving in Sabetta originate from diversified origins (Port Said, Qindao, etc.) while the vessels go on after calling at ports in northern Europe.

Due to a commercial agreement, Zeebrugge[6] has a special place within this system. Until now, Zeebrugge was used as a hub for the transshipment of modules dedicated to the construction of the LNG plant in Sabetta, explaining its third place. In the future, Zeebrugge will be the next hub for the transshipment of LNG when the ARC7 vessels will not be able to reach the Asian market in winter/spring season, and it is forecasted to manage 107 transshipments every year.[7]

The use of ARC7 vessels saw in 2018 the entrance of Chinese ports into the top ports related to Sabetta and the arrival of Montoir as a French hub for the transshipment of LNG. In 2020, 30 calls are planned for a maximum of 6 million tons per year.[8]

To conclude on this part, Murmansk appears as the main transshipment hub in the Arctic and is at the core of the Russian strategy. To support this assumption, we highlighted that the main ports in the Russian part of the Arctic are almost exclusively (Varandey, Dudinka) or strongly (Sabetta, Arkhangelsk) linked to Murmansk, which in effect makes it the main exit port of the area for now. However, in the future, the situation may slightly change. Sabetta, with the investment made by Novatek and its partner in an ARC7 fleet, shall be able to export its production directly to the final customer without using Murmansk as a transshipment

ORIGIN

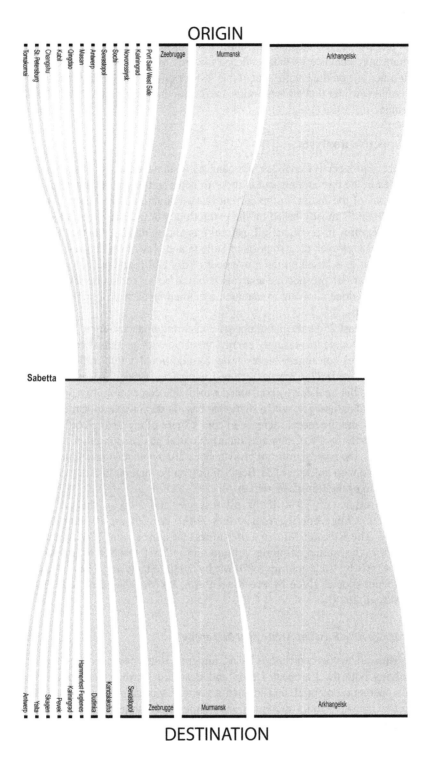

Tomakomai · St. Petersburg · Changshu · Kati · Qingdao · Masan · Antwerp · Sevastopol · Sochi · Novorossiysk · Kaliningrad · Port Said West Side · Zeebrugge · Murmansk · Arkhangelsk

Sabetta

Antwerp · Yalta · Skagen · Pevek · Kaliningrad · Hammerfest Fuglenes · Dudinka · Kandalaksha · Sevastopol · Zeebrugge · Murmansk · Arkhangelsk

DESTINATION

Figure 10.4 Destinations and origins of ships calling in Sabetta in 2017

Source: Authors (2018)

hub. Regarding Arkhangelsk, the implication of Polytechnology within its development may enhance its independence towards Murmansk and connect the port to another one on the Pacific side of the NSR or directly to the Pacific coast. Thus, we could consider that all these ports are for the time being part of the Murmansk foreland.

Prospective analysis

The art of prospective analysis first consists in an accurate use of the knowledge acquired in the past and present in order to better anticipate and participate in the evolutions of the future. In the current known situation, the Russian Arctic port development is mostly based on the extraction, storage and exportation of three main categories of products: oil, natural gas and minerals. Whether Murmansk, Arkhangelsk or even the two ports of Sabetta and Novy Port, the vast majority of tonnage traffic is based on the movement of dry and liquid bulk carriers. Yet we assumed that our prospective analysis is based on an economic scenario with a Brent barrel price allowing to maintain a defined level of profitability for hydrocarbons fields.

Over the past 25 years global energy consumption according to the BP Report (2018) has become increasingly energy intensive with an almost constant growth in the volumes consumed, representing an additional 5 000 million tons of oil equivalent since 1992 to reach a total of 13 400 Mt of oil equivalent in 2017. More than 60% of the total energy consumed worldwide comes from two primary fossil fuels, oil and natural gas, with a share that has not declined despite the progress of renewables and the recent increase in coal's share of the total global energy mix (driven mostly by PR China and India). Natural gas consumption increased by 3% in 2017, the most significant growth since 2010 with an outstanding growth in China alone with an extra of 31 Bcm (billion cubic meters) in 2017, compared to the 26 Bcm of the European market.

The Arctic, with 10% of the oil reserves and 29% of the gas reserves, represents a huge energy reserve that is the core of the Russian economic strategy. The Russian Ministry of Natural Resources and Environment estimates that the annual shipping volume on the Northern Sea Route will reach 40 to 43 Mt by 2020 and up to 70 Mt by 2030 (Staalesen, 2017). According to a recent speech given by President Putin, 80 Mt is to be targeted by 2024 (Staalesen, 2018b).

Towards a new Russian Arctic port hierarchy

The Russian Arctic coastline is being integrated into new maritime circulation involving both the European Union and East and North Asian markets thanks to its energetic potential, and in such a context Murmansk is acting as both an "Arctic Gateway" and a strategic transshipment and storage port. The same perspective seems to occur for Arkhangelsk and its advanced port of Severodvinsk, despite greater geographical constraints.

The Yamal Peninsula: the nerve center of future Russian Arctic maritime traffic

Oil and gas volumes are proven with already 4 million tons of LNG exported from Sabetta and just over 4 Mt of Novy oil (Antonov, 2018). Proven natural gas reserves in South Tambey Field are estimated at 926 billion cubic meters with processing capacity that allows for the planned export of 17 Mt annually by 2021 (Krotov, 2018). The size of Russian and international investments (1,4 billion USD confirmed) indicates that there is a perceptible territorial and strategic development of the entire Ob estuary.

Rosatomflot's commitment to maritime assistance with nuclear icebreakers is another strong signal of an integrated logistics chain of services dedicated to the Ob Estuary (Corkhill, 2018). In addition to land-based industrial infrastructures (Antonov, 2018), services linked to maritime intercontinental transportation are already operational.

In addition, the delivery of 15 giant Arctic ARC7 tankers by the end of 2020 confirms the commitment of Russian and international specialized operators to plan for the long term on the Yamal complex. These YamalMax ships have a length of 300 m and a carrying capacity of 172 600 m³ or 96 765 tons (Clarksons, 2018). Above all, with their classification by Bureau Véritas and the Russian Maritime Register, they can navigate in 2,1 m of ice (Marex, 2014). These ships are the result of a true international Arctic collaboration as they were designed by the Finnish firm Aker Arctic and built by the South Koreans of Daewoo Shipbuilding & Marine. The YamalMax ships have been chartered on a long-term basis (45 years) by four companies (Sovcomflot, Teekay, Dynagaz and Mitsui O.S.K. Lines) to ensure a business model that will serve stakeholders and shareholders, from initial extraction to maritime export to transshipments, up to and distribution in various dedicated European and Asian terminals.

From a western Europe perspective, two mid-size ports, Zeebrugge in Belgium and Montoir in France, have already positioned themselves as LNG transshipment hubs directly connected to Yamal extending the Russian port system for the next 20 years. For Montoir, the initial contract signed in 2015 with Elengy (Engie Group) covers 1 Mt of LNG per year for 23 years from 2018. For the Russian company Novatek Gas & Power, this means quickly repositioning specialized ARC7 icebreakers directly on Yamal and thus optimizing the maritime use of specialized naval capacity (Corkhill, 2018). In Zeebrugge, a Belgian port that has made natural gas its main strategic asset, the contract signed in 2015 also covers a 20-year strategic transshipment with the Belgian group Fluxys LNG. In close collaboration with the port authority, Fluxys LNG plans to increase the processing capacity of the LNG terminal to 8 million tons per year (Port Authority of Zeebrugge, 2019).

An original logistics scheme articulates such strategic development on the two western European ports which are keen to impose themselves as bridgeheads of the Russian Arctic LNG transshipment. During winter time, very expensive Yamal-Max LNG vessels use the European ports solution for strategic transshipment onto cheaper conventional LNG carriers, which mainly supply Asia markets via the Suez Canal. During the summer period, ARC7 polar-class LNG carriers can autonomously serve Asian markets directly via the Northern Sea Route. Shortening transit time and optimizing transport capacities allow regular supplies from the Sabetta facilities, reinforcing de facto this new fixing point which is a crucial component of Russian Arctic strategy according to Moscow.

The relationships between Beijing and Moscow rely on energy supplies and the consolidation of a strong and workable joint commitment. The ongoing Chinese energy policy and the development of LNG terminals on the shores of mainland China should intensify the planned connection between Sabetta and the demand requirements absorption capacities of the huge Asian markets. Beijing continues to approach Moscow to develop future contracts that would consolidate the Arctic sea route and especially the links between Russian Arctic infrastructure and their Chinese counterparts (Xin, 2018). Thus, 86% of the total amount of Yamal LNG output (secured by long-term contracts) will be shipped to Asian markets (Bogoyaslensky, 2018).

The case of the energy-industrial developments of the Yamal Peninsula constitutes an excellent illustration of the strategic consolidation of a future complex. Built from scratch, the Yamal ecosystem could become an attractive zone combining energy extraction means and the development of a future Arctic city, able to attract and fix high value-added services like R&D.

The development of entirely new or updated ports may provide safer navigation within the Arctic. The willingness to invest heavily in both airports and railroads will further support the consolidation of a unique area with multiple options to connect domestic and international Arctic business opportunities (Gunnarsson, 2017). This territorial projection is as much a matter of market pragmatism that supports Russian and international energy investors as it is a matter of a much more strategic prospective on the part of the Russian state; the latter setting a dense and productive development for decades in the heart of territories that are almost empty of population.

The gas field exploited in the Yamal Peninsula could represent up to 15% of the world's proven reserves and this implies a very long-term strategic projection with land planning and development that goes far beyond maritime lines and their port terminals. Various infrastructure projects shall connect the peninsula to the rail and road domestic networks, especially toward the western most populated areas of the country. For instance, the Russian conglomerate Transstroy wants to connect the port of Sabetta to gas reserves of Bovanenkovo by investing almost 2 billion USD (*Journal de la Marine Marchande*, 2018). An estimated extra 5 billion USD would be needed to complete the railway connectivity with the huge project of the Northern Latitudinal Railway Route (Gunnarsson, 2017). An integrated vision would probably propose a network of services eventually connecting Sabetta, Arkhangelsk, Murmansk, Moscow, St. Petersburg and the central/western European grids.

In the long term, the connection of Arctic port terminals to the east-west Trans-Siberian-Eurasian axis must also be borne in mind, especially as railways already exist and are currently being upgraded to meet the increasing number of regular services. Block trains filled with manufactured products connect the Chinese, Central Asian, Russian and European markets on a daily basis, and realistic Russian projections target a Eurasian train every hour on their territory in the foreseeable future.

Murmansk – Arkhangelsk – Kirkenes: the new western Arctic port range?

The coming years should be crucial in the industrial and port development of Murmansk, which benefits as much from its nautical accessibility as from the improvement of land connectivity. Among an extended list of projects must be put into light the confirmed major investments driven by the very powerful SUEK group (*Siberian Coal Energy Company*). A connection, via 46 km of new dedicated rail lines, will be assured to the future Lavna coal terminal in Kola Bay (Staalesen, 2018a). Scheduled for the end of 2019, the first phase of port expansion will make it possible to export 9 Mt of coal, mainly from the huge deposits in the Kusbass region. In the long term, i.e. by 2023, the Murmansk port region should offer 25 Mt of capacity through the extension of the Lavna site's capacity and the modernization of Murmansk's long-established facilities (capacity increased to 8 Mt).

The most important factor in this projection on dry bulk exports from the Murmansk port complex is the crucial role of rail-based connectivity. In such industrial-port projects, logistics and land transport are essential structuring elements and SUEK is working with the State Transport Leasing Company and the Federal Agency for Maritime and River Transport to project an integrated infrastructure, from mining area of extraction to port superstructures (RC Perret, 2013). Other structuring projects have already been confirmed at the new Lavna site, such as a fertilizer export terminal with a nominal export capacity of 6 million metric tons (Staalesen, 2018a).

Arkhangelsk appears as the other regional hub, even if it does not benefit from the same geographical advantages as Murmansk. However, with the dredging of the port as a part of the Arkhangelsk Transport Hub (ATH) project it will create a deepwater port and help make the historic port of Arkhangelsk into a major industrial complex accessible all year round.

The construction of a deepwater port 55 km from the city, financed by the Chinese group Poly Group, would accept 14,5 m draft vessels. Besides, the ATH is based on its geographical and logistical proximity to a huge amount of Russian traffic potentials, starting with the Kusbass coal deposits (in direct competition with Lavna's expansion projects previously commented at Murmansk).

The deepwater port also aims to become a strategic oil and gas supply hub for future Russian exploration and exploitation identified further to the east. The greater geographical proximity to Murmansk is being advanced with a view to a more agile and cost-effective logistics offer, as is already the case with the developments at Sabetta or the Prirazlomnoye platform north of the port of Varandey. For ATH, what is at stake is that a significant part of planned flows must stop at the Arkhangelsk facilities to meet a competitive combination between value-added logistics services and captive traffic opportunities from the extraction and storage of mining raw materials (distances and reduced costs for massive rail pre-routing).

Uncertainty of the financing and development of the various rail sections of the Belkomur project (795 km of new track to connect the port of Arkhangelsk to Russian and trans-European transport corridors) could nevertheless constrain the optimistic prediction of handling 38 Mt of freight by 2035 (The Belkomur Project, 2019). It appears impossible to concretize the great potential of ATH without efficient rail connectivity, especially for dry bulk. Consequently, one of the keys to port and industrial ATH success lies in the ability to consolidate and coordinate all the sections of the projected rail system forecasted into the Belkomur Project.

An addition to the Murmansk and Arkhangelsk ports complex is the port of Kirkenes in Norway on the immediate margins of the western Russian border (Figure 10.5). On the outskirts of the exclusive hinterland of Murmansk, Kirkenes targets more or less the same functions and markets as Russian port competitors. The heart of the Norwegian port infrastructure project is based on the future Arctic Corridor Railway Project (ACR), which would link Kirkenes to Rovaniemi in Finland, a multimodal gateway to continue to Helsinki and furthermore the three Baltic countries up to Warsaw (*Arctic Corridor*, 2018). The ACR project is the backbone of an extensive transportation network known as the Barents Euro-Arctic Transport Network which would improve rail and road

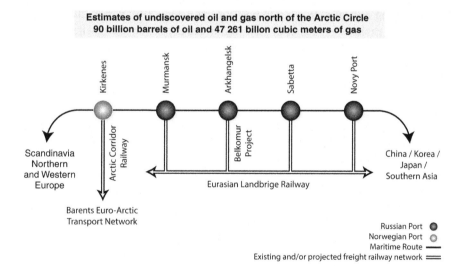

Figure 10.5 Prospective vision of the Arctic Range

Source: Alix (2018a)

connectivity between northern Europe, Scandinavia, the Baltic and the Russian existing grid.

From the Kirkenes perspective the mining potential of western Russia is combined with the natural resources located in northern Scandinavia (Lapland region in particular). Thanks to the future Arctic Railway, the deep-sea port Kirkenes complex will offer the shortest routes to export mining products from Kevitsa, Sakatti and probably Sokli (*Arctic Corridor, 2018*). Establishing connectivity with the Baltic Sea is supported by neighboring countries, and the project is divided into two parts for a total of around 500 kms and at an estimated cost of between 2,5 and €3 billion euros (Eilertsen, 2018a). Among the traffic potentials mentioned are Finnish forest reserves in Lapland and those located on the Russian side and easily "capturable" by efficient rail and logistics services.

Despite strong political commitment and willingness, some uncertainties remain with regard to the realization of such an investment by 2030 because the total volume of cargo expected and the business opportunities raised by the Northern Sea Route are still questioned (Eilertsen, 2018b). As the future facilities in Murmansk and Arkhangelsk claim, Kirkenes aims to be the first European port hub of the future Sino-Russian Polar Silk Road by locating on the shortest sea route between the western European market areas and the domestic Chinese market. For shipments from the Baltic/Western Arctic, the maritime connectivity from Kirkenes to the main consumption markets of China, South Korea and Japan are one-third shorter than the Suez route. The new western Arctic port range may be able to reduce time and expenses and include the three ports into some innovative supply chain patterns driven by Asian demand (Alix, 2018a).

Other avenues not to be neglected in future Russian Arctic port development

The exploitation of proven mineral resources including palladium, platinum, gold and diamonds will contribute to the probable future development of the Russian Arctic. In addition, it is claimed that 25% of world reserves of rare earth are potentially located in the Russian Arctic (Brigham, 2017), which means these remote territories might become an area of exploration, exploitation and export that would compete with markets that are currently not necessarily easy to exploit from a logistical and political point of view. These reserves of rare earth could justify the heavy financial commitment required to build up fully integrated land-based logistics infrastructure (Alix & Lacoste, 2013). A number of new greenfield port infrastructures could be involved serving the needs of extraction, transport and storage of mining volumes (Alix & Lacoste, 2013). The difficulty of linking port development with mining is that shipping infrastructure is dependent upon contractual conditions and the lifespan of the mines.

As the extent of ice in the Arctic retreats, this opens up a potential for fishery and fishing industry. An estimate of 10% of international fishing stocks could be found in Arctic waters according to various studies (Brigham, 2017). Although almost all of these future operations may be carried out by specialized ships requiring no land-based infrastructure, a string of small and medium-sized infrastructures could emerge in coming years along the Russian Arctic coast. The possible transformation of a huge amount of fishery resources could be used by the Russian central government to develop the as-yet uninhabited territories, particularly in the eastern part of the Russian Arctic, to supply the nearby important seafood consumption areas of Japan, South Korea and China.

Towards a future new string of pearls linking Russia and China?

It must be noted that Foreign Direct Investment combined with strong Russian commitments have been consolidated over the past ten years in several historical ports like Murmansk, Arkhangelsk and Vladivostok and much more recent infrastructures like Sabetta or Dudinka. These ports and a handful other focal strategic points constitute the backbone of a future Arctic port network that connects Asian, Scandinavian and European markets as demonstrated by AIS movement of commercial ships.

Secondary ports mostly located further east, such as Pevek and Tiksi or Provideniya, are becoming relay ports in the growing volumes shipped between the Yamal Peninsula and Northeast Asia. A fairly accurate picture emerges to the west of the Yamal Peninsula within a time horizon of ten years when the greatest opportunities could finally lie to the east of the peninsula, looking towards the immense consumption potential of China, Japan and South Korea.

Securing energy supplies is at the heart of projects in the three Asian countries, and global warming in the mid and long term could make direct maritime traffic between future industrial and eastern Russian port complexes and Asian economies a reality. From such a forward-looking perspective it is even possible that this Russian Arctic port chain could constitute a new logistics artery.

Conclusion

The Russian part of the Arctic Ocean is clearly at the core of the state strategy. The western part of the Russian coastline is a major source of oil and gas production. In order to exploit these resources and because of the harsh climate and remoteness of this area the government is implementing a port system.

This system comprises specialized ports dedicated to exportation of oil, gas or minerals and ports intended for transshipment. The necessity of transshipment hubs is due to the geographical constraints faced by ports limiting vessel size and to the climate conditions imposing the use of ice- or polar-class vessels with a higher cost and lower maneuverability within warm waters.

Our analysis stresses that while Varandey is the port that presently exports the highest volume of cargo, Sabetta, with the production coming from the Yamal LNG, will be the most important port of the system in terms of output. Shipments from both serve Murmansk. Murmansk is the main transshipment port for Russian Arctic cargoes and it is also connected to global markets thereby positioning Murmansk as an Arctic gateway.

However, if the "dominance" of Murmansk is well established, the situation may change in the future with the development of Kirkenes and the Baltic railway, the investments planned in Sabetta and the dredging of Arkhangelsk linked to the national network through the Belkomur railway.
The authors would like to thank the Fondation SEFACIL.

Notes

1 Staalesen. A. (2018). *Arctic seaports bustle as shipping on Northern Sea Route reaches new high, 18 janvier.* Retrieved from https://thebarentsobserver.com/en/arctic/2018/01/arctic-seaports-bustle-shipping-northern-sea-route-reaches-new-high.
2 Idem. www.ship-technology.com/projects/port-sabetta-yamal-peninsula-russia/.
3 Russia exports most of its crude oil production, mainly to Europe. EIA, 14 November 2017, www.eia.gov/todayinenergy/detail.php?id=33732.
4 Port of Rotterdam. (2016). *Facts & figures on the Rotterdam energy port and petrochemical cluster.* Retrieved from www.portofrotterdam.com/sites/default/files/facts-figures-energy-port-and-petrochemical-cluster.pdf?token=vHfZySB6.
5 https://belomortrans.ru/en/news/37-northern-delivery/224-launching-the-vessels-on-the-route-arkhangelsk-sabetta-arkhangelsk.
6 www.portofzeebrugge.be/en/news-events/zeebrugge-receives-first-lng-load-yamal.
7 www.portofzeebrugge.be/en/news-events/first-simultaneous-transshipment-yamal-lng.
8 www.meretmarine.com/fr/content/yamal-lng-elengy-realise-un-second-transbordement-montoir.

References

Alix, Y. (2018a). Routes of the future: shipping, corridors . . . and diplomacy. In *Prospective maritime et stratégies portuaires*. Caen: Editions EMS. 253–274.
Alix, Y. (2018b). Global supply chain dynamics & international value chain networks: General overview to feed a prospective discussion about the future of the Baltic Sea. *Concluding remarks of the International Symposium Baltic Sea: Gateway or Cul-de-sac?* Lithuanian Maritime Academy. 16th to 18th May, Klaipeda. Lithuania.
Alix, Y., & Lacoste, R. (2013). *Logistique et transport des vracs.* Collection Les Océanides de la Fondation SEFACIL. Caen: Editions EMS. 534p.
Antonov, Y. (2018). *Challenges of Artic shipping in Russia. 13th Artic shipping summit.* December 5th & 6th. Hamburg: Germany. 26p.
Arctic Corridor. (2018). *Arctic railway – Rovaniemi Kirkenes.* Retrieved from https://arcticcorridor.fi
Arctic Council report. (2009). *Arctic Marine Shipping Assessment 2009 Report. Akureyri (Iceland): Arctic Council* (Protection of the Arctic marine environment). Retrieved December 15, from www.arctic.noaa.gov/detect/documents/AMSA_2009_Report_2nd_print.pdf
Bambulyak, A., & Frantzen, B. (2009). Oil transport from the Russian part of the Barents Region. *Akvaplan Niva,* The Norwegian Barents secretariat.
Bambulyak, A., Frantzen, B., & Rautio, R. (2015a). *Oil and transport from the Russian part of the Barents Region. 2015* Status Report. The Norwegian Barents Secretariat.
Bambulyak, A., Sydnes, A. K., Milakovic, A. S., & Frantzen, B. (2015b). *Shipping oil from the Russian Arctic: Past experiences and future prospects. International conference on Port and Ocean Engineering under Arctic conditions (POAC)* June 14–18, Trondheim Norway.

Bogoyaslensky, V. (2018). Yamal LNG: A unique international project implementing in the Russian Arctic. *The Arctic Herald, 1*(24), 24–29.

BP Report. (2018). *BP statistical review of world energy*. June 2018. 54p.

Brigham, L. W. (2017). Challenges for Arctic marine transport and the Northern Sea Route. *6th International Arctic Shipping Seminar. Institute of Arctic Logistics*. Busan, December, 14th. 2017.

Bukharin, O. (2006). Russia's nuclear icebreaker fleet. *Science and Global Security, 14*, 25–31.

Cetin, C. K., & Cerit, A. G. (2010). Organizational effectiveness at seaports: A systems approach. *Maritime Policy & Management, 37*(3), 195–219.

Clarksons. (2018). *Clarksons database*. Retrieved from www.clarksons.net/portal

Comiso, J. C. (2012). Large decadal decline of the Arctic multiyear ice cover. *Journal of Climate, 25*(4), 1176–1193.

Corkhill, M. (2018). Norway transhipments to ease Yamal LNG winter logistics challenges. *The LNG World Shipping*. Retrieved October 29, from www.lngworldshipping.com/news/view,norway-transhipments-to-ease-yamal-lng-winter-logistics-challenges_55692.htm

Eilertsen, H. (2018a). Finland keeps pushing to establish an Arctic railway. *High North News*. April, 11.

Eilertsen, H. (2018b). When will Europe's Arctic railway be built? That could depend on cargo volumes. *Arctic Today*. Retrieved August 29, from www.arctictoday.com/will-europes-arctic-railway-built-depend-cargo-volumes/

Fadeev, A. M., Cherepovitsyn, A. E., & Larichkin, F. D. (2011). Industrial potential of the Murmansk Oblast in the hydrocarbon resources development of the Arctic shelf. *Development Strategy*. UDC 338.45:622.276(470.21) Retrieved from http://esc.vscc.ac.ru/article/224/full?_lang=en

Faury, O., & Cariou, P. (2016). The Northern Sea Route competitiveness for oil tankers. *Transportation Research Part A, 94*(2016), 461–469. Retrieved from http://dx.doi.org/10.1016/j.tra.2016.09.026. 0965–8564/ 2016 Published by Elsevier Ltd.

Figuereido De Oliveira, G., & Cariou, P. (2011). A DEA study of the efficiency of 122 iron ore and coal ports and 15/17 countries in 2005. *Maritime Policy & Management: The Flagship Journal of International Shipping and Port Research, 38*(7), 727–743, doi:10.1080/03088839.2011.625989

Grigoriev, M. (2015). Oil and gas: Russian arctic offshore. *11th Annual Arctic Shipping Forum 24–26* February 2015 / Finland, Helsinki.

Gritsenko, D., & Efimova, E. (2017). Policy environment analysis for Arctic seaport development: The case of Sabetta (Russia). *Polar Geography, 40*(3), 186–207.

Gritsenko, D., & Kiiski, T. (2016). A review of Russian ice-breaking tariff policy on the Northern Sea Route 1991–2014. *Polar Record, 52*(2), 144–158.

Gunnarsson, B. (2017). Arctic shipping from Norwegian perspective. *6th International Arctic Shipping Seminar. Institute of Arctic Logistics*. Busan, December, 14th. 2017.

IES Report State Institute of Energy Strategy. (2010). *Energy strategy of Russia for the period up to 2030. M.: Institute of energy strategy, 2010*. 172 p. Retrieved from www.energystrategy.ru/projects/docs/ES-2030_(Eng).pdf

IMO. (2014). *Resolution MSC 385(94) of 21 November 2014 and resolution MEPC 264(68) of 15 May 2015, international code for ships operating in polar waters (*polar code*)*. Retrieved November 10 from, https://edocs.imo.org/Final Documents/English/MEPC 68–21-ADD.1 (E).doc

Le Journal de la Marine Marchande. (2018). Une zone d'intérêts multiples. Dossier spécial Arctique: de nouvelles routes maritimes ? N°5091. *Journal de la Marine Marchande*, Novembre, 14–25.

Kitagawa, H., Izumiyama, K., Kamesaki, K., Yamaguchi, H., & Ono, N. (2001). *The Northern Sea Route, the shortest sea route linking East Asia and Europe.* Tokyo: Ship and Ocean Foundation.

Krotov, I. (2018). Yamal LNG Project: Production & transport plan. *6th international Arctic shipping seminar. Institute of Arctic logistics.* Busan, December, 14th. 2017.

Lasserre, F., & Têtu, P. L. (2017). Extractive industry: The growth engine of Arctic shipping? *Whole of Government through an Arctic Lens*, (pp. 239–268).

Le Guyader, D., Brosset, D., & Gourmelon, F. (2011). *Exploitation de données AIS pour la cartographie du transport maritime. M@ ppemonde, 104*(2011.4). Retrieved from http-mappemonde

L'évêque, L. (2016). Les signaux AIS pour la recherche géoéconomique sur la circulation maritime. In A. Serry & L'évêque (Eds), *Short sea shipping, myth or future of regional Transport I* (pp. 189–210). Caen: EMS.

Marex, S. (2014). SCF Sovcomflot: Yamalmax LNG Tanker Steel-Cutting. *The aritime Executive.* Retrieved September 30, from www.maritime-executive.com/corporate/SCF-Sovcomflot-Yamalmax-LNG-Tanker-SteelCutting-2014-09-30

Mitchell, K. N., & Scully, B. (2014). Waterway performance monitoring with automatic identification system data. *Transportation Research Record, 2426*(1), 20–26.

Mulherin, N., Eppler, D., Proshutinsky, T., Proshutinsky, A., Farmer, L. D., & Smith, O. (1996). *Development and results of a Northern Sea Route transit model* (CRREL Research Report 96–3). US Army Corp. of Engineers, Hanover, NH.

Perez, H. M. (2009). Automatic Identification Systems (AIS) Data Use in Marine Vessel Emission Estimation. *18th Annual International Emissions Inventory Conference*, Baltimore.

Port Authority of Zeebrugge. (2019). Retrieved from www.portofzeebrugge.be/en/port-authority

Ragner, C. L. (2000). *Northern Sea Route cargo flows and infrastructure – present state and future potential* (FNI report, 13, 2000).

RC PERRET. (2013). *Turning orders into reality. A summary of Russian 2030 transport strategy 2030.* 7p.

Rodrigue, J. P. (2017). *The Geography of transport systems* (4th Ed.). New York: Routledge, 440 pages. ISBN 978–1138669574.

Rosmoport Report. (2013). *Strategy of development of sea port infrastructure of Russia up to 2030.* Retrieved December 10, from www.rosmorport.com/seastrategy.html

Salameh, M. G. (2009). Russia: An aspiring energy superpower with feet of clay. *Oil Market Consultancy Service.* Working paper for United States Association for Energy Economics.

Serry, A. (2017). Automatic Identification System (AIS) as a tool to study maritime traffic: The case of the Baltic Sea. In *Proceeding of the International Conference on Marine Navigation and Safety of Sea Transportation (Trasnav)*, Gdynia, Poland, June 21–23. doi:10.1201/9781315099132-2

Staalesen, A. (2017). New era starts on Northern Sea Route *The Barents Observer.* Retrieved December 8, from https://thebarentsobserver.com/en/arctic/2017/12/new-era-starts-northern-sea-route

Staalesen, A. (2018a). Biggest Arctic port ties future to coal. *The Barents Observer.* Retrieved November 21, from https://thebarentsobserver.com/en/ecology-industry-and-energy/2018/11/biggest-arctic-port-ties-future-coal

Staalesen, A. (2018b). It's an order from the Kremlin: Shipping on Northern Sea Route to reach 80 million tons by 2024. *The Barents Observer.* Retrieved May 15, from https://thebarentsobserver.com/en/arctic/2018/05/its-order-kremlin-shipping-northern-sea-route-increase-80-million-tons-2024

The Belkomur Project. (2019). *Belkomur.* Retrieved December 2 from, www.belkomur. com, © JSC Interregional Company Belkomur, 2007.

Thorez, P. (2008). La Route maritime du Nord. *Le Courrier des pays de l'Est*, (2), 48–59.

Von Bertalanffy, L. (1972). The history and status of general systems theory. *Academy of Management Journal, 15*(4), 407–426.

Xin, Z. (2018). First privately-run LNG port opens. *China Daily.* Retrieved August 11, from www.chinadaily.com.cn/cndy/2018-08/11/content_36746773.htm

11 Free Ports as a tool to develop the navigation in the Arctic

Alexandre Lavissière and Olivier Faury

Introduction

The Arctic region is a developing area of trade that recently benefited from better sailing conditions yet challenges still exist. Among them is the lack of port infrastructures which slows the potential of growth. Hence local governments look for new opportunities.

Today, oil and gas represent the majority of goods shipped from the Arctic region. Construction material for extraction facilities and supplies for the population amount for the rest of most flows (Humpert, 2014). As Lasserre and Têtu (2017) highlight, the Arctic has so far been mainly been an oil and gas deposit so far. Hence, ports of the area aim to load liquid bulk.

The Northern Sea Route (NSR) and the Northwest Passage (NWP) are the main shipping routes within the Arctic and are mainly used for destinational traffic (Doyon et al., 2016; Lasserre & Têtu, 2017).

The AMSA report (Ellis & Brigham, 2009) considered that the NSR needs to handle 40 million tons to be profitable. Regarding the global trend of goods shipped along the Russian coast, this goal appears to feasible. As an example, flow coming from the LNG plant on the Yamal Peninsula represents about 40% of the 40 million tons. Yet, regarding this area, Nalimov and Rudenko (2015) emphasize that a new system has to be found for a social and economic development of this region, raising the question of resource sustainability.

The economic development of the Arctic is based on hydrocarbon and mineral extraction fields and mines with a finite lifetime (Nalimov & Rudenko, 2015) and highly impacted by markets, which brings limits and risks to the Arctic routes. Moreover, fishery and tourism are only emerging sectors. Coastal states are, therefore, facing challenges of route sustainability due to the volatility of these markets. Thus, the potential next step in the development of the Arctic would be to develop a way to settle population and economic revenue and to obtain as much independence from the oil and gas industry as possible, as the United Arab Emirates did with Dubai or Sharjah (Jacobs & Hall, 2007) or southern Europe, with the use of heavy industrial complexes into transshipment container hubs (Ducruet, Itoh, & Joly, 2015).

The use of Free Zones (FZ), among other opportunities, could settle and sustain economic development of the area and act as a catalyst in the development of ports (Fedi & Lavissière, 2014). Around the world, 3 500 FZs employ 70 million people (Lavissière, Mandják, & Fedi, 2016). For instance, the isolated island state of Mauritius benefited from the creation of 64 000 jobs between 1971 and 1977 thanks to FZs. When successful, an FZ has a positive impact on both host region and international trade development (Baissac, 1996).

The topic of FZs remains however complex. Several types coexist with various goals (Lavissière & Rodrigue, 2017): production, import, transshipment, export, IT service, industry. As any business infrastructure, FZs, and especially free ports (FPs), serve the objectives of different actors: economic, social and environmental development for hosting states, profitability for investors and developers of the zone and business facilitation for operators (Lavissière et al., 2016).

FZs exist in most trading routes (Fedi & Lavissière, 2014), but are still at an early stage in the Arctic. The present chapter grounds its analysis on a prospective approach, aware that such a larger implementation requires large investment combined with the capacity for the Arctic to become a transit waterway.

As far as we know, until now, only the port of Murmansk has implemented an FZ. Besides, when dealing with the infrastructures and the economic development of the Arctic, numerous articles highlight the need to invest in icebreakers, the issue of port governance and the development of hinterland but not one, as far as we know, focuses on free trade, except for one thesis (Sorokina, 2014) that underlines this lack of FZ in the area and calls for more investigation on the topic.

Firstly, we define precisely what an FZ and more specifically what an FP is. Secondly, based on that precision, we analyze the context of the Arctic routes and their suitability for FPs. Thirdly, we present our prospective approach with three types of FP infrastructure that should emerge in the Arctic route and at its periphery.

A Free Port is a logistic Free Zone

The concept of FPs is almost as old as trade itself. Phoenicians, Romans and those Chinese of bygone empires developed concepts of storage exempt from taxes in their trade empires (Thoman, 1956). The number of FPs as well as the specificities of these zones developed historically with the several waves of acceleration of globalization of economies (Lavissière & Rodrigue, 2017) and a widening geographical range (Bost, 2010).

Since it has evolved over time and space, the concept of FPs can become confusing. First of all, the term FP tends to present a port which is free. In fact, an FP is both narrower than a port, since it is in general only one part of the port area that is free; and larger than a port, since it is sometimes a free airport or free river port. Second, there is no universal definition of what an FP is. It is up to the discretion of each state to define an FP in its legal provision. The Kyoto Convention on Customs is the only international text mentioning FZ (Fedi & Lavissière, 2014). Third, terminology of FPs covers different realities and sometimes more than one concept is regrouped under the same denomination. In fact, Bost (2010) listed 45 different names related to the concept of FZs, resulting from path dependency as well as marketing purposes of the developers of FZs.

The historical perspective provides a sense of what the essence of the concept of FPs is. A good example is American Congressman Emanuel Celler's use of an analogy to define what is at stake in the use of an FP and, therefore, the main function of the FP for an international company, the role of buffer: "A Free Trade Zone is a neutral, stockaded area where a shipper can put down his load, catch his breath, and decide what to do next" (Emanuel Celler quoted by Tiefenbrun, 2012).

Mc Elwee (1926, quoted in Thoman, 1956, 6), develops this idea with different steps and possible processes for goods within the FP.

> The modern FP is an area of a port separated from the customs area of a nation by a stockade. Ships may enter such a port, discharge, load, and depart without customs formalities. The goods may be stored, repacked, manufactured, and re-exported without customs formalities. Only when the goods pass the barrier to reach the consuming public of the country do they undergo customs revision and pay the necessary duty. A FP is a "Customs Outland" with the political boundary of a country.
>
> (Mc Elwee, 1926: 381)

However, the above definition focuses on the spatial aspects of the status by summarizing an FP as a 'Custom Outland.' A French statesman of Louis XVI, Charles Gravier, Count of Vergennes, already explained why a shipper could 'catch his breath' and the taxes mechanisms that enable this.

> A place where can be imported all merchandises, either foreign or domestic, and from where one can re-export them freely. Prohibitions and imposed duties to foreign merchandise would apply only in the case of some people willing to introduce merchandise subject to one or the other into the interior parts of the kingdom.
>
> (Lorot & Schwob, 1987: 11)

The FP is often defined as an area or a place, or a zone, or part of a larger area such as a port. This area is specific because it provides time as seen by Celler. The combination of these two dimensions lead to the 'buffer effect' of the FP, as this is an area that gives the supply chain time. The FP is seen as a tool for the management of time; it is meant to passively optimize logistics. However, while this characteristic is mentioned, it is never identified as the core of the definition, and this is the reason why scholars take Celler's remarks into consideration.

Following early attempts to define FPs by individuals, Thoman (1956) highlights the definitions provided by states in industrial Europe and then in the USA. The first one is a German definition that takes into consideration the separation of the port area and the FP. This definition is modern because it focuses on that part of the port that has custom extra-territoriality. This is the change from the concept of a wide FZ area, including the city, to a smaller area with a more functional concept of the FP. The French definition concentrates on the differences between the specific status of the FP and the interior of the country. The French approach reflects the vision of FP as a privilege after the French Revolution. Therefore, there is a complete freedom of operations whatever the origin of the merchandise as long as it does not enter the domestic area and compete with domestic companies. The Swedish definition provided by the author is more pragmatic and explains the role of regulation of the zone, but does not give any more clues to the essential nature of an FP other than that of a customs extra-territoriality useful for trade and industrial activities. On the contrary, the United States Tariff Commission definition provides a very clear summary of the concept as it is used for the Foreign Trade Zone system implemented in the USA. Finally, the author provides his own definition covering most of these concepts:

> A FZ may be defined as an isolated, enclosed, and policed area, in or adjacent to a port of entry, without resident population, furnished, with the necessary facilities for loading and unloading, for supplying fuel and ship's stores, for storing goods and for reshipping them by land and water; an area within which goods may be landed, stored, mixed, blended, repacked, manufactured, and reshipped without payment of duties and without the intervention of customs officials. It is subject equally with adjacent regions to all laws relating to public health, vessel inspection, postal service, labor conditions, immigration, and, indeed, everything except customs.
>
> (Thoman, 1956: 7)

After World War II, we observed the acceleration of globalization leads to a diversification of the types of FZs. We can also identify a global spread, starting with the US Foreign Trade Zone Development, the Shannon Airport example, and then the Asian Zones. Definitions and perspectives concerning FPs have changed during this period.

From this point, there is a distinction made between two main models of FZs. First the Model of Villefranche, based on the Middle Age cities that were exempt from taxes by local lords in order to attract trade in their kingdoms and therefore generate activities. The other model is the model of Piraeus that is based on the ancient port of Piraeus where goods to be re-exported were stored behind a wall and separated from goods to be shipped to Athens (Lavissière, 2014). The World Bank made the same distinction with the wide area zones that cover whole cities and small area zones they call Special Economic Zones.

For our present study, the first step consists in understanding what the different terms compiled by Bost (2010) refer to. From the 45 referenced, no more than a dozen are used by scholars and institutions to make their typologies. The other ones are declinations or local names. See the main terms in Table 11.1.

Some of the research reviewed for the present study states that there is only one reality on FZs (Figure 11.1). In this perspective, all of these terms would

Table 11.1 Table of the main acronyms

Acronym	Designated term
FP	Free Port
FZ	Free Zone
FTZ	Free Trade Zone
EPZ	Export Processing Zone
SEZ	Special Economic Zone
EZ	Enterprise Zone
IPZ	Industrial Processing Zone
SFZ	Single Factory Zone
FE	Free Enterprise
SZ	Specialized Zone

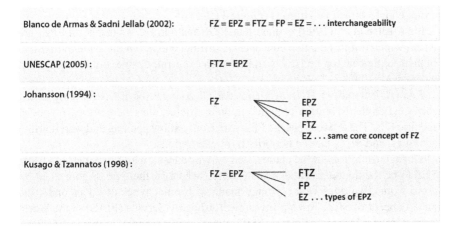

Figure 11.1 First typologies of Free Ports

be interchangeable, meaning the terminology refers to the same phenomenon (Blanco de Armas & Sadni Jallab, 2002). A UNESCAP research paper (Zengpei et al., 2006) approaches FTZs with the definitions provided by academic literature covering the concept of EPZs.

From another standpoint, Johansson (1994), states that they are different phenomena, but that they refer to the same concept. In addition, Kusago and Tzannatos (1998) explains that all zones are related to EPZs. As a consequence, the two researchers only developed their study on this concept. While their study implicitly means there are differences, these differences are not however explicitly defined or explored in the cited work.

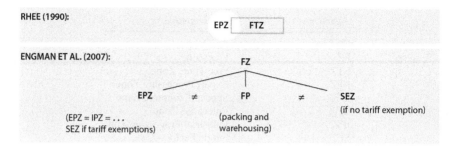

Figure 11.2 Rhee's and Engman et al.'s typologies

Some literature reviewed proposes typologies and classifications of types of zones or at least a terminology referring to zones. These typologies can be arranged into three main groups (Figure 11.2).

First, Rhee et al. (1990) explain that FTZs include EPZs but not all EPZs are FTZs, which implies the two concepts are distinct and not in the same dimension. In fact, for this author, an FTZ is an EPZ with exporting feature policies as quoted by Madani (1999).

Second, Engman et al. (2007) consider all zones to be EPZs (as long as the zones match the definition provided in their article); then there are two types of specific FZs. These two types are FPs, which only allow packing and warehousing activities, and SEZs that do not offer tariff exemptions.

Third, the majority of the authors, led by World Bank working papers, consider SEZ to be the main term to designate an FZ, whatever the type (Figure 11.3). In these works, we observe a typology made with other types of zones under the meta-concept of SEZ. Foreign Investment Advisory Service (FIAS) of the World Bank Group (Akinci & Crittle, 2008) makes a distinction between FTZ, EPZ, enterprise zone, Freeport, single factory EPZs, and specialized zones. These are all grouped under the broader concept of SEZ. We also note that the term, *Free-ports*, is defined as a large zone including tourism resorts, resorts facilities, on-site residences, etc. This is a different definition than usual as well as a different spelling.

According to FIAS approach, two World Bank studies led by Farole (Farole, 2011; Farole & Akinci, 2011) conserve the same typology and make it more precise by merging single-factory EPZ and enterprise zones. These two terms are two ways to designate the same concept of a single company with a special economic regime outside a designated zone.

Bost (2007) makes the same distinctions (Figure 11.4), but takes a broader view. He acknowledges the existence of Free Trade Areas/Unions but excludes them from the FZ concept. He also excludes Urban FZs that have emerged in developed countries in the last few decades and added a more economic zone, comparable to an SEZ. This third type lies between EPZs; manufacturing-oriented

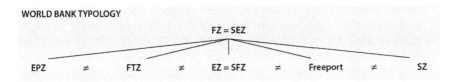

Figure 11.3 World Bank's typology

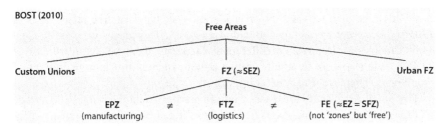

Figure 11.4 Bost's typology

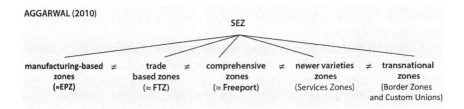

Figure 11.5 Aggarwal's typology

FZs and FTZs; logistic-oriented FZs; and finally, free enterprises, which are not zones.

With the same kind of distinction, Aggarwal (2010) creates a typology of zones depending on their functions (Figure 11.5). Under the SEZ concept therefore we find trade-based zones, manufacturing-based zones, comprehensive zones, newer varieties zones (mainly based on services), and transnational zones, on a border. He also excludes Customs Unions and enterprises zones from the SEZ concept.

Some different typologies of zones utilize a historical perspective to underline the appearance of one term which replaces or adds precision to another; some are more geographical, highlighting the various terms used from one country to another. A final distinction, from World Export Processing Zone Association (Wepza) and quoted by Farole (2011), differentiates zones by their size. This definition distinguishes between *wide area zones* and *small area zones* (more or less than 100km², and thus, fenced or not), which seems consistent because *wide area* zones refer to the *Freeport* definition as a wide area special economic zone and *small area zones* refer to EPZ and FTZ as defined by FIAS.

We therefore have different typologies, all of which use five or six of the 45 terms describing zones. Within these typologies, FP appear with two different spellings ('Freeport' and 'FP') and two very distinct meanings, one being a type of FTZ/EPZ similar to the Piraeus type and the other being a wide area zone, similar to the Villefranche type.

Our proposition for a typology, in order to analyze and propose prospective solutions for the Arctic situation and that would reflect the evolution of terminologies is found in Figure 11.6.

In this typology, we take into consideration all types of free areas, as Bost (2010) did, except we include the wide area zones. This means we classify Customs Unions and Urban FZs as different and separate; then, we identify two types of FZ, wide (large as an administrative region, such as in China or India) and small ones. This level is a structural level.

The Small Area Zones are divided into four types: manufacturing (EPZ), trade (FTZ), service (SFZ), and zones that are constituted by a single company (FE). This is a functional typology at this level.

In the literature reviewed, SEZ is the generic term. Only the Chinese use it for a different purpose (the Wide Area Zones); we consequently preferred to follow the main stream of classification and use SEZ as a synonym of FZ. These are choices to make because the same reality has several names and vice versa, several names cover the same reality.

Then, we included Custom Unions because they are often presented in the literature as a type of FZ. The purpose is mainly to highlight the distinction and through this major difference, discard them. We followed the same process for the inclusion of Urban Zones, although this could be discussed, since Bost (2007), for instance, includes them in his analyses of FZs.

FPs, however, do not appear in this typology, because historically, they were the only type of FZ (before the 20th century), and they have had a transversal function.

When we incorporate FPs into our typology, we can once again make a connection with the two main historical types we identified (Figure 11.7). We can also distinguish a transversal aspect of the concept of the FP.

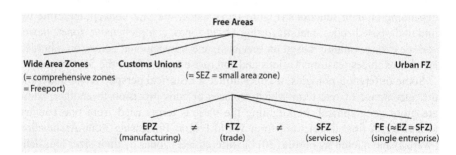

Figure 11.6 Typology of Free Ports

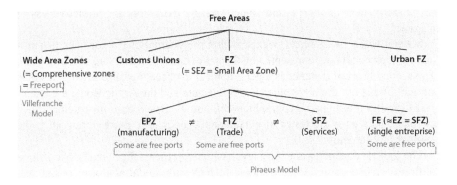

Figure 11.7 History of Free Ports

A Free Port (FP) reduces trade distances

The objectives of an FP depend on the actors involved in the infrastructure. Considering the state that created the FP, the objectives are at macro level. The FP is created in order to produce economic growth and create employment. For the private sector, the FP is a logistic cluster and as such it should provide premium quality service for the companies involved. This premium service includes logistics infrastructures, route connections, IT services, but also qualified workers, marketing services, and sometimes financial services. The FP is both helping to optimize logistics chains and reducing constraints to it (Lavissière, Fedi, & Cheaitou, 2014).

FPs achieve these objectives because they reduce frictions of international trade and specifically those related to crossing borders. Three main factors intervene in the process (Lavissière & Rodrigue, 2017). The first being the jurisdiction and regulatory system of the host country; because the stricter the border and/or domestic provision is, the more the FP will bring fluidity to the supply chain. The second factor is the clustering effect of the FP with not only logistic and warehousing services, but also supply chain services including door-to-door management of flows, tracking and tracing, customs facilitation, banking and marketing services as well as all the services that can bond actors of the port community and facilitate border crossing. The third factor is the orientation of flows, either sequential or multidirectional. This factor is intrinsically linked to the crossing of borders, because either the FP acts as a buffer in order to cross borders smoothly or it enables to incorporate added value in the supply chain, so as to cross other borders, without even having to cross the domestic border of the FP's host country.

In that sense, the FP reduces distances. In fact, the main goal of an FP for international operators is to reduce distances and then, as a consequence, this ability brings in companies, foreign direct investments, qualified employees, and added value, which aggregated represent the macro objectives of the host state. This is the attractiveness of the FP and sometimes, by extension, the attractiveness of the port.

Several levels of distances coexist within the international trade. The first distance is a physical one represented by the travel distance when cargos are shipped. The second level of distance is a geographical distance, because often a physical straight line is not the best route. The Silk Route and the Arctic Route are examples of routes that bypass geographical difficulties. Based on infrastructures such as roads, they ease the flows of persons and goods and, more importantly, the number of kilometers.

The logistic distance is the third level, which represents the human organization of flows. Transportation organizations, such as multimodal platforms or hub and spoke systems, help reduce the burden of transportation. Sometimes the shorter pathway is not the most direct one.

The fourth level is financial. Transnational firms optimize their global supply chains on a financial basis. Border frictions such as quotas, excise, customs, certificates of origin are considered in the process of designing the chain. Nodal points of international transports such as Dubai, Hong Kong and Singapore, are clusters in which high levels of services are provided to companies.

The last level is the business distance. More than financial optimization of flows, what is at stake in international trade is facilitation of interactions. Places such as Mauritius offer a business ability, enabling trade and diverting it from the usual route from Asia to Europe who benefit from the expertise of Mauritius companies in business network management (Mandják & Lavissière, 2014). Languages, cultural differences, and trade agreements are among the facilitating factors that save time and energy for transnational companies and create value for the supply chain. Reducing this distance is the ultimate goal of global supply chain managers.

FPs facilitate distance reductions, provide the possibility to firms and states to reach their social and economic development, thanks to the reduction of distance.

FPs act as a catalyst when embedded with local business networks (Mandják & Lavissière, 2014). Along major international trade routes FPs that offer such services flourish. Hence, the Arctic zone should see the implementation of new FPs. Yet, the difficulty to respect schedules hinders the transit of containers (Pelletier & Lasserre, 2011). The use of FPs as a buffer would avoid such an issue, thereby allowing to save time and money. Besides, Lavissière & Rodrigue (2017) explain that the next potential step in the evolution of FP would be their integration within a network of FZs.

Port system and maritime strategy in the Arctic

The lack of port infrastructure is the major constraint to the development of shipping in the Arctic. (Ragner, 2000; Lasserre & Têtu, 2017; Humpert, 2014; Ellis & Birgham, 2009; Kitagawa, 2000). The race between the Arctic states to capture projected flow and gain in geopolitical influence is, however, fierce and crucial for their development. Russia develops ports in the Kamchatka and Kola Peninsulas as potential hubs. Norway, supported by Finland, posits Kirkenes (Staalesen, 2018), whose mines collapse in direct competition with the Russian ports of the area. Iceland, thanks to its position at the exit of the Transpolar Sea Route and between the Americas and Europe, is a serious challenger (Ómarsson, 2010). Canada, which lost its main deepwater port in the Arctic in 2016 further to the closure of its Port of Churchill, is preparing its new polar strategy. In the Subarctic area, the USA with Dutch Harbor and Nome are working on benefiting from the opportunities provided by the Arctic. China and North Range countries, close to the Arctic gates, are also interested by the NSR and NWP.

The case of the Belkomur project and Arkhangelsk's port, funded by a Chinese company, is an example of the importance of hinterland for ports (Chernov, 2014) and social development. Hence, one of the main elements is the creation of value and the capacity to deliver goods to the population and to open up the region (Lasserre & Têtu, 2017).

Because ports in the Arctic primarily sustain the exportation of raw materials, the economic development of the Arctic is strongly associated with ports and their hinterland. Yet, the harsh climate conditions and the remoteness of some ports render complex and costly their implantation. Besides, an oil field or a mine is not perpetual. Basing the development of a region on this potential is quite hazardous in the long term.

The Arctic is surrounded by six countries: the USA, Canada, Iceland, Denmark (Greenland), Norway, and Russia. If they all consider the development of their Arctic coast as paramount, the development is unequal. The European part, with Norway and Russia, is well developed and subject to important investments. Besides, the majority of flows happen along their shores and implies their ports.

On the contrary, the western part of the Arctic does not have ports with nearly the scale of the European ones. Even if they are located in strategic areas, the important lack of basic infrastructures for some of them and the low level of population render economic development, and thus the implantation of an FZ, highly hypothetical according to us.

Russia

The Arctic development is strategic for the Russian government. The Russian part is a huge oil and gas deposit and most of the reserves are within the Exclusive Economic Zone of Russia. To support the exploitation of these resources, the federal government has implemented upgraded ports and increased their capacities. Besides, the connection of ports with their hinterland has been upgraded. Among the numerous existing projects, Murmansk, Arkhangelsk, and Sabetta mega project are at the core of the Arctic development Kinossian (2016) and should provide the possibility to transport 80 Mt along the Russian shore by 2025.

Murmansk is the port with the largest output of the area with 51,29 Mt of coal handled in 2017, an activity supported by a population of 295 200 inhabitants, that is slowly declining due to the lack of opportunity (Kinossian, 2016). It is also the only ice-free port all year long with an FZ: the Murmansk Transport Hub (MTH). The depth of the port allows the call of VLCC with 15 m draught (CHNL, 2018). The fact that Murmansk is ice free on a yearlong basis provides the possibility for vessels with no ice class to call in as in any other ports.

In order to counterbalance the loss of population, new investments are done to develop the port activity within the port and its hinterland. Regarding the port, the big investment is the implementation of the MTH which should give the possibility to Murmansk to reach 70 Mt per year. The implementation of such a project is vital for the economic development of the Murmansk Oblast. Besides, thanks to tax exemptions, more than 110 billion rubles were invested in the area, representing a 30% increase compared to 2016 and positioning the area as the sixth region for investment in Russia.

Arkhangelsk faces a population challenge with 351 300 inhabitants, possibly due to the lack of economic attractiveness and opportunities. Thus, the refurbishment of Arkhangelsk's port would create 9 000 jobs: 16% dedicated to the port itself and the rest between the various companies operating the port or working within the port.

If Arkhangelsk faces a general decrease of cargo handled (2,6 Mt in 2017), this situation may change with the investment of the Chinese company Polytechnology within the port and the Belkomur project. The aim being to affirm Arkhangelsk as a future container hub and to reach the target of 30 Mt imposed by the IES report (2010) by 2030, for a cost of 1,05 billion USD (Nielsen, 2017).

The Belkomur railway is one of the most important infrastructure projects related to the dredging of Arkhangelsk. According to Bambulyak and Frantzen (2009), the modernization of this 1 161 km railway, with 715 newly built kilometers, should cost around USD 16,5 billion and supply 22 Mt of cargo per year to Arkhangelsk and link Arkhangelsk to the rest of Russia and also to the European economic center, and hence is a key to sustain the economic development of the Republic of Komi.

If Murmansk and Arkhangelsk are benefiting from investments to upgrade their infrastructures, it is not the case of Sabetta built from scratch in order to export the LNG produced by the Yamal LNG, a joint venture between Novatek (51%), Total (20%), CNPC (20%), and the Silk Road Fund (9,9%).

The 27 billion USD investment was dedicated to the building of a port, an airport, and a railway connecting this port to the Russian network and its clients. Sabetta will export 36 Mt per year when both plants (LNG Plant and Arctic LNG 2) will be producing.

Because as stressed by Glukhavera (2011), an outdated railway may act as a bottleneck and hamper the economic development of the area, an update and construction of a 707 km railway is underway in order to connect the productions areas with the consumption territories to ease the supply of goods into the Yamal Peninsula.

The lack of repair yards along the NSR challenge the safety of navigation. Because of its remote position Sabetta may not be able to receive parcels for vessels damaged that called in the port, yet the railway shall solve this issue. This infrastructure will supply the cargo terminal for the population, ease its development and export of Polar-Ural minerals (after transformation, the minerals may be worth USD 1,5 billion). This railway will connect the Port of Novy dedicated to the exportation of crude oil extracted by Gazprom Neft (Gazprom's subsidiary).

The € 3 billion investments for this strategic railway come from a private-public partnership between Gazprom and a Russian railway national company. The SShKh consortium should start its construction by 2019 for completion in 2023, so as to load 24 Mt per year of mainly crude oil and LNG.

The Northern Latitudinal Railway appears as a game changer and eases exportation of raw materials and manufactured goods from this region.

Due to its oil and gas reserves, the Yamal Peninsula is strategic for the Russian economy. Besides, its position between Europe and Asia offers the possibility to reach both markets with the ARC7 ships. The implantation of the Yamal LNG plant and Arctic LNG 2 will require the implantation of an oil and gas industry to sustain the development of this area over the long term. Thus, the integration of an FZ would make the investment more profitable for private investors.

In conclusion, the development of the port of Sabetta, dedicated to become along with Murmansk and Arkhangelsk one of the most important in the Arctic, relies on the supply of parcels for the repair of vessels, the exportation of manufactured goods, the cargo for the development of a petrochemical industry in the Sabetta port, all of it being conditioned by the ice melting and the investment in general cargo vessels.

Norway

Norway with the port of Kirkenes competes with Russian ports in the race for an Arctic hub connecting Europe to Asia. As Murmansk, Kirkenes is ice free all year long and able to manage containers. Besides, the connection with the European market is underway with the building of a railway between Norway and Estonia via Finland (Staalesen, 2018).

The oil price collapse impacted negatively the Norwegian economy with a loss of thousands of jobs, stressing the risk represented by a strategy exclusively based on raw material exploitation. Thus, in order to sustain a model of socio-economic development, the implementation of a hub connected with consumption and production areas in Europe and with a transshipment capacity appears as the optimal solution. Yet, such a hub is not only strategic for Norway but also for Finland and the rest of Europe.

Kirkenes is located at the extreme north of Norway, close to the Russian border. Although it is smaller than Murmansk, Lukoil used to transship its crude oil in Kirkenes instead of Murmansk.

As Murmansk, Kirkenes can load vessels without ice class, provide yearly ice-free passage and a depth of 13m. If both ports can be rivals, they are also partners at only three hours' drive from each other.

The closure of the Sydvaranger mine has curbed the development of the port. The investment of the Tschudi Group within its infrastructure, because of its geographical position, gave the port a second life. The new hub of Kirkenes would have a 550 000 container capacity, and 200-meter long vessels would call by 2040 and connect with the Arctic Ocean Railway.

Bareksten et al. (2018) consider that Kirkenes is one of the best options for an Arctic hub. The strategy is to connect Berlin to the Arctic, via the Rail Baltica, for an investment between 10 and 16 billion euros. This would make Kirkenes the main gateway for exportation of goods from European countries to Asia via NSR. Moreover, the connection of Finland to the port of Kirkenes would give the opportunity for Baltic countries to avoid the issue presented by the shallow water depth of the Danish Straits and the matter caused by the ice and to enhance the connectivity of the European continent with Asia.

Canada

Canada had three main nodes in the Arctic with the Port of Churchill, the Straits of the Northwest Passage, and the Beaufort Sea Area, next to Alaska. The Port of Churchill was sold in 1997 to the American company OmniTRAX who also runs the Arctic railway connecting the North American continent to Arctic routes. There was also an agreement between Canada and Russia for an air link. Despite the deep-sea capacities of the port, the ice constraint lowered profitability, and the port, which was the main and only gateway to Arctic, was shut down in 2016 but may be plan to reopen (Malone, 2018).

The second node integrates ports like Nanisivik and operated part of the year, distant from population, production areas, and services. The third node pools ports such as Tuktoyaktuk next to the Alaskan border. This area benefits from extraction areas, but the ports are still modest and the hinterland is reached with pipelines which leave no room for value-added production and consequent economic development.

United States

The USA's presence in Arctic is of two natures. Firstly, ports in northern Alaska including Prudhoe Bay, Barrow, Kivilina, and to some extent Nome are next to mines and gas and oil fields similarly with Canadian ones and are connected with a pipeline to the south in order to avoid going through the Bering Strait. Secondly, ports in southern Alaska (Dutch Harbor, Kodiak Island, Anchorage, and Valdez) have a Foreign Trade Zone.

Greenland and Iceland

Greenland is developing few mining projects leading to the creation of wider ports, but today, the main port able to link Greenland to an Arctic route is Nuuk Port and Harbour on the Labrador Sea, with an entrance restricted by the tide and the ice during much of the year.

In Iceland, the Port of Reyarfjörur is dedicated to container transshipment thanks to Chinese investments. The backing of China within the economic life of Iceland has created tension. The other main port in Iceland is Akureyi.

Other countries with involvements

The Artic port system depends also on other countries that are linked to the area. We could quote Finland that appears as a land gateway to the North Sea Route. Moreover, Finland has FPs and railroad systems that connect it to markets. Finally, China and countries of the North Range in Europe have an indirect role to play with the production and consumption markets that need alternative routes to route the goods.

In the Arctic there are several types of Free Ports

Among the six coastal countries of the Arctic, there is, of course, no harmonized regulation on FPs. There is a project of the Arctic Free Trade Zone covering the entirety of the Arctic, but such vision seems however quite difficult to set up politically and administratively. In terms of local regulation dedicated to FZs and FPs, Iceland and Norway have no such provision. Some private actors, especially mining companies are mentioning the opportunity to create a regulation and the subsequent infrastructures; however, such a project is not on the political agenda of one or the other country yet.

Denmark and Canada have a regulation for FZs, but no FP implemented in the Arctic zone. Denmark has an FP in Copenhagen, a legacy from the Hanseatic League. Canada has a Foreign Trade Zone in Winnipeg connected to the port of Churchill and offers the possibility to implement Free Enterprises.

The USA is the country with the highest number of FZs in its territory as well as the leading one in terms of FPs. The USA created this status in the early 1930s, copying European examples. The reason for this status was to create ways to diminish the impact of the protectionist tariffs set up in 1930 under the Smoot-Hawley Tariff Act. If the Foreign Trade Zone Act of 1934 had only a minor impact, the step was made in the 1950s to promote subzones that were no longer FZs, but free enterprises, as it is now the case in Canada.

After the 1973 oil crisis, American companies started to go global due to a slowdown of the domestic market. Combined with the decrease of the tariff barriers induced by the General Agreements on Tariffs and Trade, American companies faced competition from Asian firms. From this point on, the number of FTZs kept growing from around 50 in 1979, to more than 200 in 1993. There are four FTZs in Alaska and three of which are FPs: FTZ 108 – City of Valdez; FTZ 160 – Port of Anchorage; and FTZ 232 – Kodiak Island Borough. These three FPs are all located outside the Arctic, but at its gate. The main reason is the pipeline linking the fields of the north coast of Alaska with the south coast. In 2016, only FTZ 160 – Port of Anchorage was exclusively operating, with 24 warehouses and storage facilities plus Tesoro Alaska Company Oil facility's oil products.

Russia started the implement FZ in 1988 to increase the competitiveness of Soviet companies abroad. Public-private companies could develop in these zones following the Chinese model of FZs. These FZs were islands of capitalism within the system. Two years later a new wave of FZs started with a wide range of objects: tourism, logistics, technological, and industrial zones among others. In 2010 Bost (2010) listed 15 major FZs with two of them located in ports: Kaliningrad in the Baltic Sea and Magadan in the Okhotsk Sea. Today, there are six Industrial and Production Zones (EPZ), five Technology and Innovation Zones (SFZ), 14 Tourist and Recreational Zones (SZF), and three Special Port Economic Zones (FPs). The third FP created is Murmansk. Apart from transportation and bulk handling, the Special Port Economic Zone of Murmansk offers the opportunity of oil rig assembling, which successfully supports the development of offshore oil and gas fields. This FP is located in the vicinity of the major transit corridors and gateways toward both far east and central regions of the Russian Federation. The location, at the gateway of Arctic, with yearlong ice-free facilities is a major advantage. The only zone in the Arctic area has been in existence for a period of 49 years.

Finally, there are three FPs in Finland on the Baltic Sea planned to be linked by rail to the Barents Sea. Cooperation between Finland and Russia and/or Norway could create value within these FPs as well as in the FPs on the Barents Sea.

The future of Free Ports in the Arctic region

FPs are mostly present on the periphery of the Arctic, with the exception of Murmansk. The main limitations to developing FPs today is the lack of existing flows and the fact that existing flows are mainly bulk flows requiring less value-added operations than containerized goods. Moreover, the population rate in the area is low. There is neither a demand on the production side, nor on the consumption side. The Arctic routes are however developing and should benefit from major investments, thus FPs could become catalysts of economic activity.

The second factor to implement an FP in this prospective approach would be the routes. Arctic hinterlands are mostly deserted and there are only a few inland corridors that lead toward industrial or populated areas such as Alaska, via the pipelines; Iceland; and the Peninsula of Kola, leading to Norway, Finland, and to some extent Saint Petersburg.

Another prospective aspect is the development of other markets. Cruise tourism is among emerging activities, especially in the Canadian part of the Arctic. Seafood could become another one, copying the experiences developed in countries such as Mauritius that has developed a seafood hub in its FP.

Another prospective element is the characteristic of the FP. Free trade zones are in general developed to import, transform, and re-export goods. This is a business model that could come in addition to another activity, but not sufficient to justify the creation of an FP in itself. Export processing zones are industrial zones in which manufacturing can be developed and integrated within the Yamal projects as long as there are other activities creating value around the initial project.

Finally, what is important is the port itself. First, an efficient port needs to be open on a yearly basis; therefore, it has to be ice free yearlong. Second, insurance companies generally make the use of ice-class vessels mandatory above the 70th or 72nd north parallel. However, ice-class vessels lose efficiency in warm waters involving the need for transshipment at the border of Arctic routes where most free trade zones are already. Third, the port should be efficiently run with deep-sea access. Fourth, there should be a network of FPs, enabling relationships and trade between the Arctic zone and South East Asia, North America and the North Range. This last point is a way to reduce the frictions of international trade and should be one of the focusing points of the next generation of FPs (Lavissière & Rodrigue, 2017).

Conclusion and discussion

We can therefore conclude there should be two types of FZs in the Arctic: the *route gateway FPs* and the *route market FPs*. The *route gateway FPs* should be able to act as transshipment nodes where one can enter or exit in this specific area of the Arctic. Most probably they should be of a free trade zone type. Services around this transshipment facility should be developed, such as manufacturing and storage. The *route market FPs* should be export processing zones in which a production zone or a consumption zone are the point of origin or point of destination of the flows in the Arctic. Typically, oil field bases are of this type. A third type is a *route mixed FP*, in which there is no exclusive transshipment, but also incorporation of market goods into the flows (Figure 11.8).

Being ice free on a yearly basis, outside the exclusion zone of insurance companies, and a deepwater for the call of non-ice class or polar vessels are three main parameters to welcome an FZ (Figure 11.9). However, it has to be at the limit of

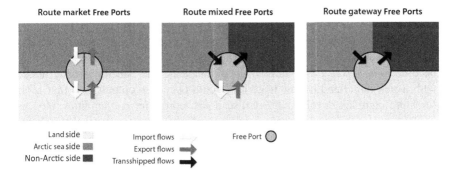

Figure 11.8 Free Ports and routing

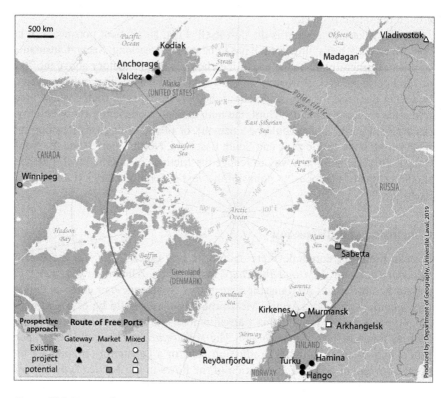

Figure 11.9 Route of Free Ports

the area so the use of ice or polar-class vessels would be optimized. Yet, we made an exception within our approach with Vladivostok. We assume that its proximity to the Chinese market, combined with the strong relation maintained between China and Russia shall place this port as a gateway for the Chinese to export their production via the NSR.

With the exception for Sabetta, which was built from scratch to ease the exportation of LNG, we assume that ports such as Murmansk (with coal and consumer commodities), Arkhangelsk (with timber and consumer commodities), Vladivostok (with consumer commodities), Kirkenes (with consumer commodities) may become *route mixed FPs*. Murmansk, Arkhangelsk, and Sabetta, already linked with a rich hinterland of raw materials, could use these outputs as a first layer for more complex development (cruise liners, consumer commodities, etc.) as in Murmansk. This dual activity purpose reinforces our hypothesis that FZs are relevant for the economic development of those ports.

The FP status brings advantages during the building phase of the industrial zone and its operation phase. It also enables the development of other activities that could piggyback on multinational projects.

References

Aggarwal, A. (2010). *Economic impacts of SEZs: Theoretical approaches and analysis of newly notified SEZs in India. Munich personal RePEc archive.* Retrieved November 11, 2012, from https://mpra.ub.uni-muenchen.de/20902/2/MPRA_paper_20902.pdf

Akinci, G., & Crittle, J. (2008). *Special economic zones: Performance, lessons learned, and implications for zone development.* Washington, DC: The World Bank.

Baissac, C. (1996). A critique of cost-benefit analysis in the evaluation of export processing zones. *Journal of the Flagstaff Institute, 2*(1), 28–38.

Bambulyak, A., & Frantzen, B. (2009). *Oil transport from the Russian part of the Barents Region. The Norwegian Barents Secretariat and Akvaplan-niva, Norway. 97 pages.* Retrieved February 6, 2019, from http://barents.custompublish.com/getfile.php/908406.900.qpqreacrqx/Oil_transport_2009.pdf

Bareksten, H. S. Karamperidis, S., Valantasis-Kanellos, N., & Song, D. W. (2018). An exploratory study on the Northern Sea Route as an alternative shipping passage. *Maritime Policy & Management, 45*(4), 495–513.

Blanco de Armas, E., & Sadni Jallab, M. (2002). *A review of the role and impact of export processing zones in world trade: The case of Mexico.* Post-Print halshs-00178444_v1, HAL. Retrieved February 6, 2019, from https://econpapers.repec.org/paper/haljournl/halshs-00178444.htm

Bost, F. (2007). Les zones franches, interfaces de la mondialisation. *Annales de géographie, 6*, 563–585.

Bost, F. (2010). *Atlas mondial des zones franches.* Paris: La Documentation française.

Chernov, V. (2014, December 19). Phantoms of Russian infrastructure in 2014. *Port News.* Retrieved July 1, 2018, http://en.portnews.ru/comments/1888/

CHNL. (2018). *Center for High North Logistics.* www.arctic-lio.com

Doyon, J. F., Lasserre, F., Pauline, P., Têtu, P. L., Fournier, M., Huang, L., & Beveridge, L. (2016). Arctic routes opening up: Strategies and perceptions of the bulk shipping industry. *Géotransports, 8*, 5–22.

Ducruet, C., Itoh, H., & Joly, O. (2015). Ports and the local embedding of commodity flows. *Papers in Regional Science, 94*(3), 607–627.

Ellis, B., & Brigham, L. (2009). *Arctic marine shipping assessment 2009 report.* Oslo: Arctic Council.

Engman, M., Onodera, O., & Pinali, E. (2007). Export processing zones: Past and future role in trade and development. *OECD trade policy papers 53.* Paris: OECD Publishing.

Farole, T. (2011). *Special economic zones in Africa: Comparing performance and learning from global experiences.* Washington, DC: The World Bank.

Farole, T., & Akinci, G. (2011). *Special economic zones: Progress, emerging challenges, and future directions.* Washington, DC: The World Bank.

Fedi, L., & Lavissière, A. (2014). Les régimes d'exploitation des ports francs au début du 21ème siècle. *Droit maritime français, 759*, 766–774.

Glukhavera, E. K. (2011). Prospect for the production and transportation of oil and gas resources from the western Russian arctic. *Studies of Russian Economic Development. 22*(5), 507–514

Humpert, M. (2014). Arctic shipping: an analysis of the 2013 Northern Sea Route season. *Arctic Year Book.* Retrieved July 1, 2018, from https://arcticyearbook.com/arctic-yearbook/2014/2014-briefing-notes/111-arctic-shipping-an-analysis-of-the-2013-northern-sea-route-season

IES Report (2010). Energy strategy of Russia for the period up to 2030. Retrieved July 1, 2018, from www.energystrategy.ru/projects/docs/ES-2030_(Eng).pdf

Jacobs, W., & Hall, P. V. (2007). What conditions supply chain strategies of ports? The case of Dubai. *GeoJournal, 68*(4), 327–342.

Johansson, H. (1994). The economics of export processing zones revisited. *Development Policy Review, 12*(4), 387–402.

Kinossian, K. (2016). Re-colonising the Arctic: The preparation of spatial planning policy in Murmansk Oblast, Russia. *Environment and Planning C: Government and Policy 35*(2). doi:10.1177/0263774X16648331

Kitagawa, H. (2000). *The Northern Sea Route – The shortest sea route linking East Asia and Europe.* Tokyo: Ship Ocean Foundation.

Kusago, T., & Tzannatos, Z. (1998). Export processing zones: A review in need of update. *Social protection group, human development network.* Washington, DC: The World Bank.

Lasserre, F., & Têtu, P. L. (2017). Extractive industry: The growth engine of Arctic shipping? In W. Lackenbauer, & H. Nicol, (Eds.), *Whole of government through an Arctic lens* (pp. 239–268). Antigonish, Nova Scotia, Canada: Mulroney Institute of Government.

Lavissière, A. (2014). Les ports francs en Méditerranée et l'exception Marseillaise. *Annales de l'Institut Méditerranéen des Transports Maritimes.* Marseille: CMCI.

Lavissière, A., Fedi, L., & Cheaitou, A. (2014). A modern concept of FPs in the 21st century: a definition towards a supply chain added value. *Supply Chain Forum: an International Journal. 15*(3), 22–28.

Lavissière, A., Mandják, T., & Fedi, L. (2016). The key role of infrastructure in backshoring operations: the case of FZs. In *Supply Chain Forum: An International Journal. 17*(3), 143–155.

Lavissière, A., & Rodrigue, J. P. (2017). FPs: Towards a network of trade gateways. *Journal of Shipping and Trade, 2*(7).

Lorot, P., & Schwob, T. (1987). *Les zones franches dans le monde. La Documentation Française.* Paris: DILA.

Mc Elwee, R. (1926). *Port development.* New York: McGraw-Hill.

Madani, D. (1999). *A review of the role and impact of export processing zones.* Washington, DC: The World Bank.

Malone, K.G. (2018). 'We are free:' Churchill celebrates return of train service with prime minister. *Canada's National Observer* (November 2nd). www.nationalobserver.com/2018/11/02/news/we-are-free-churchill-celebrates-return-train-service-prime-minister

Mandják, T., & Lavissière, A. (2014). The Island that should be isolated from trade routes: The paradox of FPs. communication: *30th annual industrial marketing and purchasing conference*, Bordeaux, 4–6th September.

Nalimov, P., & Rudenko, D. (2015). Socio-economic problems of the Yamal-Nenets autonomous okrug development. Communication: *International Conference on Applied Economics*, ICOAE 2015, 2–4th July 2015, Kazan, Russia.

Nielsen, T. (2017). Railway, port on agenda for China's Vice Premier in Arkhangelsk. *The New Barentz Observer.* Retrieved March 27, 2019, from https://thebarentsobserver.com/en/industry-and-energy/2017/03/railway-port-agenda-chinas-vice-premier-arkhangelsk

Ómarsson, S. A. (2010). *An Arctic dream: The opening of the Northern Sea Route: Impact and possibilities for Iceland* (Doctoral dissertation). Bifröst University, Island.

Pelletier, S., & Lasserre, F. (2011). Polar super seaways? Maritime transport in the Arctic: an analysis of shipowners' intentions. *Journal of Transport Geography, 19*(6), 1465–1473.

Ragner, C. L. (2000). *Northern Sea Route cargo flows and infrastructure – present state and future potential*. (FNI report, 13, 2000).

Rhee, Y. W., Katterbach, K., & White, J. (1990). *Free trade zones in export strategies*. The World Bank Industry and Energy Department.

Sorokina, Y. (2014). *Special economic zones of Russia alternatives for development of Transport Hub SEZs* (Master Thesis). Helsinki Metropolia University of Applied Sciences.

Staalesen, A. (2018). Barents town envisions Arctic hub with link to China. *The Barents Observer*. Retrieved February 6, 2019, from https://thebarentsobserver.com/en/arctic/2018/02/barents-town-envisions-arctic-hub-link-china

Tiefenbrun, S. (2012). *Tax free trade zones of the world and in the United States*. Cheltenham, UK: Edward Elgar Publishing.

Thoman, R. S. (1956). *FPs and foreign-trade zones*. Cambridge, MA: Cornell Maritime Press.

Zengpei, X., Cho, J.-W., Proksch, M., & Duval, Y. (2006). *Asia-Pacific trade and investment review*. United Nations Economic and Social Commission for Asia and the Pacific (UNESCAP).

12 The opportunities and challenges of developing the Arctic area and shipping in Canada

Mawuli Afenyo, Yufeng Lin, Adolf K.Y. Ng and Changmin Jiang

Introduction

In recent decades, there has been an increase in economic activities in the Arctic area, where both Arctic (e.g., Canada, Russian, US) and non-Arctic countries (e.g., China) have emerged as active players. Although the Arctic area attracts much attention due to (expected) vast reserves of natural resources and the prospects of fully exploiting the potential of Arctic shipping, many have argued that the risks are too high. According to this view, we are still not adequately prepared for the accompanying consequences of such activities. The Arctic environment remains fragile and may become a big contentious issue. Admittedly, many questions that are key to prepare for an 'Arctic take-off' remain unanswered.

In this regard, even less known is the Canadian federal government (CFG)'s (and other levels of governments') visions for the Arctic area. Although public opinion is still being sorted (CFG, 2017), the initial steps to develop an Arctic policy framework for Canada are already in place. Arctic shipping has become a prominent topic in both the research community and for the general public. Cruise ships and pleasure yachts increasingly venture into Arctic waters, including the Northwest Passage (NWP). Industry news recently noted a large number of ships are being built for the Arctic area. The cruise industry could witness a significant boom moving forward. Although some vessels will not be ready until 2020, a sizable number are already in operation within the Arctic waters (Anon, 2018). At the same time, ship operators are actively looking for shorter routes connecting Europe via the eastern North American coast to Asia (Lasserre, 2011). Considering canal fees, fuel costs and other factors influencing freight rates, Arctic shipping routes could reduce the cost of a single voyage by a large container ship from $17,5 million to $14 million (Borgerson, 2014). Regardless of costs, these routes can save much time, making just-in-time (JIT) deliveries more available. Indeed, sailing distance, costs, and risks are important factors that determine the revenues of shipping corporations. With shorter routes via Arctic waters, we may even witness a new phase of globalization – possibly explaining why even non-Arctic countries are getting more interested in the Arctic area than before. For example, China has recently published a guidebook for freight vessels navigating through the NWP across northern Canada, thus putting more pressure on the CFG to step up and do something similar (Mei, 2016).

In the past decade, vessels that sailed through CFG-monitored waters in the Arctic area have risen by 45% – from 86 in 2009 to 125 in 2018 (Naomi & Friedman, 2019). Nowadays, there are 49 oil and gas fields in Mackenzie River Delta (15 located along the Canadian Arctic Archipelago). Canada's unexplored territorial north, not only the Arctic area but also the roadless (permanent roads) northern hinterlands in many provinces (e.g., northern Manitoba) possesses substantial potential. In 2016, the offshore Arctic development restrictions were revisited at the Arctic Oil & Gas Symposium (held in Calgary, Alberta) (Office of the Prime Minister of Canada, 2016). Recently, the US President, Donald Trump, attempted to re-open the Alaskan Arctic to drilling (Thanawala, 2019). Although his attempt was blocked by federal judges, it illustrated the interests and ambitions of the US in regulating and drawing revenues from the Arctic area. Facing such threats, there are views that Canada is falling behind the exploitation of the Arctic area due to the ban, while the Minister of Northern Affairs, Dominic LeBlanc, regards the ban as a required step to ensure that the environment is explored and exploited in an environmentally-friendly way (National News, 2019). Also, he said that CFG is consulting with northern people and communities, with governmental and industrial efforts to come up with a science-based report on this issue. On the other hand, the Minister of Finance, Bill Morneau (2019) earmarked more than $700 million over a decade for Canada's Arctic and northern communities initiatives, including $400 million for cleaner energy in the north, $400 million for transportation infrastructure, and $84 million over five years for climate change research. Taking actions to tackle the gaping infrastructure deficit in Canada's north is corresponding to Canada's Prime Minister Justin Trudeau's 2016 commitment to co-develop the *Arctic and Northern Policy Framework* with local residents and stakeholders. However, the fact that a highly anticipated long-term development strategy for the region is only starting suggests that Canada still has much catching up to do with its Arctic counterparts.

All these illustrate that there are still many questions on how to open up the Canadian Arctic, but simultaneously indicate the numerous opportunities that researchers can investigate. Understanding such, by focusing on Canada, the chapter seeks to raise such questions by discussing the opportunities and challenges posed by the development of the Arctic area, including shipping. The rest of the chapter is structured as follows. The second section consists of the *marine* aspect that addresses the prospects of shipping and natural resource exploration and production in the Arctic area, with a special focus on oil spills and how to deal with them. The third section consists of the *land* aspect that discusses the impacts of opening up the Arctic to northern communities, including a case study on the town of Churchill, Manitoba. The conclusion, including the suggestions on future research, can be found in the last section.

Shipping and natural resource exploration in the Arctic: the dilemma of harnessing potentials while protecting the environment

Natural resource exploration and shipping in the Arctic have attracted attention lately. This is due to the huge economic benefits such activities are likely to bring to the local communities and countries involved (Østreng, Eger, Fløistad, Jørgensen-Dahl, Lothe, Mejlænder-Larsen, & Wergeland, 2013). As mentioned earlier, even non-Arctic countries have identified this potential, where, for example, since 2018, China has made Arctic shipping a key part of its Belt and Road initiative (Schach & Madlener, 2018). In addition, the current US administration have stepped up their effort to push for oil exploration and drilling in the Arctic. This has resulted in the issuing of licenses for the Italian oil giant, ENI S.p.A., for Arctic oil exploration in the US Arctic waters (BOEM, 2017). Despite such, there is a huge community that questions if there is even a need to engage in Arctic shipping, as well as natural resource exploration and production in this region. Their main argument is that other countries and regions can still do without exploiting Arctic resources. In this way, the pristine Arctic environment could be preserved and transition gradually to open water status. Moreover, this would minimize oil spill, while the traditional livelihoods of the indigenous population can be preserved (see the third section).

Owing to the nature of the Arctic and the scattered nature of the communities, one question that keeps popping up is whether the Arctic communities (governments and local people) have the capacity to respond to oil spills should they happen. Oil spills, whether from drilling or shipping remain (and are perceived as) a serious problem. It is a fact that most Arctic countries, including Canada, do not have adequate equipment to deploy in case of an emergency. Booms, skimmers, dispersants, or igniters remain some of the relevant response equipment that can be deployed in the Arctic in case of an oil spill. Also, there is a situation whereby some equipment is available in the communities, but the local people cannot deploy them. Apart from availability, it is equally important on how and where to position such equipment at strategic points: is there any strategy or guidelines for the location of this equipment? It is pivotal that there is coordination between federal agencies, such as the Canadian Coast Guard, local people, and between Arctic countries. The latter is critical because an oil spill that occurs in one jurisdiction may affect others so many miles across the border. Arctic international response units might be required at selected strategic locations. This does not only help to protect the Arctic marine environment, but also ensures that trade and other economic activities can be implemented without the fear of potentially disastrous pollution. Should a disaster happen, there would be timely and effective response that could minimize/control the negative impacts.

In addition, timely deployment is equally important. For a harsh and difficult terrain like the Arctic area, it is very difficult to deal with oil spills. Darkness and the presence of ice are two key factors that hinder any responses in a timely manner. Depending on the time of the year, it could be more complicated. For example, if it happens in the extreme cold season, it might even be impossible to undertake any responses. Apart from timeliness, most oil might become encapsulated by ice and so it might become further complicated. In addition, some of the oil might also be under the ice, in between leads and engulfed in snow (Afenyo, Khan, & Veitch, 2016). Each of these scenarios requires specialized techniques to deal with. Currently, this is not helped by the issue of sovereignty. If an oil spill occurs in one jurisdiction and spreads to another, who is responsible for dealing with it? This is further worsened by the ambiguity between Arctic countries as it involves sovereignty. For example, there is a dispute between the US and Canada regarding the sovereignty of NWP. While the US argue that it is international waters, Canada insists that it is domestic Canadian waters. At the same time, Russia and Norway have similar disputes over Svalbard (Todorov, 2017; Østreng, Eger, Fløistad, Jørgensen-Dahl, Lothe, Mejlænder-Larsen, & Wergeland, 2013). Such disputes add complexities to cooperation among Arctic countries and require extra efforts for them to work together so as to respond in the right manner to avert potential environmental disasters.

Many researchers, especially in science and engineering, argue that the single most important issue when it comes to dealing with oil spills in the Arctic is the understanding of the behaviour of oil in ice-covered waters (Afenyo, Khan, & Veitch, 2016). Despite progress made in this regard, many questions remain about the interaction between oil and ice. In this regard, the recent *Joint Industrial Project* (JIP) has generated substantial knowledge base. However, there is still more that needs to be done. For example, the oil spill models that are currently available have not really been tested for Arctic waters as no such spill has occurred. Even though some meso-scale experiments have been carried out, it remains to be seen how these models perform in practice when an oil spill actually occurs in the Arctic area. This means that resources need to be committed to creating an artificial environment that will mimic the Arctic to test these models. In addition, some processes are not well understood when they take place within the Arctic area (e.g., oil emulsification, evaporation, encapsulation, de-encapsulation). In this case, the Norwegian consulting organization, SINTEF, has done extensive work, but much still needs to be done (Afenyo, Khan, & Veitch, 2016; Lee et al., 2015). Of course, another important factor to be considered is the need to develop a reliable method to accurately assess the socio-economic impacts of oil spills (both shipping and exploitation of oil) if and when it takes place in the Arctic area. Hitherto, difficulties remain on how such impacts should be quantified: 1) What are the criteria? 2) Are there any relevant documents and guidelines? While documents and guidelines exist for conducting (e.g., environmental impacts) of an oil spill for Arctic drilling, such as the report published by the National Energy Board (NEB, 2011), until now, there is a lack of similar documents and guidelines in assessing socio-economic impacts to the Arctic area due to oil spills from shipping and other resource exploitation activities. Recognizing such scarcity, the authors of this chapter have developed a model to address the problem, namely the *Socio-Economic Model for the Arctic* (SEMA). The details can be found in Afenyo, Ng, & Jiang (2019) and Afenyo, Jiang, & Ng (2019).

Finally, the use of drone technology, geographical information systems (GIS), and remote sensing would be helpful to deal with oil spills in the Arctic area. Much advancement has been made, especially in the use of high technology gadgets to address pollution problems. For example, the drone technology is far advancing and could be used to deliver dispersants and collect potential data for oil spill modelling works. With 5G technology already functional, much can be learnt from the advancements of other sectors, so that oil spills could be dealt in a timely and efficient manner. In this way, the effects on the marine fauna and flora would not be immensely affected.

Issues in the Canadian Arctic and northern communities

Apart from the *marine* aspect, the development of the Arctic area, including shipping, involves a substantial *land* aspect. Here is noted that shipping is part of the global supply chain system that involves different transportation modes and poses substantial regional impacts (Ng & Liu, 2014). After all, with the global warming debate still a rather controversial question, not everything may be negative. Indeed, natural resource exploration and shipping can be silver linings. However, the question remains on how prepared we are for the many negative consequences, including flooding of settlements and damaging transportation and other critical infrastructures. These often incur huge costs on the governments of these countries and destroy families, as some might lose their lives. Moreover, further oil spills from Arctic shipping can result in trauma, divorce, and mistrust. For example, this is still the case ten years after the *Exxon Valdez* incident. People have lost family members and others are been tagged as traitors. This is because the local people who have joined the polluting companies for cleaning jobs are often perceived as endorsing the disaster and thus betraying the local communities (Ritchie, Gill, & Long, 2018). Understanding such, this section is further divided into two sub-sections. The first part discusses how the local population can potentially benefit from natural resource exploration in the Arctic area. The second part illustrates a case study, namely the town of Churchill, Manitoba, Canada, notably how it tried (and is still trying) to overcome the negative socio-economic impacts posed by the disruption of key transportation infrastructures in 2017 and 2018.

The prospects for local populations

Being one of the major Arctic countries, most of the Arctic lands and waters in Canada are governed by the four constitutionally backed *Inuit Land Claim Agreements*. This means that the indigenous people get to experience their culture being preserved in the face of the fast-developing Arctic. However, enacting the laws does not necessary mean that they will be implemented effectively. Another challenging issue is that the First Nations consist of different groups and so sometimes governments (including the CFG) find it difficult to deal with the scattered groups. A recent article (CBC, 2019) suggests that indigenous people are gradually getting involved in the development of the Arctic. In fact, they are advocating more involvement. It is the responsibility of the government and other businesses about to work or already working in the Arctic to engage the local population.

Also, there is another critical question: how would the indigenous people benefit the most from natural resource extraction? Has the government set aside a quota of employment for local people? If there are not enough local people with the right skills for the jobs (e.g. oil drilling and other oil related activities), what are the legislations in place to ensure that the local population can benefit from these activities? More often than not, companies fly in expatriates to come to these communities to do such jobs instead of training locals. If locals are trained to do the same jobs, there is technical knowledge addition to the communities. The community loses a lot in the case of the former, except for few jobs and some royalties where there are some available. In the long term, there is a necessity to develop a program to ensure that the bulk of the workers are local people so as to address unemployment. Even if a company finishes its projects and programs, the skills remain in the communities and this helps beneficiaries in the long term (e.g., start a similar business of their own).

In fact, the personnel for a response is as equally important as time, position, and the number of equipment available. Should such a disaster occur, there is a need to have pre-trained and pre-identified people that can be called upon. It is even better if a majority of such personnel come from local communities that could be directly impacted by such oil spills. Oil spills affect their culture and economic activity, and so the commitment level, as well as the understanding of the terrain, would be unparalleled to others recruited from elsewhere. Indeed, in northern Canada, it is common knowledge that there is often a spiritual connection between the indigenous population and the Arctic area, and that only local people would likely thoroughly understand such connections. To some, their gods and ancestors 'live in these areas' and so it is only proper for them to be the ones to deal with issues related to their spiritual home. That notwithstanding, it is equally critical to ensure that the rightly trained personnel are on site to deal with the pollution irrespective of where they are coming from. It is pivotal to examine the worst-case scenarios to be encountered during shipping, oil and gas exploration, production, and mining. Finally, understanding the worst-case scenarios that could occur would go a long way to help putting together contingency plans and other response efforts.

The case of the town of Churchill, Manitoba, Canada

To understand the problem of the quality of supporting infrastructures, like rail and port, an illustrative example will be the Churchill Railway washout in northern Manitoba, Canada. Parts of the rail tracks of Churchill Railway were 'washed out' by a severe flood in May 2017 (Figure 12.1), resulting in hardship on residents physically and mentally. Connecting other parts of Canada, Churchill is part of the country's diverse and rich history. As a natural landmark that showcases some of the most beautiful Arctic wildlife (e.g., polar bears, beluga whales), Churchill

Figure 12.1 Photo illustrating part of the damage of the rail tracks connecting the town of
Churchill, Manitoba and southern Canada

Source: Authors, 2017

should not only be explored but preserved. Also, the town is home to families that
need reliable food, supplies, and work, being a key player in delivering items to
the northern communities and in the future the rest of Canada.

However, the then rail operator, OmniTRAX refused to fix the rail tracks,
claiming that it was not their responsibility and did not have the money to repair
the damages, notwithstanding that it closed down the operations of the port of
Churchill in 2016, largely due to the loss of the Canadian Wheat Board (CWB)'s
monopoly in handling the country's grain exports (equivalent to about 90% of all
of the port's cargo throughputs). However, as the rail tracks served as the only
permanent land connections to Churchill (there were no permanent roads connecting Churchill with other regions in Manitoba), if left unchecked, the town
of Churchill, with a population of about 900, could be cut off from any reliable
supplies, even basic necessities. This was a serious social problem requiring an
economic solution. As the old adage goes "a rising tide lifts all boats", so the
best plan was to make Churchill's economy grow and be strong thereby helping
the residents of Churchill. By revitalizing the railway, business should not shy
away from using Churchill's port due to lack of southern transport. Rebuilding
ports that can handle more goods and raw materials will bolster traffic through the
region with intermediacy. Furthermore, implementation of a free trade zone will
boost imports and exports.

A total of $100 million provided by the government was only for the acquisi-
tion, repairs, and an annual operating subsidy required by the Hudson Bay Railway Company, the Hudson Bay Port Company, and the Churchill Marine Tank
Farm (Morneau, 2019). These funds helped to restore rail services along the Hudson Bay Railway Line. However, it did not offer a future plan for the Churchill
railway or the port of Churchill. As the only deep-water port in northern Canada

to date, the port of Churchill has the potential to be 're-born' and grow into a key transportation and logistical hub. However, except the repair costs and operation subsidies, the necessary facility upgrade is not included in the Canada 2019 budget. Again, the question is whether the CFG and the Manitoban Provincial Government draw up any blueprints for Churchill, or even northern Canada. On the other hand, the cost of living in northern Canada is very high (and hard) due to the shortage of infrastructures and facilities that can build a reliable supply chain system. The lack of (permanent) roads means more expenses on travelling and supply of basic necessities by air (ice roads were possible in winter but not a permanent solution). For companies or government executing projects, there is an additional layer of expenses, as roads, ports, railways, and/or airstrips need to be constructed (Naomi & Friedman, 2019). Finally, there are more challenges to overcome if responsible Arctic shipping is to be achieved, including the physical accessibility, social-economic feasibility, indifferent (or even negative) attitudes of shipping stakeholders and the scarcity of quality infrastructures. In this case, Ng, Andrews, Babb, Lin, and Becker (2018) have provided a detailed account on such challenges.

As mentioned earlier, a major concern for Canada's Arctic development is how to convince the local communities, especially the indigenous population, on the benefits so as to get them involved. Hitherto, much of the indigenous population struggles to adapt to the changing social environment with the desire to maintain their distinct identity. They have to cope with rapid environmental changes, notably rapid melting ice brought by the shifting climate. Recognizing that indigenous people's culture offers valuable contribution to humanity's diversity and heritage, we argue that their involvement in Arctic shipping and development is not only necessary, but pivotal. The study of indigenous knowledge that has successfully avoided ecological collapse in the long term should not only benefit the theory and practice of modern management, but also satisfy the urgent needs of climate change adaptation (Ulturgasheva, Rasmus, Wexler, Nystad, & Kral, 2014; UN, 2009; Whiteman & Cooper, 2000). Importantly, it addresses indigenous people's concerns about the increased exploitation of an environment and disaster prevention system (Banuri & Marglin, 1993).

Conclusion

In recent decades, there has been an increase in economic activities in the Arctic area. However, the Arctic environment remains fragile and so may become a big contentious issue as well. Understanding such, the chapter discusses the opportunities and challenges of developing the Canadian Arctic area and shipping, including both the *marine* and *land* sides. The chapter illustrates that many questions and challenges remain, where the development of the Arctic area should not be merely treated as a takeaway. Nevertheless, it also lays out numerous opportunities for further collaborative and interdisciplinary research. Apart from further scientific and engineering research in the improvement of resource exploration, exploitation, and production, research on the influence of

Arctic development is the very first step to earn the trust of the northern communities. The debate of Arctic development is significant in that it highlights issues of social and cultural diversity, which are often neglected in discussion of the 'Public-Private-People Partnership' (P4). It is a component of vast, complex technological, and economic systems that entail far-reaching changes, about which the northern communities try to make their concerns known and heard. Research that focuses on the profitability (i.e., economic and financial benefits) and environmental implication of activities in the Arctic area has received much attention. This is currently not the case for the social and cultural impacts posed by increasing activities in the Arctic area and further efforts are needed to address this deficiency.

Finally, data on the influence of increasing human exploring and exploiting activities, the costs of building, repairing or upgrading infrastructures, and subsidies for the local (especially indigenous) communities, should be encouraged as they would help the CFG, provincial/territorial, and local governments to establish better visions and approaches on how the Arctic area should be developed. Further steps by researchers should be undertaken to help other governmental agencies (e.g., Transport Canada, Manitoba Infrastructure and Transportation, Canadian Coast Guards) to design better management structures dedicated for Arctic community involvement and engagement. The project *Genomics Research in Oil Spill Preparedness and Emergency Response in an Arctic Marine Environment* (GENICE) that involves close collaboration between major Canadian universities (e.g., University of Manitoba, University of Calgary, McGill University) with scholars and researchers from diversified disciplines (genice.ca) and international collaborative networks on Arctic research (e.g., International Forum on Climate Change Adaptation Planning for Ports, Transportation Infrastructures, and the Arctic (CCAPPTIA)) (ccapptia.com) can be illustrative examples on how interdisciplinary, collaborative research on the Arctic area can be conducted. We are confident that the chapter provides useful insight on setting up a future research agenda for the well-being of the Arctic area, especially Canada and its northern communities.

Acknowledgements

The study is supported by the project *GENICE: Genomics Research in Oil Spill Preparedness and Emergency Response in an Arctic Marine Environment* funded by Genome Canada, the project *Climate Change Adaptation Planning for Ports* funded by the Social Science and Humanities Research Council of Canada (SSHRC)'s Insight Grant (project no. 47360 and sponsor award no. 435–2017–0735), and CCAPPTIA (ccapptia.com).

References

Afenyo, M., Khan, F., & Veitch, B. (2016). A state-of-the-art review of fate and transport of oil spills in open and ice-covered water. *Ocean Engineering. 119*:233–248.

Afenyo, M., Jiang, C., & Ng, A. K. Y. (2019). Climate change and Arctic shipping: A method for assessing the impacts of oil spills in the Arctic. *Transportation Research Part D: Transport and the Environment* (in press). doi:10.1016/j.trd.2019.05.009

Afenyo, M., Ng, A. K. Y., & Jiang, C. (2019). A method for assessing the socio-economic impacts of oil spills generated by Arctic shipping. *Proceedings of the Annual Conference of the International Association of Maritime Economists (IAME) 2019*, Athens, Greece, 25–28 June.

Anon (2018). *Expedition market report. Cruise industry news. Special report*, Retrieved December 21, 2018, from www.cruiseindustrynews.com/store/product/digital-reports/2018-expedition-report/

Banuri, T., Apffel-Marglin, F., & Research, W. I. (Eds.). (1993). *Who will save the forests?: Knowledge, power and environmental destruction*. London: Zed Books.

Borgerson, S. G. (2014). Arctic Meltdown: The Economic and Security Implications of Global Warming, *Foreign Affairs*, *87*, 63–77.

Bureau of Ocean Energy Management (BOEM) (2017). *BOEM Approves Eni Beaufort sea exploration plan. Communiqué*. Retrieved December 7, from www.boem.gov/press07122017/

CBC. (2019, February 06). *Inuit making recommendations on Arctic shipping routes*. Retrieved from https://ca.news.yahoo.com/food-security-top-mind-inuit-100000741.html

CCAPPTIA website: ccapptia.com. Retrieved from 13th July, 2019.

Canadian federal government. (CFG) (2017). *Canada's Arctic policy framework: Discussion guide*. Retrieved from www.rcaanc-cirnac.gc.ca/eng/1503687877293/1537887905065

GENICE project website: genice.ca/. Retrieved from 20th April, 2019.

Lasserre, F. (2011). Arctic shipping routes. *International Journal*, *66*(4), 793–808.

Lee, K., Boufadel, M., Chen, B., Foght, J., Hodson, P., Swanson, S., & Venosa, A. (2015). *Expert panel report on the behaviour and environmental impacts of crude oil released into aqueous environments*. Ottawa, ON: Royal Society of Canada. Retrieved October 01, 2018, from https://rsc-src.ca/sites/default/files/pdf/OIW%20Report_1.pdf

Mei, Y. (2016). China reveals plans to ship cargo across Canada's Northwest Passage. *Globe and Mail*. Retrieved April 20, from www.theglobeandmail.com/news/world/china-reveals-plans-to-ship-cargo-across-canadas-northwest-passage/article29691054/

Morneau, W. F. (2019). *Investing in the Middle Class, Budget 2019*. Department of Finance Canada. Retrieved from www.fin.gc.ca

Naomi, P., & Friedman, G. (2019). "We're not getting it": Liberals sprinkle $700 million in Arctic but a strategic plan remains elusive. *Financial Post*. Retrieved March 22, 2019 from https://business.financialpost.com/news/economy/were-not-getting-it-liberals-sprinkle-700-million-in-arctic-but-a-strategic-plan-remains-elusive

National Energy Board (NEB). 2011. The past is always present. Review of offshore drilling in Canadian Arctic. Preparing for the future. Ottawa. 54 pages.

National News (2019). Canada 'falling behind' other nations because of Arctic moratorium: CAPP, *APTN News*. Retrieved March 14, from https://aptnnews.ca/2019/03/14/canada-falling-behind-other-nations-because-of-arctic-moratorium-cap/

Ng, A. K. Y., Andrews, J., Babb, D., Lin, Y., & Becker, A. (2018). Implications of climate change for shipping: Opening the Arctic seas. *Wiley Interdisciplinary Reviews: Climate Change*, *9*(2), E507.

Ng, A. K. Y., & Liu, J. J. (2014). *Port-focal logistics and global supply chains*. Basingstoke: Palgrave Macmillan.

Office of the Prime Minister of Canada (2016). *United States-Canada joint Arctic leaders' statement*. Retrieved from https://pm.gc.ca/eng/news/2016/12/20/united-states-canada-joint-arctic-leaders-statement

Østreng, W., Eger, K. M., Fløistad, B., Jørgensen-Dahl, A., Lothe, L., Mejlænder-Larsen, M., & Wergeland, T. (2013). *Shipping in Arctic waters: A comparison of the Northeast, Northwest and trans Polar passages*. Chichester: Springer.

Ritchie, L. A., Gill, D. A., & Long, M. A. (2018). Mitigating litigating: An examination of psychosocial impacts of compensation processes associated with the 2010 BP Deepwater Horizon oil spill. *Risk Analysis, 38*(8), 1656–1671.

Schach, M., & Madlener, R. (2018). Impacts of an ice-free Northeast Passage on LNG markets and geopolitics. *Energy Policy, 122*, 438–448.

Thanawala, S. (2019). Judge blocks Trump's attempt to open up Arctic, Atlantic areas to oil and gas leasing. *Global News*. Retrieved March 30, from https://globalnews.ca/news/5113867/trump-arctic-atlantic-oil-gas-judge-order/

Todorov, A. A. (2017). The Russia-USA legal dispute over the straights of the Northern Sea Route (NSR) and similar case of the Northwest Passage. *Arktika i Server, 29*, 62–75.

Ulturgasheva, O., Rasmus, S., Wexler, L., Nystad, K., & Kral, M. (2014). Arctic indigenous youth resilience and vulnerability: Comparative analysis of adolescent experiences across five circumpolar communities. *Transcultural Psychiatry, 51*(5), 735–756.

United Nations (UN) (2009). *State of the world's indigenous peoples*. Department of Economic and Social Affairs, UN, New York, NY, *9*, 52–77.

Whiteman, G., & Cooper, W. H. (2000). Ecological embeddedness. *Academy of Management Journal, 43*(6), 1265–1282.

Conclusion

Frédéric Lasserre

Climate change triggered a renewal for Arctic shipping in the late 1990s. The idea was not new: it laid at the basis of the European's quest for the Northwest and Northeast Passages from the 16th century. It was revived with plans for cargo submarines transit in the 1930s (Popular Mechanics, 1931). Several research projects have been conducted since the turn of the 21st century to try and demonstrate shipping along the shorter Arctic routes was cheaper and would thus experience a significant expansion in the forthcoming years.

The reality seems more complex: first, depending on the parameters, more recent models tend to depict a more nuanced picture of the profitability of Arctic commercial shipping. Second, climate change appears to impact sea ice with significant variations from year to year, from region to region, and also triggers other phenomena that do not necessarily make traffic easier, such as the concentration of sea ice depending on prevailing winds, the increased frequency of icing spray, fog and growlers. Third, shipping companies themselves have assessed Arctic shipping opportunities. Their analyses showed that cost per transit may prove to be lower, depending on the origin/destination couple, but that this factor is not paramount in the decision to develop shipping in the Arctic: this business decision rests on the perceived strategic opportunity perceived by shipping companies.

In Canada, as well as in Russian Siberia, destinational traffic dominates a very significant expansion of Arctic shipping, especially in Russian waters: ships come to the Arctic to perform an economic activity, rather than just to transit. Along the NSR, the number of transits and trade volume both increased from 2011 to 2013 and declined in 2014 and 2015, before recovering slightly in 2017 and 2018, indicating an unstable and vulnerable shipping environment up to now. However, total traffic amounted to 9,7 Mt in 2017 and 18 Mt in 2018. The NSR seems to be more appealing to bulk and general cargo transportation, while container shipping companies have not displayed a significant interest for Arctic shipping, despite Maersk's test transit in September 2018 (Lakshmi, 2018). Most activities are still domestic and destinational in nature. This expansion of destinational traffic is partly sustained by the expansion of community resupply in Canada; however, in both countries, especially in Russia, it is the construction of infrastructure and the development of natural resources exploitation that fuels the present strong growth.

Similarly, traffic is dominated in Siberia by Russian shipping companies and in the Canadian Arctic by Canadian companies, for natural resource transportation as well as for the community resupply market. Canadian shipping companies in particular have adapted to the poor infrastructure of the Canadian Arctic villages and to the numerous barriers of entry to this niche market (Giguère, Comtois, & Slack, 2017). If natural resource exploitation picks up in Canada, it could prove more attractive for foreign corporations. This is in line with past Russian declarations to the effect they did not expect transit traffic along the NSR to develop to large volumes (Pettersen, 2013; Barents Observer, 2015), while President Putin officially set the objective for total traffic along the NSR to expand to 80 Mt by 2024 (Digges, 2018; Staalesen, 2018).

The melting of sea ice may act as an enabler, but it may not in itself be sufficient to trigger the development of massive traffic along Arctic seaways, nor of single-voyage cost-effectiveness: it does not drive the expansion of Arctic shipping since its evolution is contrasted between regions and between market segments, except for a few market niches like community resupply in Canada where demand is consequent. Shipping companies display a very limited interest for transit traffic, being more interested in the natural resources market. They stress that entering the Arctic market is a strategic diversification move that implies much broader considerations. It continues to be seen as a risky choice, both operationally and commercially, and implies business strategy choices that involve the global picture of the positioning of the company in its regional or global market (Lasserre & Pelletier, 2011; Lee & Kim, 2015; Beveridge et al., 2016; Lasserre, Beveridge, Fournier, Têtu, & Huang, 2016).

The future of Arctic shipping is thus likely to rest, in the coming decades, on the development of destinational shipping and its integration with global traffic. The expansion of resource extraction in Siberia, but also in northern Norway, Greenland and northern Canada could lead to a very significant expansion of total traffic in Arctic waters, underlining the need for clear and stringent regulations to prevent human and environmental disasters, since Arctic shipping will keep taking place in remote, dangerous waters for many more decades. For this expansion to take place, world resources prices must remain at a high level for the extraction to be profitable, but a port system in the Arctic could also develop to sustain traffic expansion. Extractive industries could opt for the setting up of local ports to handle the extraction of natural resources, with transshipment at major Arctic hubs where resources would be shipped to global markets on larger, open water and more affordable cargo ships, as can already be envisioned in Western Siberia with a system revolving around Murmansk.

Should such a process further develop, it would complete the globalization of the Arctic. Climate change is acting as an enabler of Arctic shipping, and is a global phenomenon. Increasing world prices triggered a renewed interest for extractive industries for Arctic minerals and oil and gas, themselves being the reflection of the globalization of resources markets. The Polar Code was a global, coordinated answer to the expansion of Arctic shipping, designed to propose a set of rules that would help control risks associated with the expansion of cargo shipping in polar waters that will remain risky for many years to come despite melting sea ice. Beyond the media hype about the Arctic, the interest of several non-Arctic states for the region is real, as China, Japan, South Korea, India, Germany, the UK, the European Union, among others developed Arctic strategies that have triggered heated debates about their political objectives among Arctic states. In the frame of this ongoing globalization, Arctic shipping may not be booming along transit routes as some observers may claim. It is certainly set, however, to keep expanding and structuring the future of the Arctic economy.

References

Barents Observer. (2015, October 17). Northern Sea Route – focus on domestic projects. *The Barents Observer*. Retrieved April 12, 2019, from http://barentsobserver.com/en/arctic/2015/10/northern-sea-route-focus-domestic-projects-17-10, a. Jan. 22, 2018; also at www.rcinet.ca/eye-on-the-arctic/2015/10/19/nsr-russia-to-focuses-on-domestic-projects/, a

Beveridge, Leah, Mélanie Fournier, Frédéric Lasserre, Linyan Huang, & Pierre-Louis Têtu (2016). Interest of Asian shipping companies in navigating the Arctic. *Polar Science*, *10*(3), 404–414.

Digges, C. (2018, May 16). Putin decrees an increase in Arctic traffic. *Bellona*. Retrieved April 10, 2019, from https://bellona.org/news/arctic/russian-nuclear-icebreakers-fleet/2018-05-putin-decrees-an-increase-in-arctic-traffi

Giguère, M. A., Comtois, C., & B. Slack (2017). Constraints on Canadian Arctic maritime connections. *Case Studies on Transport Policy*, *5*(2), 355–366.

Lakshmi, S. (2018, September 28). Maersk Tests Russian Arctic Route. *Maritime Logistics Professional*. Retrieved April 10, 2019, from www.maritimeprofessional.com/news/maersk-tests-russian-arctic-route-321976

Lasserre, F., Beveridge, L., Fournier, M., Têtu, P. L., & Huang, L. (2016). Polar seaways? Maritime transport in the Arctic: An analysis of shipowners' intentions II. *Journal of Transport Geography*, *57*(2016), 105–114.

Lasserre, F., & Pelletier, S. (2011). Polar super seaways? Maritime transport in the Arctic: An analysis of shipowners' intentions. *Journal of Transport Geography*, *19*(6), 1465–1473.

Lee, T., & Kim, H. J. (2015). Barriers of voyaging on the Northern Sea Route: A perspective from shipping companies. *Marine Policy*, *62*, 264–270.

Pettersen. T. (2013, December 19). Northern Sea Route no alternative to Suez – Deputy Minister. *Barents Observer*. Retrieved January 15, 2018, from http://barentsobserver.com/en/business/2013/12/northern-sea-route-no-alternative-suez-deputy-minister-19-12

Popular Mechanics. (1931). To Europe via the North Pole. *Popular Mechanics Magazine*, *55*(4), 529–532.

Staalesen, A. (2018, May 15). It's an order from the Kremlin: Shipping on Northern Sea Route to reach 80 million tons by 2024. *The Barents Observer*. Retrieved April 10, 2019, from https://thebarentsobserver.com/en/arctic/2018/05/its-order-kremlin-shipping-northern-sea-route-increase-80-million-tons-2024

Index

Note: Numbers in *italics* indicate figures and in **bold** indicate tables on the corresponding pages.

Printed in the United States
by Baker & Taylor Publisher Services